8TH AIR FORCE
AT WAR

Patrick Stephens Limited, an imprint of Haynes Publishing, has published authoritative, quality books for enthusiasts for more than a quarter of a century. During that time the company has established a reputation as one of the world's leading publishers of books on aviation, maritime, military, model-making, motor cycling, motoring, motor racing, railway and railway modelling subjects. Readers or authors with suggestions for books they would like to see published are invited to write to: The Editorial Director, Patrick Stephens Limited, Sparkford, Nr Yeovil, Somerset, BA22 7JJ.

8TH AIR FORCE
AT WAR

Memories and missions, England 1942-45

Martin W. Bowman

Patrick Stephens Limited

First published in 1994

British Library cataloguing-in-publication data:
A catalogue record for this book is available
from the British Library

ISBN 1 85260 444 1

Library of Congress catalog card no. 93 80186

Patrick Stephens Limited is an imprint
of Haynes Publishing, Sparkford,
Nr Yeovil, Somerset, BA22 7JJ

Typeset by MS Filmsetting Limited,
Frome, Somerset BA11 3EG
Printed and bound in Great Britain
by Butler & Tanner Ltd
of London and Frome

CONTENTS

CAST OF CHARACTERS

Adams, Marjorie, Englishwoman
Anderson, Carl L.
Arcaro, Lt Anthony, pilot
Ayers, May, Englishwoman
Bailey, Mike, Norwich schoolboy
Baker, Sgt George, cartoonist creator of 'Sad Shack'
Baker, Sgt Marshall E., 368th BS, 306th BG
Balsma, Mickey
Bank, 1/Lt Raymond M., 357th FG
Becchetti, Fred, 445th BG.
Beck, Father Gerald, Base Chaplain, 389th BG
Belovich, Lt Col Tom S., 446th BG
Bendiner, Lt Elmer, navigator, *Tondelayo* 379th BG
Betz, Lt Franklin L., navigator, 379th BG
Bing, Richard, radio operator, 561st BS, 388th BG
Bishop, Capt Bob, navigator, 44th BG
Boileau, Mrs Angela, Englishwoman
Borne, Melvin, 453rd BG
Brock, Kim, 882nd Chemical Warfare Co, Attlebridge.
Browne, 2/Lt Robert W., pilot, 487th BG
Bruce, William, 445th BG, Kassel, 27 September 1944
Butler, S/Sgt John W., gunner 389th & 93rd BGs
Cameron, Col William, 44th BG,
Campbell, Claude, pilot, 303rd BG
Caniff, Milt, artist
Capp, Al, artist
Capicotta, Joe, 8th Combat Camera Unit
Carleton, Bill, 351st Squadron Engineering Officer
Carrow, 1/Lt Raphael E., 445th BG

Carson, Capt Leonard 'Kit', 357th FG,
Casey, William J., Head of OSS
Cherry, Clarence F., gunner, 100th BG
Chipman, F/O Vance, 25th BG
Clark, S/Sgt Forrest S., gunner, 67th BS, 44th BG
Clark, G. Marden, 458th BG
Clark, Lt Col William C., 357th FG
Clingan, Wilbur, 453rd BG Operations Officer
Colby, Lt (later Capt) Franklin H. 'Pappy', 94th BG
Collar, George M., 445th BG
Collins, Father Joe Chaplain, 94th BG
Cooper, Alan, Schoolboy
Cordery, Henry C., co-pilot, 306th BG
Cose, Wayne E., top turret gunner/engineer, 486th BG
Cotner, Frank, 466th BG
Coward Noël, English playwright
Cromarty, 1/Lt Arthur, 453rd BG
Crosby, Maj Harry H., 100th BG
Cross, Elvin O., 445th BG tail gunner
Crowley, Clyde, bombardier, 95th BG
Darrah, Harry H., 389th BG, artist
Day, Philip G., co-pilot, 467th BG
DeKeyser, Henry A., 576th BS, 392nd BG
deLancey, 1/Lt Lawrence, pilot, 398th BG
Dewey, William R., pilot, 701st BS, 445th BG
Dolim, Abel L., navigator, 94th BG
Doyle, Charles 'Bud', 389th BG
Dregne, Col Irwin H., 357th FG
Dugger, Lt/Col Dick, 448th BG
Eaker, Lt Gen. Ira C.
Easthaugh, Brian, schoolboy
Elias, Jacob, 44th BG
Elliott, Christopher, English historian

Nairn, Roland 'Lefty'
Nasch, Ralph L., co-pilot, 92nd BG
Natvig, Orlo, radio operator, 91st BG
Newmark, Ray, bombardier, 388th BG
Noble, Wiley S., 3rd SAD, Watton-Griston
North, Tony, Norwich schoolboy
O'Brien, Maj Jim, pilot, 44th BG
O'Hara, Sgt E. W., Mail Call, *Yank* magazine
O'Hearn, Bob, 306th BG
O'Neill, Cpl James, Mail Call, *Yank* magazine
Parker, Lt Col George H., Station Engineer, 466th BG
Parker, Ted, waist gunner
Peal, Sheila, Englishwoman
Peaslee, Col Budd J., CO, 384th BG
Peck, General, 2nd Air Division
Peiffer, Kenneth M., tail gunner, 491st BG
Perry, Richard E., pilot, 390th BG
Petty, George, artist
Pickstone, T/Sgt Norman R., engineer, 493rd BG
Pollitt, 1/Lt Byron, B-17 pilot, 652nd BS, 25th BG
Preston, Gen Maurice 'Mo', CO, 379th BG, 41st Wing
Pye, Mr, Chief Foreman of Trades
Ramirez, S/Sgt Joe, 467th BG
Ramm, Pat, Norfolk schoolboy
Reed, Vince, 466th BG
Renwick, Lt Col Donald R., Dean of 'Clobber' College
Richards, Connie, Bedfordshire schoolgirl
Richardson, Sgt Wilbur, gunner, 94th BG
Rogers, Julian P., pilot, 100th BG
Rose, William, B., pilot, 326th BS, 92nd BG
Rudd, Perry, pilot, 457th BG, 29 April 1944
Saling, Pfc Joseph H., Mail Call, *Yank* magazine
Sanner, Dean H., Mosquito pilot, 25th BG
Sears, Capt Ray L., pilot, 453rd BG
Schaumberg, Chum, radio operator, 453rd BG
Schreck, Martin H.
Schröeder, Ernst, pilot, II.Sturm/JG 300
Schultz, Harold, Aircrew Mess, Attlebridge
Schuyler, Keith C., pilot, 44th BG 'Elusive Horizons'
Seale, Emmett D., 446th BG
Shahbaz, Lt Calvin, 491st BG, Metfield
Shanker, Herbert, 359th BS, 303rd BG
Shields, Ray, British bandleader
Shoens, Robert, pilot 100th BG
Shower, Col Albert J., CO, 467th BG
Skaggs, Capt Alvin D., pilot, 448th BG
Skitterall, Les, schoolboy
Smales, Phyllis, Rackheath teenager
Smetana, S/Sgt Adolph J., tail gunner, 351st BG

Smith, Ben Jr, radio operator, 360th BS, 303rd BG
Smith, Lloyd T., lead pilot, 93rd BG
Spaatz, Gen Carl 'Tooey'
Spengler, 1/Lt Bruce, P-51 pilot, 83rd FS, 78th FG
Spivey, Col Delmar
Spredbury, Ann K., Norwich schoolgirl
Stack, Phil, artist
Stanforth, John, 713th BS, 448th BG
Starek, Rocky, gunner, 712th BS, 448th BG
Starzynski, S/Sgt Robert J., 306th BG
Steller, Al, 709th BS, 447th BG
Sterrett, William B., bombardier, 100th BG
Stewart, Walter, pilot, 93rd BG
Stewart, William C., 92nd BG
Strong, Russell A., 306th BG
Stubbs, Lt Harry C., 44th BG
Sublett, Lt John L., pilot, 357th FG
Sullivan, 2/Lt Robert F., 453rd BG
Sutton, Beryl M., Englishwoman
Sweatt, S/Sgt Robert H., 389th BG.
Tarcza, Henry, 95th BG
LeMay, Gen Curtis E., 305th BG & 3rd Bomb Division
Taylor, Billy, Suffolk schoolboy
Tays, Col Robert H., pilot, 392nd BG
Tenneberg, Lt Robert H., pilot, 490th BG
Thatcher, Leo, 44th BG
Thomas, Col Larry, CO, 453rd BG
Thomas, Frank, radio operator, 453rd BG
Thompson, Mary, Englishwoman
Timberlake, Col Ted
Tipton, Ralph, 25th BG
Vanden Heuvel, 1/Lt George R., 376th FS, 361st FG
Vargas, Alberto, artist, *Esquire* magazine
Vorhees, Edith, GI bride
Vorhees, Keith, USAAF
Walker, George M., Carpetbaggers
Wandtke, Gilbert 'Gibby', engineer, 44th BG
Watts, 1/Lt Lowell, pilot, 388th BG
Weatherwax, Lt, navigator, 44th BG
Wegner, Lt Col George, 490th BG
Wendel, Karl W., navigator 447th BG
Weston, Linda, Englishwoman
Whitehead, Lt Kaylor C., pilot, 453rd BG
Whitehouse, Arch, *True* magazine
Wilson, John N., crew chief, 734th Squadron, 453rd BG
Worthen, 'Dusty', bombardier, 93rd BG
Wroblewski, 1/Lt Joe, pilot, 351st BG
Wysoki, 1/Lt Mike, 94th BG
Zimmerman, Earl, radio operator, 389th BG

SUPPORTING CAST

Adams, Steve
Aubrey-Cound, Rupert
Avis, Jim
Barnes, the late Marvin
Betcher, Ray
Bowman, Paula
Colborn, Mrs Muriel
Crawford, M/Sgt Hugh K., 94th BG
Ferguson, Andrew
Gann, Harry, McDonnell Douglas
Gilbert, Lt Col Laurence
Giles, Molly
Hall, Cliff
Hannant, Robert
Hawkins, Ian
Henry, Pete
Jefferson, Steve
Jessop Photo Centres
Johns, Claire
Krause, Jake, 458th BG
Lea, Alfred R., 452nd BG
Livingston, Art, 446th BG

Lockheed Aeronautical Systems Co
Mabee, S/Sgt Floyd H., 93rd BG
MacLachlan, Ian
Mayor, Dave
McGlone, Dr. John
National Geographic
Natvig, Orlo, 91st BG
Nekvasil, Charles 'Chuck'
Nicholls, William B.
Page, John
Richards, Gordon
Robertie, Bill
Roberts, Pfc Dave
Sesler, George R., 25th BG
Sheehan, Francis X.
Thorpe Abbotts Tower Memorial Museum
Tootell, Jim, 446th BG
Warman, Robbie
USAF Official
Ward, Geoff
Winston, Dan
Woodall, Truett
Woolnough, the late Lt Col John H.
Young, Sam

EXTRAS

Abner, L'il
Sad Sack, Pfc

'They never flinched or failed. It is to their devotion that in no small measure we owe our victory.'

Winston Spencer Churchill, speaking of the USAAF.

Flying in the heavens, only imagine can I
The duelling of strangers in the raging sky.
All so young, so aspiring, each belonging to a name,
Woven patterns of vapour, like a picture frame.
From the sleeping dawn to the revealing of dark night,
Twisting and turning in formation, they fought the fight.
A few did return, to live a life, the remainder will forever fly,
As the guardian angel of skylight, kissed them goodbye.

by KARINA WILES

AUTHOR'S INTRODUCTION

American troops, or GIs as they were known because of their own derisive term of 'General Issue', began arriving in war-weary Britain in the months immediately after Pearl Harbor. Bomber and fighter groups made an especial impact. The young Americans with their well-cut uniforms, new accents and money, created a colourful heroic chapter in the lives of the British people that is still remembered today.

The American 8th Air Force and the villagers and towns folk of East Anglia shared a close attachment that only wartime can create. England 1942–45 was a battle front. The civilians were all involved in the war effort – as shipyard and factory workers, Red Cross and Land Army, farmers and firemen. Above all they were stubborn, determined fighters who had already endured more than three years of war. Into these lives came the sights and sounds – particularly the jargon – of the men from Idaho, New York, California and the rest as they went on flak leave, R&R, and pubbing missions. The impressions they made were profound.

Stirring deeds of these gladiators of the air filled the newspapers and magazines of the period. They were crystallized in the minds of the population with movies such as William Wyler's wartime epic *Memphis Belle*, a poignant feature screened on both sides of the Atlantic, about the lives of a B-17 crew who flew the ship on 25 missions. Half a century after the war this immortal period of Anglo-American history is still being commemorated, with new films, books and magazine articles about the period, and with celebrations for the returning US veterans and the English families who had opened their hearts and homes to them so long ago.

Those Second World War years are recalled here by a cast of characters no movie director could ever hope to assemble. They tell of laughter, friendship, death, fear, exhilaration, stupidity, superstitions, discipline and indiscipline, lust and love, respect, disrespect, and outrage. Also of course the sheer horrors faced mission after mission by the 'boys in the sky', together with the personal deprivations experienced by the British men, women and children. These are their memories.

PASSAGE

'Come and join the Air Corps
It's a grand bunch so they say,
We never do no work at all,
Just fly around all day!
While others work and study hard
And so grow old and blind,
We take to the air, without a care,
And you will never mind.'

'They came out of the wheatfields, the factories in the cities. They were guys just off the street. Some of them only had a few weeks' training, a few months' at the most. As soon as the commander said, "I think I can make it," they sent him out.'
Gen. Lewis Lyle, 379th BG

'I was a mining engineer in Nicaragua. I made many flights in Ford Tri-motors and Lockheed Vegas. On 7 December 1941 a farewell cocktail party was held in my honour, as I was departing for America. I told my fellow miners that I would not be returning to Nicaragua after my vacation, but returning to Panama, the land of my birth, to work in the construction industry. We were arranging bottles for the party when the local radio put out by a Costa Rican station announced that Costa Rica had declared war on Japan! Everyone who came to the party just sat around listening to the tragic news, stunned with disbelief. Everyone had one thought: how would this affect each and every one of us? One of the immediate effects was that the Nicaraguans swiftly imprisoned the German and Japanese workers.'
Bill Rose

'I wanted wings, 'till I got the god-darn things
Now, I don't want them anymore!'

'Two Royal Navy ships were in dock at Mare Island Naval shipyard for repairs to damage sustained in the battle for Crete. One ship still had 60 men sealed into the bow. The bodies were later removed. A short time after that I decided that I was not going to be just another shipyards' worker, and I took examinations for pilot training in the Air Corps.'
Carl L. Anderson

'Our squadron loved to sing as we marched, so we made up a song about squadron 'H' to the tune of 'Mademoiselle from Armentieres, Parlez Vous'. It went thusly:

'Squadron H is always late, Parlez Vous
Squadron H is always late, Parlez Vous
Squadron H is always late
They lay in bed and Masturbate
Hinky Dinky Squadron Parlez Vous'

John W. McClane Jr., AAF Aviation Cadet, Squadron G, Nashville AAF Classification Centre

---

'While training in the States, my pilot's wife, Donis Campbell, a tall nice-looking girl, and four other pilots' wives, followed their husbands from base to base in an old beat-up car loaded down with what

Our squadron loved to sing as we marched, so we made up a song about squadron H to the tune of 'Mademoiselle from Armentieres, Parlez Vous.' (John W. McClane Jr.)

'Wendover Field wasn't the kind of base that you might look forward to being assigned to. It was a dreary base, with no shrubs or trees of any kind. The only thing green on the whole base was the airplanes and they were olive drab. The town of Wendover was nothing more than a watering stop, with a gas station, a couple of houses, and a hotel straddling the Utah-Nevada State Line. The State Line ran down the centre of the hotel so it was possible to gamble on the Nevada side, but not on the Utah side.'
S/Sgt. Gene Gaskins, trainee B-24 gunner

'Despite the intensive training at Wendover, there was still an occasional moment for recreation. Some relaxed at the State Line Hotel, where half the bar was in Utah and half in Nevada. When midnight closed Utah, the bar patrons simply moved a few steps west. There were nurses to be impressed in Elko, Nevada. [In those days a buzz-job in a B-17 had a way of attracting a lady's attention!] Those unmarried and in search of excitement had to travel the 120 miles to Salt Lake City, or go west to Kimberley, Nevada.'
'First Over Germany', Russell A. Strong, 306th BG

'He was flying a light bomber somewhere in the States and had a forced landing outside Syracuse. This time he allowed the mechanics to work on the trouble and went into town for a meal. While he was there he suddenly remembered he once knew a girl in an office nearby, so he called her up. In exactly 90 minutes he had proposed to her and they were married. He saw his bride for exactly eight hours! After that he flew away and before he could return, his Liberator group was heading across the North Atlantic for Britain – and the war. He didn't mind that. He figured that night that with any luck he would soon complete his operational war missions and get a chance to go home for instruction work.'
Arch Whitehouse, writing in 'True Magazine' about Capt. John B. McCormick, 389th BG pilot

possessions they could get in. They were at the gate the morning we left the States to tell their husbands good-bye. Donis Campbell was the only one of the five to have her husband return.'
Howard E. Hernan, gunner, 303rd BG

'Pvt. John Doe, after a long and tiresome journey, the last part of which was across "No Man's Land" (the Great Salt Lake desert), arrives at a railroad station at the west extremity of Utah, at perhaps nine a.m. He glances curiously out of the coach, and it's not the train that makes him wonder, "What in hell have I done to deserve this?"'
Sgt. Marshall E. Baker, first squadron clerk for the 368th BS, 'First Over Germany', by Russell A. Strong, 306th BG

'Off we go into the wild blue yonder,
Climbing High, into the sun.
Here they come, zooming to meet our thunder,
At 'em boys, give 'er the gun.
Down we dive, spouting flame from under,
Off with one hell of a roar.
We live in fame, or go down in flame,
For, nothing can stop the US Air Corps.'

The US Air Corps Song

Wendover Field wasn't the kind of base that you might look forward to being assigned to. (USAF Official)

'In January 1944, we wallowed in latrine rumours about what theatre we would go to – England or Italy, or, some said, Norway.'
Allan Healy, 467th BG

'Satisfied with the formation flying, the POM inspectors gave the go ahead signal and in a few days all 'planes were on the way to Morrison Field, West Palm Beach, Florida, which was the shoving-off base.'
Allan Healy, 467th BG

'Many crews added weight to their 'planes by loading on cases of the plentiful native rum, and the not so plentiful Scotch and bourbon.'
Allan Healy, 467th BG

SECRET

Note: THIS ENVELOPE CONTAINS SECRET DESTINATION ORDERS FOR THE ABOVE NAMED PERSONNEL AND IS NOT TO BE OPENED UNTIL ONE (1) HOUR AFTER DEPARTURE FROM THE CONTINENTAL UNITED STATES. THE DOCUMENTS CONTAINED HEREIN ARE TO BE SAFEGUARDED IN ACCORDANCE WITH AR 380-5.

'The crew came together at MacDill AFB, Tampa, Florida and we went to Savannah, Georgia, to pick up a brand new B-17. After picking up all the kit in an assembly line process, we took off at two a.m. We went to Bangor, Maine, stayed there a day, and then on to England via Labrador. A tremendous storm at Goose Bay set in. Winds blew at 100 kts

Satisfied with the formation flying, the POM inspectors gave the go ahead signal. (the late Allan Healy)

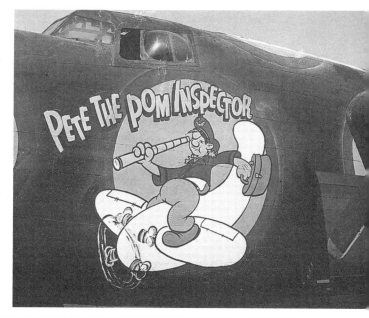

Marrakech has a unique history. Its walls were built with the remains of thousands of captives whose bodies were thrown into the lime kilns and baked into bricks that served as fortifications. (Col. William Cameron)

and blew two B-17s into the sea. Then on to Bluey West 3 at Greenland. At the end of the runway abutted a 1,000-ft glacier. We stayed there a week until the storm abated. We played poker, slept, and ate. We had to use a rope between our barracks and the Mess hall in order to stop us being blown away. We then flew on to Keflavik, Iceland, on to Valley, Wales, and our 'plane was taken from us. The crew was assigned to various bomb groups.'
John A. Holden, navigator, 452nd BG

'After crossing the Equator, right on the banks of the Amazon River, the next stop was Belm, Brazil, where all personnel below the grade of field officer were restricted to the base. From Belm, part of the 'planes flew to Fortaleza and others to Natal where most crew members acquired a pair of the well-known Natal boots, and bought stockings to be mailed home to wives and girl friends.'
Allan Healy, 467th BG

'We were laying on our bunks in the barracks and someone said: "Dopko's crew went down today on their first mission." Flight Officer Dopko's crew were our room mates and had flown a B-17 over the African route. Replacement crews always had brand new equipment, plus Dopko's had a much cherished item: custom-made leather boots from Africa. There was a mad scramble as 25 men reached for the brand new equipment and the leather boots.'
Larry Goldstein, radio operator, 388th BG

'From Marrakech to Prestwick, Scotland; Valley, Wales, and Mawgan, Wales, crews kept guns loaded and maintained a sharp watch for German planes as they skirted Portugal and Spain and passed by the Brest Peninsula.'
Allan Healy, 467th BG

'March 7 1944: All set to fly to England. We were to fly up past Spain, Portugal and France and into England. Take-off was at 23:45 hrs. At altitude it soon became colder as we neared the northern climes, so out came our woollies. The navigator had to make sure he stayed on his meridian. Too far east, and Jerry might come up and give us a going over. Too far west, and we are liable to run out of fuel.'
Philip H. Meistrich, 453rd BG

'The day we brought our *Snoozy II* in, the English tower master said on open radio: "I say there, American aircraft, this is your field; you are cleared to land." Lord Haw Haw must have been listening, for that night on radio he said: "Welcome to England, 306th Group!"'
Al La Chasse, bombardier, 306th BG

'Over There, Over There,
We're going over, Over There.'

OVER HERE

'All our past errors, all our omissive sins,
Must be wiped out. This war no nation wins.
Remember that when you are over here.'

Lines to An American Officer. Noël Coward

'The first thing I recall on arrival was checking into our squadron living site and the hut which was to be home for the next year or more. I noticed that someone was cutting off a piece of the beams in the hut to make firewood.'
S/Sgt. Forrest S. Clark, gunner, 67th BS, 44th BG

'These lines are dedicated to a man
I met in Glasgow, an American.
He was an Army officer, not old,
In the late twenties. If the truth were told
A great deal younger than he thought he was.
I mention this ironically because,
After we'd had a drink or two, he said
Something so naive, so foolish, that I fled.
This was December, Nineteen Forty-Two.
He said: "We're here to win the war for you."'

Lines to An American Officer. Noël Coward

'When we arrived at our Quonsett hut at Deopham Green, so many officers had been killed there was no room to hang our clothes. One door was blocked with piles of uniforms. In the interim, our crew borrowed a wheelchair from supply and moved clothing and footlockers out. It took us two days to empty the barracks.'
John A. Holden, navigator, 731st BS, 452nd BG

'We arrived April 11th with three other crews. Later in the Mess Hall we learned that four crews failed to return on this day from Poznan, Poland. Such news to hear on arrival. For the month of April, 25 crews were lost. What would our fate be?'
Wilbur Richardson, gunner, 94th BG

'Finally, it was our turn. We did not fly to our base, we took the train from Bovingdon to a station near Molesworth and were ignominiously carried there in trucks. When we came to our squadron area, we were not greeted by the familiar, "You'll be sorry," which was the customary greeting on Stateside.The men we saw gave us only a few incurious

When we arrived at our Quonsett hut at Deopham Green so many officers had been killed there was no room to hang our clothes. (Alfred R. Lea)

glances and said nothing to us. Our hearts sank. We were assigned a barracks shared by two or three other crews. Six empty cots gaped at us. These had been occupied by a crew that had not returned from the mission the day before. We were not prepared for this sobering reality.

In progress was a non-stop poker game. The players did not look up or acknowledge our presence in any way. (Bill Robertie)

'In progress was a non-stop poker game. The players did not look up or acknowledge our presence in any way. We were accorded a few glum nods from some others who were lying in their sacks reading. About that time the door flew open and a bevy of uproarious drunks fell inside. It was the lead crew – Lt. Brinkley's crew. I had seen many drunks but this was a different kind of drunkenness. These men were veterans of the great missions of Schweinfurt and Oschersleben. They had seen too much and it showed. I had the sudden feeling that things were far different from what I had been led to believe. I was right.

'We were not referred to as Lt. Cecchini's crew. Instead, we were called the "new crew", which continued to be our status until we had flown about eight combat missions. New crews were given the most vulnerable places in the formation and had a way of disappearing after a few missions. We heartily resented this callous treatment, but after winning our spurs, we were as bad as the rest.'
Ben Smith Jr., radio operator, 360th BS, 303rd BG

'When we asked, "Why the empty beds?" we were told they were left by the men who had gone down recently. This was rather discouraging.'
Larry Goldstein, radio operator, 388th BG

'We settled in. We were restricted the first month until we became operational. We learned to drink warm English beer and "cyder" at the Officers' and NCO clubs. We sang around the piano about Pete the POM Inspector. We learned about English money – a little. It always seemed as if a pound note was a dollar and in poker and dice games pounds were flipped about like confetti. It was cold – the wet North Sea cold that was as nothing we had experienced before. It cut through six blankets at night and lay about the small coke stoves like wolves about a dying doe. We struggled and sweated over those stoves to warm, in part, our huts. It took an hour with wood to get the coke started and aglow, and the wood had to be stolen somewhere first.'
Allan Healy, 467th BG

We learned to drink warm English beer and 'cyder' at the Officers' and NCO Clubs. (Rackheath Memories)

It always seemed as if a pound note was a dollar and in poker and dice games pounds were flipped about like confetti. (Rackheath Memories)

'The quarters did receive a ration of coal for the fires. We all, or most of us, including myself, wore warm socks even in bed and were seldom without them. The floor was always wet. Yet the dampness seeped into the beds and into the quarters and the wind across the Norfolk Broads and the Fens rattled against the huts. The cold was the same damp chill that invades the English cathedrals and in a country without central heating in the 1940s, it was most difficult to avoid.'
Forrest S. Clark, gunner, 67th BS, 44th BG

'Around 3,000 men arriving in our small village, all with film star accents and many with suntans. I am only glad I was a small child at the time!'
Patricia Everson

'The weather is going to be very hard to get used to. It's very damp and you seldom see the sun . . . '
USAAF Sgt. in a letter to his wife in California, October 1944

'We were a little suspicious of them at first, but they seemed to take to children . . . they gave me a set of sergeant's stripes, (which I wore on the arm of my raincoat), and a flying helmet . . . '
Pat Ramm, Old Buckenham schoolboy

The wet North Sea cold . . . was as nothing we had experienced before. It cut through six blankets at night and lay about the small coke stoves like wolves about a dying doe. (Floyd H. Mabee [seated, left])

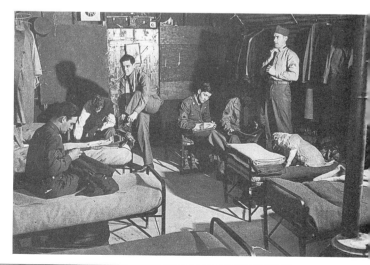

Left: *Around 3,000 men arriving in our small village, all with film star accents and many with suntans. I am only glad I was a small child at the time! (Pat Everson)*

Below: *The weather is going to be very hard to get used to. It's very damp and you seldom see the sun. (392nd BG)*

Bottom: *We were a little suspicious of them at first, but they seemed to take to children (Pat Ramm centre, with stripes). (USAF Official)*

'There used to be a gnome-like Irishman who came around to the barracks with fresh eggs for sale. One night he appeared with a bottle of Jameson's Irish whiskey, which he sold us for $10. After he had gone, we poured ourselves a drink in our mess cups and, to our chagrin, found out it was cold tea. Needless to say we never saw the little Irishman again.'
George M. Collar, 445th BG

'We were treated like long-lost relatives. They didn't have much, but they cooked eggs and toast and made a pot of tea. The tea kettle hung on a hook over a raised stone hearth, which contained a peat fire.'
George M. Collar, 445th BG

'I travelled to Aberdeen, Scotland on a three-day pass to see my grandparents, whom I had not seen since I was four. How their eyes lit up when I had

unpacked 5 lb of sugar, a large tin of Spam and three pounds of butter – through the courtesy of a friendly mess sergeant. They hadn't seen food like that since wartime rationing started in 1940.'
Douglas D. Walker, 'Carpetbaggers'

'The old men of the village were standing around the pubs, hands up to their mouths: "The Yanks are coming, have you heard?", "I suppose you've heard them old Yankees are coming," and similar comments punctuated their games of darts, skittles or pints of beer. "They'll be after our women – they are all oversexed." The men seemed despondent.'
Connie Richards, Bedfordshire teenager

'You people were brave and so very hospitable to us "Yanks".'
Al Steller, 709th BS, 447th BG

'First came the GI trucks and jeeps, then we started seeing the Americans themselves, good-looking men in uniforms. "What will life be like now," I thought. "Maybe I'll marry one of them when I grow up and go to live in America." They were good to us then, as we were the 'Chewing Gum Kids'. One of the Americans used to come to my home for dinner and my mother did washing for them.'
Connie Richards, Bedfordshire teenager

Malcolm Smith the maltster, who had been bombed out of his house in East Dereham, invited us for dinner almost every Saturday night. We would bring oranges and butter, etc. He would always have Scotch salmon, partridge and other unrationed food. He had a plentiful supply of Scotch and a unique cellar of old wines. He loved to talk. He lived in a house near the airfield at Attlebridge.'
Lt. Col. George H. Parker, Station Engineer, 466th BG

'I had never seen an orange before and didn't know what to make of it.'
George Evans, on receiving an orange from WAAC Mary Frances Elder at Ketteringham Hall

'One lecture that stands out was the one on the evils of VD. This was a Flight Surgeon giving the talk who said, flat out, "avoid all sex". He paused, then said: "Now after you've done it, here is how you use your profolactics." '
Lt. John W. McClane Jr., navigator, 44th BG

First came the GI trucks and jeeps, then we started seeing the Americans themselves, good looking men in uniforms. (Col. William B. Cameron, 44th BG)

'After the drab colours of the camouflaged RAF bombers, the Liberators with their different colours seemed fantastic to us boys. Being a school which took boys from all over the city, we had quite an intelligence service. Hardly a 'plane took off, or crashed, without us knowing about it. If we knew they'd set off on a mission from St. Faith's in the morning, we wouldn't go home after school. We'd cycle straight to the base to watch them come back. We were old enough to know what was going on, but not old enough to have to worry about it. It was all excitement as far as we were concerned.'
Tony North, Norwich schoolboy

'Our house was directly on the flight path as they took off, mostly each day on their bombing missions in Europe. I used to watch them go out – each one painted with a figure of a girl or other symbol and barely clearing our chimney pots as they flew out.'
Neville Firman

'Watching Liberators going up in the mornings on missions, with pencil and paper I would make a list of each one. Then, watching them return home in the evenings, sadly not all were ticked off my list to return.'
Beryl M. Sutton

'Early in the mornings we would hear the drone of the 'planes overhead as they assembled, layer upon layer, ready for their attack on the enemy. When they returned, often shot to pieces and limping home with sometimes only one engine left functioning, our thoughts would be with those men.'
May Ayers

'Remember I'm a Britisher.
I know my country's faults. Its rather slow,
Superior assumptions; its aloof
Convictions in its destiny. The proof
Of its true qualities. I also know –
This lies much deeper. When we stood alone,
Besieged for one long agonising year,

When they returned, often shot to pieces and limping home with sometimes only one engine left functioning, our thoughts would be with those men. (the late Allan Healy)

The only bulwark in our hemisphere
Defying tyranny, in this was shown
The temper of our people. Don't forget
That lonely year. It isn't lease or lend,
Or armaments, or speeches that defend
The principles of living. There's no debt
Between your land and mine except that year.'

Lines to An American Officer. Noël Coward

THE MISSION

'They were scheduled a mission to fly,
The crew was unhappy for they were sure to die.
With a grunt and a groan it took to the air,
and those on the ground all whispered a prayer.'

'The barracks are dark. Each man was in his bed and knows there is a mission today because we had been alerted the night before. At 3:30 a.m. the light is switched on. The CQ reads off the names of the crews for the mission and adds, the briefing

100 Octane fuel between you and the pilot plus eight 500-lb HE bombs in the same compartment. We wondered what made us join the Air Corps. (the late Allan Healy)

is at 06:00.'
Larry Goldstein, radio operator, 388th BG

'There were many cigarettes glowing in the dark. There was not much sleeping going on. In the early hours of 18 April the door flew open and this cheery CQ named "Fluke" came in, switched on the lights and started calling off the crews who were to fly on the day's mission. He yelled, "Cecchini's Crew!" and my heart sank within me. I felt like a condemned man.'
Ben Smith, 360th BS, 303rd BG

'Breakfast at 04.30.
Briefing at 05.00.
Start Engines at 05.30.
Taxi out at 06.00.
Take-off at 06.30.
What's the gas' load?
"Thirty-one hundred gallons!"'
'That is the gallonage we did not like to hear. It meant a long and rough mission. And bomb-bay tanks. Five hundred and fifty gallons of 100 Octane fuel between you and the pilot plus eight 500-lb HE bombs in the same compartment. We

wondered what made us join the Air Corps.'
Russ D. Hayes, gunner, 389th BG

'What a life. Up at 14.00 and the only sleep we got was in the afternoons and also, we were only getting two meals a day.'
Howard Herman, 92nd BG

'We tumble out of a warm bed, dress warmly, shave in cold water and board a GI truck in darkness to the Mess Halls for a breakfast we are not sure we can eat because of our nervous stomachs. Each man was wondering, "Will we make it back today?"'
Larry Goldstein, radio operator, 388th BG

'I soon learned to shave close because high-altitude flying necessitates an oxygen mask and facial hairs can cause a good deal of irritation. Also, it could get awfully cold. The temperature varied from a −10 to a 70. Because of this there was little or no food or water. Our "blue bunny" heated suits did not always work efficiently.'
Wilbur Richardson, gunner, 94th BG

'We donned our flying coveralls, heated suits and boots and headed to the Mess Hall down the road where the cooks were putting on a mission breakfast. The chefs were very solicitous − seemingly

We donned our flying coveralls, heated suits and boots. (Frank Thomas)

sion, and I found their jollity very disquieting and out of place. I could eat none of the breakfast anyway. Even to this day I have butterflies before breakfast.'
Ben Smith, radio operator, 303rd BG

'The thoughts of what awaits me in the Officers' Mess is not heart-warming. Those same damned powdered eggs, cooked three tons at a time, the greasy bacon that would slide off a gravel driveway and that steaming black coffee with the hard English rolls. Oh well, I bet the Roman gladiators were fed better than this "but there's a war on Mac."'
Lt. Robert L. Ferrell, 20-year-old lead navigator, 458th BG

'Combat crews were entitled to bacon and fried eggs on the morning of a mission, but there were

jovial. We could have pancakes, eggs sunny side up, or any way we wanted them. Sort of like, "It's your last meal – you can have what you want."
'To me it seemed a somewhat macabre occa-

The chefs were very solicitous – seemingly jovial. We could have pancakes, eggs sunny side up, or any way we wanted them. Sort of like, 'It's your last meal – you can have what you want.' (Rackheath Memories)

not enough to go around. Sometimes we had powdered eggs and if they had been prepared right you couldn't tell the difference.'
Howard E. Hernan, gunner, 303rd BG

'The Mess Hall seemed virtually empty as we had our usual breakfast of dried eggs, spam, coffee, toast and good old orange marmalade with vast amounts of good American butter to go on that wonderful dark English bread.'
Lt. Bob Hughes, pilot, 100th BG

'At six a.m., tired crew members assembled at squadron briefing. A white sheet covered the wall at the far end of the room. Behind its cleanness was a map of Europe and our dirty work for the day. Hopefully, we prayed, it was a short run to France. Allied armies were on the outskirts of Paris and, just maybe, they needed some help. After Brux, we needed a break.'
Richard Bing, radio operator, 561st BS, 388th BG

Sometimes, we had powdered eggs and if they had been prepared right you couldn't tell the difference. (USAF Official)

'I saw the room-size map of Europe on the front wall. There was a red ribbon on the map, held by pins, showing the route to be flown. The target on the map was Dresden. I had never heard of that German city before.'
William C. Stewart, a ball turret gunner in the 92nd BG

'To say the least, shivers always ran up and down our spines to see this mission appear on the map. Like Schweinfurt and others, this was the one mission one could count one's blessings if you returned unharmed.'
Herman L. Hager, 398th BG Nutty Hussy, describing a mission to Meresburg

'All of the crews, officers and non-commissioned officers, were briefed together. The radio operators were also given a separate briefing, at which time they received a canvas packet with coded data in it called a "flimsy". In the main briefing hall, the target remained covered until the Intelligence Officer came in. He was a dapper individual, sporting a moustache, and quite hearty in manner – for a good reason: he didn't have to go. These

Left: *I saw the room-size map of Europe on the front wall. There was a red ribbon on the map, held by pins, showing the route to be flown.* (Ray Betcher)

Below: *At the revetment while we waited to board our aircraft, all of us constantly watched for a flare shot from the control tower scrubbing the mission.* (Author's Collection)

Bottom: *We were on board and soon taxiing out in trail until we reached the end of the runway.* (USAF Official)

Intelligence Officers were non-flying personnel with some useful information and a lot more that was useless.

'His first move was to peel back the cover from the map, which act was always met with a loud groan from the assembled crews. They were a lively bunch, and time had to be allowed for them to get over the initial shock, sound off, and cuss a little while. After a time they subsided and he began. We could see that the red lines pinned on the map went deep into Germany. The target was the Heinkel plant at Oranienburg in the suburbs of Berlin. We were told we could expect heavy fighter opposition, with flak at the target described as "intense." In other words, the target was heavily defended.

'We could see from the diagram that we were flying "Tail-end Charlie" in the high squadron. There would be a lead squadron and a high squadron.

'Briefing over, we got up and started out. We climbed onto lorries and headed out for the hardstands where the Forts were parked. The ground crews swarmed over our B-17 getting it ready. The armourers were arming the bombs in the bomb bay. It was still pitch dark.

'We put our machine guns into their casings and attached the gun belts. When this was done, we went to the dispersal tent and lay down on the canvas cots which were there for that purpose. We tried to log a little sack time before "Start Engines". The signal for this was a red flare from the control tower.

'These quiet moments in the dispersal tent were always the worst part of the mission for me. I was always inflicted with an unbearable sadness at this time. I can still hear the clanking coughs of the aircraft engines as they struggled manfully in the damp mist and then caught up.'
Ben Smith, radio operator, 303rd BG

'At the revetment while we waited to board our aircraft, all of us constantly watched for a flare shot from the control tower scrubbing the mission. It never came.'
Larry Goldstein, radio operator, 388th BG

'We were on board and soon taxiing out in trail until we reached the end of the runway. Every 30 seconds a Fort would gun its engines and hurtle down the runway into the black darkness. Finally, it was our time. We always sweated take-off as we were heavily laden with gas and bombs.

'We climbed through the mist on a certain heading until we reached a predetermined altitude. At 10,000 ft, Chick told us to go on oxygen. Thereafter, we had periodic oxygen checks with each position checking in. We learned the value of this on a later mission when the ball turret gunner did not check in. We pulled him out of the turret unconscious and almost dead. His hose had become disconnected.

'During all this time there was complete radio silence, as the German interceptor stations were monitoring constantly. Looking back, I doubt if we ever fooled them. The planners would go to extreme lengths to conceal the mounting of a mission, but I doubt if they could conceal something of that magnitude. I imagine the Germans had ample notice from their own agents in England of every mission we flew. I don't remember their ever being asleep when I visited Germany.'
Ben Smith, radio operator, 303rd BG

'We took off in beautiful CAVU weather topped with high cirrus clouds. On VHF I heard a weird chatter unfamiliar to me. Phrases like "Fireball," "Vampire Violet," "Clambake Yellow," "Hotshot Red," (our group code) and "Rotate" (our squadron code) badgered the radio waves. As we assembled over the "splashers" and "bunchers" the sky became dotted with coloured flares, signals and doubles, while hundreds of aircraft tacked on to flights, squadrons and groups. Finally, after more than an hour of forming, we took our place at the lead of the 4th Combat Wing and proceeded at 150 m.p.h. indicated airspeed. Our fighter escort of P-47s and P-38s picked us up just north of Imjuiden on the Dutch coast. There were no reports of enemy fighters as we turned at the IP and opened our bomb bay doors for the bomb run. From the IP onward there was absolutely no evasive action.

'So far I was fine. It was a bright, clear day marred only by the contrails of the bombers ahead of us in formation. I can recall a certain amount of exhilaration and pride. The great battle formations were something to see! As far as the eye could see there were B-17s, some of them olive drab F's, others the new silver G's.'
Ben Smith, radio operator, 303rd BG

'I recalled at briefing that we were told we would be the last group in. We had crossed the Zeider Zee. I observed large formations of aircraft forming to the rear. I called the navigator:
"Aren't we supposed to be the last group in?"
'He said: "Yes."

'I said: "Someone is lost or we are in for a lot of trouble."'
Henry C. Cordery, 423rd BS, 306th BG

'He that outlives this day and comes safe home
Will stand a tip-toe when this day is named
And rouse him at the name of Crispian.'
Henry V

'The 11th of each month always seemed to be my day for missions. I was picked to fly with a new crew that had just arrived at Polebrook. This was usually standard procedure to take a new pilot and his crew on their first mission. We went to Arniswalde, Germany, which was our secondary target near the Polish border. We flew at 15,000 ft, descending to 12,000 ft at the target. That gave the German anti-aircraft gunners a field day. They got their share of B-17s over Hannover. Bombers were blowing up, burning and falling out of

It did keep me occupied, however. Just before 'Bombs Away' a moving shadow caused me to look up and through the open radio hatch. A bomber had moved directly above us. Horrified, I was looking directly into his bomb bay. (Cliff Hatcher)

control all around us. We all got scared as hell when a four-inch piece of flak came right through the nose and cut the oxygen line on the right side. The whooshing sound of the escaping oxygen under pressure made plenty of noise.

'The new pilot grabbed the controls from me and about pulled us out of formation in panic. I almost had to beat his hands off the yoke. I told him that if we did get out of formation by ourselves the enemy fighters would be on us like a pack of wolves. Some of our crew members had to use portable oxygen bottles after losing half our supply. Enemy fighters did not bother us although we could see other groups under heavy attack.'
Joe Wroblewski, pilot, 351st BG, 11 April 1944

'. . . I heard it before I saw it. Whomp-Whoosh. Simultaneously, the bombardier shouted, "Flak, 12 o'clock. Christ look at it!" 'By then we were at the IP and turning on the bomb run. A rush of cold air blasted the radio room as the bomb bay doors came open. The 'plane began to lurch and reel with the continuous explosions. Now I could see it. Oily, black bursts with crimson blossoms in the centre. Everywhere there were literally thousands of bursts as far as the eye could see. I was throwing chaff out of the chute. I couldn't see that it did any good at all. They had our range perfectly. It did keep me occupied, however.

'Just before "Bombs Away" a moving shadow caused me to look up and through the open radio hatch. A bomber had moved directly above us. Horrified, I was looking directly into his bomb bay. I called Chick and we slid over in the nick of time. The bomber lurched as the bombs went away. I stood up in the door of the bomb bay to see if the bombs had all gotten clear. As soon as I did, a jagged piece of shrapnel sliced the command radio set in two and struck me directly in the chest. I was wearing a metal flak vest which was all that saved my life. It spun me around and stunned me momentarily. I saw that I was bleeding. A piece of spent metal had lodged in my neck, and this was where the blood was coming from. I was not badly hurt and I felt no pain at all, but I had had a close shave.'
Ben Smith, radio operator, 303rd BG

'My ears began to ring from the engine noise. Either the extreme cold at −40°C or the tension caused me to pass water frequently. I discovered that no-one used the relief tube in the bomb bay for two good reasons. First, the trip with an oxygen bottle was too much and second, if one

We saw the flak before we spotted the target. The 88 mm explosions looked like double black mushrooms as though the shell exploded in the middle and worked itself out at both ends vertically. (the late Russ D. Hayes)

used it but did not notify the ball turret gunner to rotate at six o'clock, his windscreen was very neatly frosted. We used empty bomb fuse containers, with which we were very generously supplied by the armourer-gunners. The filled cans froze quickly, then they were stacked alongside a bulkhead until they were thrown out during the bomb run.

'We saw the flak before we spotted the target. The 88 mm explosions looked like double black mushrooms, as though the shell exploded in the middle and worked itself out at both ends vertically. The railroad marshalling yards at Hamm, the choke-point to "Happy Valley," was $3\frac{1}{2}$ miles long, the largest in Germany; so large that we bombed in combat wing formation – three groups abreast. Flak was not too accurate and we were lucky to be the first over the target. Our bombs blanketed the yard; only a few appeared to go astray.

'As we turned off to the rally point, I looked toward five o'clock and saw a sky full of flak with two B-17s in trouble, one in a shallow dive afire and the other exploding after a short vertical dive. I watched several parachutes descend to German soil, then looked for my chest pack – it was not within reach. I made a note to stack it between my position and the emergency hatch against the bulkhead next to my navigation table. The trip

back was uneventful, the 94th suffering no losses.'
Abe Dolim, navigator, 94th BG, 22 April 1944

The railroad marshalling yards at Hamm, the chokepoint to 'Happy Valley,' was $3\frac{1}{2}$ miles long, the largest in Germany. (Ray Betcher, 467th BG)

Above: When we got home we found that we were one of only five ... to return. (Art Livingston, 446th BG)

Below: My first mission – holding out the cup of coffee and trying to smile. I was so scared you wouldn't ... smile back. (USAF Official)

'On the way home we had some more excitement. We strayed over Brunswick which was not on our itinerary and got flakked again. We eventually crossed the enemy coast and started letting down from altitude. It was a relief to take off the oxygen mask and relax for a bit. I ate a Clark bar and felt better at once. We had been on oxygen for about eight hours.

'The hydraulic system was damaged; so we knew we were going to have some problems getting down. Fortunately, we were using the long runway. We touched down; after slowing a bit, Chick headed her off the runway onto the grass. We circled to the right, kept circling, slowing gradually; and finally she gave up the ghost and stopped. We got out and looked her over. It was unbelievable. She was one more lacerated lady. That morning she had been a lovely girl without a blemish. The ground crews could do wonders with a shot-up B-17, but they had their work cut out for them with that one. Sometimes, when one was shot up too badly, they made her a "hangar queen" and cannibalized parts off her. I remember the ground crew laid some rueful looks on us.'
Ben Smith, radio operator, 303rd BG

'When we got home we found that we were one of only five B-17s to return to Thorpe Abbotts. We had lost 15 airplanes. To say the least, we were upset, as was everyone on the base. Col. Turner, the Squadron Commander, met us as we parked the airplane. He was in tears. Most of the losses had been from his squadron. It was hard to take, but this was what we had been trained for.'
Robert Shoens, pilot of Our Gal' Sal, *100th BG*

'When we returned, the left waist gunner, a bombardier from another crew on his last mission, hit the ground, kissing it.'
Lloyd Murff, pilot, 491st BG

'My first mission – holding out the cup of coffee and trying to smile. I was so scared you wouldn't want to smile back. I remember straining to see through the clouds, counting. Then trying not to let anyone see me wipe away a tear when the last one appeared.'
Mary Carroll Leeds, American Red Cross girl, Attlebridge, June 1944 to May 1945

'Oh, this is number ten,
And we're at it once again.
Roll me over,
Lay me down,

And do it again.'

'When I stand on some old abandoned runway or control tower and look out across an English flying field or old base I hear many sounds, engines warming up, the squeal of landing wheels and the roar of take-offs. However, above all these sounds there are the faint words of a song that comes back with the wind across the English fields like a whisper from our youth. That song, a favourite of bomber crews, still haunts me and is to me the essence of my combat flying experience in World War Two. We would be coming back from a mission, tired, disgusted, many times ill from the cold and high-altitude flying. Suddenly, over the intercom, silent on most returns from a mission, we would hear a voice starting with the words, "Roll me over, roll me over, lay me down and do it again ... "'
Forrest S. Clark, gunner, 67th BS, 44th BG

'Your Son, my Lord, has paid a soldier's debt;
He only lived but 'till he was a man;
The which no sooner had his prowess confirmed
In the unshrinking station where he fought,
But like a man he died.'

William Shakespeare

BOYS IN THE SKY

'Our thoughts go back to long ago
When you came over to fight the foe
Some old, some young, some in between
Good looking guys in uniform green
Your way of life had us in whirls
Let alone the hearts of English girls
You flew your missions and then departed
So many were left broken hearted
As memories drift and years roll by
You're still thought of as Boys in the Sky'

Pedar Larsen, 96th BG

'They were wonderful boys. At first we weren't sure what to expect. But in a few weeks it was like having one big family. They didn't like our bitter to start with, but they soon got used to it. It was

They were wonderful boys. (USAF Official)

the same with darts. Most had never played before so we had to teach them. Then it became their game. Our pub is in the path of what they called "Bomber Alley". All the 'planes used to fly overhead to get to the airfield after bombing the Germans. But not one of our "regular" boys got killed. One 'plane went down in Switzerland, but they all got back later. The nearest thing we came to losing anybody was Scottie. We were all sitting around with long faces when we heard that he hadn't got back to the airfield. Nobody had a drink. Nobody spoke. It was like a funeral. Then the door burst open and in walked Scottie with a huge bunch of carnations. All he said was, "I'm back". Some of the boys married the local girls they were going out with.

They came in no uncertain fashion, with their jeeps, their superior uniforms, their big mouths, their big hearts. (William B. Cameron [left])

But most of the evenings we spent round the piano singing all the old songs like ''Roll out the Barrel'' and ''Daisy, Daisy''.'
The late Mrs Daisy Elmar, with her husband Jimmy, publicans of the Three Nags *at Fritton, Norfolk in the Second World War*

'They came in no uncertain fashion, with their jeeps, their superior uniforms, their big mouths, their big hearts.'
George Greengrass, a soldier at Gibraltar Barracks, Bury St. Edmunds

---

'There was a faint drumming in the air, a far-off buzzing and we knew they were coming. When the Yanks arrived us youngsters stood open-mouthed as these huge aircraft filled the skies overhead. The noise was tremendous, it was very daunting and quite an awesome sight. We hopped on our bikes and rode off following them to the airfield, to their dispersal point. The end of the aircraft opened as it landed and these crewmen threw out chewing gum and candies for us. They had heard these terrible stories that the English were starving and on rations; we didn't mind playing on it a little bit. Then they threw out a bundle of 10-shilling notes and there was a right free for all.'
12-year-old Jim Matsell on the arrival, at Deopham Green, of the 452nd BG in January 1944

'When the Fortresses came back we saw them taking out the guns and we used to have the chance to climb in as long as there were no wounded aboard ... All the fliers were really friendly and used to give us gum and sweets, but we also got to be good friends with the ground crew. They had to camp out near the planes and not leave the base. Sometimes we used to nip to the Cherry Tree pub and fetch a jug of beer for them.'
Alan Cooper, Eye schoolboy

'Those boys used to come to our house at any time. They knew where my mother left her spare key and would let themselves into the house knowing that my parents would never mind. They called No. 79 their Norwich home. I had a lovely 21st birthday party at home, which wouldn't have been possible without the little luxuries they sneaked from their bases.'
Muriel Lawrence

'We would meet the local people in the pub and

All the fliers were really friendly and used to give us gum and sweets, but we also got to be good friends with the ground crew.

there were ladies who would do our laundry, and everyone was just as gracious as could be.'
Wilbur Clingan, 453rd BG Operations Officer

'I remember Giroux, a bomb loader from Chicago, who ''liberated'' a large can of fruit cocktail from the canteen for me (I cycled home with it expecting at any moment to be stopped by a stern policeman – or worse still, a ''Snowdrop''!).'
Marjorie Adams

'A great many families in the city used to have Americans to stay with them at weekends. We had one called 'Joe'. He would play football with us in the street and sleep in our Morrison shelter. He'd bring with him a supply of tins of food. They never had labels so we never knew what we were going to find until we opened the cans.'
Tony North, Norwich schoolboy

'We were organizing Saving Week for the benefit of the war. My wife was secretary. We invited local folk to give all kinds of articles which I would

I visited Flixton airfield as a humble 16-year-old with two friends – an ATC cadet and another naval cadet ... and, after a casual word with the Snowdrop at the guard post, we ... were assigned ... a flight. (Author's Collection)

auction in the village hall. On one occasion I auctioned a duck and twice a little boy bought it, but his father wouldn't let him have it. So I put it up again and a Yank bought it. He said: "If the little boy wants it, he shall have it." '
J. Gogle

'Life at Old Buckenham was good for a while, but then "Dear John" letters started arriving from wives who had got fed up with waiting. I got mine

They stood me on an ammo box and taught me how to strip down the .50 calibre guns. It got so I could do it with my eyes closed. (Russell Foster)

on Thanksgiving Day 1944. My morale dropped sharply. Of 36 men in my barracks, 14 received "Dear Johns". I was lucky in a way as I had no children. The older men had pictures of their children by their bunks and they lived for the daily mail call.'
Melvin Borne, 453rd BG

'I visited Flixton airfield as a humble 16-year-old naval cadet with two friends – an ATC cadet and another naval cadet. We had cycled from Lowestoft and, after a casual word with the Snowdrop at the guard post, we proceeded to the control tower and were assigned to a flight on B-24 *Little King* (pilot, F. G. Drake). 'After several hours, we returned in late evening, too late to return home, having no lights. We were shown to the mess hut where food such as we had never seen was on offer. We were driven in a jeep to a hut with 10 empty beds (a missing crew).

'Next day, after eggs, bacon and hash browns, we took off again in *Hustling Hussy* (pilot M.O. Reid), for another long flight. Memorable days, great guys! The courtesy and generosity the three of us received will never be forgotten.'
Les Skitterall, ATC cadet

'The crew of this aircraft which had been shot at

We wonder if they're mice or men/Decided they're wolves, we avoid the den. (Ray Betcher, 467th BG)

on its mission had bailed out apart from the pilot, who nursed it back to Metfield. When he got out of the 'plane after he landed safely, he just cried.'
Brian Easthaugh, Suffolk schoolboy

'They stood me on an ammo box and taught me how to strip down the .50 calibre guns. It got so I could do it with my eyes closed. I also had rides in a Liberator around the taxiway from the hangar to the hardstands. Sometimes I was allowed to sit in the gun turrets and rotate them.'
11-year-old Russell Foster, whose house bordered Old Buckenham airfield and the 732nd BS area

ANGELS WITH DIRTY FACES

'Yankee officers cause us to smile,
With their light pants, you see them for miles,
We wonder if they're mice or men,
Decided they're wolves, we avoid the den.'

The GIs, *by a WAAF at Shipdham*

'When the Americans arrived, they became my heroes ... I decided that GIs were the closest

thing to angels I'd ever met.'
Ann K. Spredbury, Norwich schoolgirl

'Instead of doing our homework, we would sit at the runway threshold in the evenings and at weekends, and watch the bombers land. We were called "little limeys". I got to know three crews in the 730th very well. They were billeted in the field across from my parents' house. One hut had paintings of a B-17 and half-naked women on the walls behind their beds. My friend, Pfc Dave

My friend, Pfc Dave Roberts, an armourer in the 730th Squadron, was a great artist. He painted names on the B-17s and drew my portrait, complete with lieutenant's forage cap. (Pfc Dave Roberts, 730th BS, 452nd BG)

Roberts, an armourer in the 730th Squadron, was a great artist. He painted names on the B-17s and drew my portrait, complete with lieutenant's forage cap. I virtually lived on the base. I sat on the edge of their bunks and listened speechless to tales of exciting combat. One crew I visited were there one day. Next day they weren't. I was a 12-year-old kid. I was bewildered. "Are they shot down? Are they dead?" I asked. Men were stripping the hut of their belongings and moving them out.

'I collected washing and cycled home to my mother with it in bags perched on the handlebars and front basket of my bike. My mother would discover bars of soap and chocolate, and cigarettes for my dad, who mended their shoes, among the washing. I would check the crew status board for them to see if they were flying next day. I crawled under barbed wire to steal coke for their fires, which I would light before they returned from a raid, and stood in line for meals at the EM Mess in my lieutenant's forage cap, coat with sergeant's stripes, and "my" mess kit. Dave even painted a Fortress on my cup. The meals were better than at home – steak, spuds and sprouts, rice pudding, fruit juice – all on one big plate! The orange juice mingled with the meat and gravy but I didn't care!

'At the base cinema one evening the air raid sirens sounded. We had been used to air raids since 1940 and just stood in amazement, wondering what all the panic was about as the Americans ran to the shelters! One pilot, who wore his pistol on the base, fired into the moonlit sky at the Ju 88 as he ran!

'My best American pal was a 19-year-old ball turret gunner from Utah called "Junior". One day, me and my friends watched the B-17s return when a badly damaged Fort' flew over, landed, and taxied quickly to one side. Being "blood-thirsty", curious kids, we wanted to see who was injured. I wondered if it was one of the crews I knew. "Was it Junior?"

'The ball turret had not been retracted. The guns were still in, pointing forward. The glass was cracked and shattered. It had taken a direct hit. Trapped inside, the ball gunner was giving blood-curdling screams. I can hear them to this day. "Christ, how could anyone survive in a position like that?" They levered the jammed ball turret door open. His arm was just hanging off. Still screaming, they put him on a stretcher. His oxygen mask dangled over the side. They took him away to hospital. The inside of the turret was soaked in his blood. It was as if four or five bottles of milk had been poured into the turret.

I had guarded a fifth of Seagrams V.O. from Texas across the north Atlantic, through a crack-up and through buzz bombs, only to have it swiped from my B4 bag at Stone. (the late Allan Healy)

'I was friendly with Netzley, a cook at the base hospital, and went around the wards with him and his fat spaniel next day, but the gunner was not there. Overnight he had been taken to hospital at Ely.'
12-year-old Jim Matsell, Deopham Green

'One Sunday, when I went to visit my uncle at Sprowston, he told me about an American gunner who bailed out during assembly after the group took off from Horsham St. Faith. He landed in his garden and my uncle helped him. He called him Joe. The American said: "How did you know my name was Joe?" He said he called all Americans "Joe". Later, the MPs came and took him away.'
Mike Bailey, Norwich schoolboy

'We had a young boy in the armament shop on the base who had never had a woman before. It was decided that he wasn't going back to the States a virgin. We plied him with quite a few drinks and then took him to the village to see "B . . . . Lil". He didn't come back for two days.'
8th Air Force groundcrewman

'If we wanted to take a shower on the base we had to go about half a mile to the showers. There was never any hot water. It was just too much trouble and a very punishing experience, so nobody bothered. Sponge baths had to do. After a time we couldn't smell ourselves; or we thought we smelled alright, because everybody smelled that way! We never wore uniforms on base. I can recall wearing my flight coveralls for days at a time without taking them off. I would sleep in them too. We cleaned our OD's (wool uniforms) in aviation gas'. Consequently, we smelled like gasoline when we dressed to go on pass.'
Ben Smith Jr., radio operator, 303rd BG

'We had an armourer who never washed because he said the showers were always cold. It got so bad we called him "Stinky"; then we could stand it no more and scrubbed him down, clothes and all.'
8th Air Force groundcrewman

'After a preview of wartime London blackouts, buzz bombs and rationing, we were sent by train to the replacement pool at Stone. I had guarded a fifth of Seagrams V.O. from Texas across the north Atlantic, through a crack-up and through buzz bombs, only to have it swiped from my B4 bag at Stone. [V.O. was selling for $50 a fifth in England.]
John E. Greenwood, 401st BG

'When we sneaked off the hospital for a trip to the cinema, we used to splash aftershave onto our plaster casts to try and cover the smell. Because the casts were made of real plaster of paris it left no chance for the skin to breathe, so not surprisingly we could be smelt a mile off. Despite our best efforts we still had to sit apart in a special section of the cinema.'

Roland 'Lefty' Nairn, patient, 65th General Hospital, Redgrave, Suffolk, after being wounded in action on a mission to Handorf where he was hit in the shoulder but still managed to drop his bombs — 'on instinct I guess, like a boxer who keeps fighting after being hit.'

'I only got through by smoking 60 cigarettes and drinking a bottle of whisky each day.'
B-17 pilot

Just an encounter with a group of them on the street was an adventure, full of wisecracks and compliments. (Col. William B. Cameron, 44th BG)

Left: *World War Two airmen will remember the refrain of a lusty song, 'He took out his tally-whacker.' (379th BG)*

'World War Two airmen will remember the refrain of a lusty song, "He took out his tally-whacker." The object of this song was to see how quickly the airman could consummate the love act with his girl. The airmen I knew could sing this song the night before a mission, yet on the mission they could pray and think of home and their mothers.'
Sgt. Forrest S. Clark, gunner, 44th BG

'Just an encounter with a group of them on the street was an adventure, full of wisecracks and

To go 'cycle riding with them was a hilarious event. (the late Lt. Col. John H. Woolnough)

compliments − and to go 'cycle riding with them was a hilarious event. My father was very strict − and of course, I was young − so no fabled dances at the lovely Samson & Hercules, or the exciting liberty truck runs out to parties at the airbases for me; but there were picnics, afternoons on the river, and strolls around the parks while we gradually became used to one another's funny accents.'
Marjorie Adams

LIBERTY RUN

'They moan about our lukewarm beer,
Thinks beer's like water over here,
But after drinking one or more,
You'll find them on the floor.'

The GI's, *by a WAAF at Shipdham*

'A liberty run of trucks went into Norwich every night, parked at the cattle Market and brought home those who had visited the flicks, the Norwich pubs, or their girls. The Red Cross clubs in Norwich were excellent, the Maddermarket players gave good theatre, the Lido, Blackfriars or Samson & Hercules had dances. We fell easily into English ways, or at least, we got about on the wrong side of streets with odd money, and suffered not too much with pubs for drugstores ... The Motor Pool was always busy with jeep or six-wheeler, weapons-carrier or motorbike checking in or out, or lined by the bicycle repair shop near a great Norfolk straw stack hard by the farm. The trick of driving on the left side of the road was soon learned though English roads were narrow and twisting. Driving a six-wheeler through a Norfolk hamlet made an incongruous picture; the house walls leaned over the truck, the people scurried back onto their three-foot sidewalks and all traffic gave way to let the lorry through.'
Allan Healy, 467th BG

'One of the most dangerous activities while sta-

Above: *A liberty run of trucks went into Norwich every night, parked at the cattle Market and brought home those who had visited the flicks, the Norwich pubs, or their girls. (Rackheath Memories)*

Below: *An English country road is not like anything known in America.*

tioned at Shipdham had nothing to do with flying combat missions. This perilous event was something forced upon us by necessity, i.e. the need to catch a ride to town. The transportation was furnished free by the USAAF. This courtesy came by way of a 2½-ton GI truck and drivers with nerves of steel. The vehicle had a wild west covered wagon tarpaulin stretched over hoops. There were canvas end flaps that secreted what little view there was for the hapless passengers.

'At a designated place and time, the tail gate was lowered; a climb of approximately 3½ ft allowed us to get aboard, usually with a little assist from a helping hand from above. There was a hard wooden bench seat on either side that could comfortably accommodate perhaps six men, eight maximum, but we always managed to get two or three more than there was really room for. An English country road is not like anything known in America. The nursery rhyme that told of the

Children from six to 12 who liked candy and chewing gum were there to greet them with chants of 'Any gum chum?' and, 'I've got a sister mister!' (Rackheath Memories)

crooked man who walked a crooked mile, was no lie. The only difference was that in our case, it was wild maniacs driving down these crooked miles. The truck would weave back and forth, travelling at excessive speeds, tossing its passengers around like corks on the sea. The only thing that kept us in any semblance of order was that sardines were never packed so tightly.

'The 15-mile ride seemed like an eternity. I wanted to get on my knees and pray for deliverance but there was not room. All an airman could do was close his eyes and hope for the best. Somehow or other we always managed to arrive safely, even if our nerves were in a state of shock. Jumping off the tail gate was like being born again. The pleasures of leave in town were always overshadowed in the back of our minds that somehow, we had to get back to base via the same means. The only difference being that it was difficult to schedule one's activities with enough discipline to be in shape to make the deadline of the last trucks. It was always pitch dark in the blackout, the trucks had almost no headlights, the drivers were tanked up on mild 'n' bitter ale and some of us were not in such good shape ourselves. The Transportation Personnel did a fine job. They got us there and

back and I never heard of a casualty. I never had grey hair before these rides.

'My disembarking point was at the Red Cross building in Norwich. Here, we had a place one could relax, get coffee and doughnuts and keep extra clothing or supplies. There was also an area that I could keep a bicycle in town which was a great convenience. The Red Cross girls were always friendly and cheerful. I can't say enough for the efforts of the Red Cross.'
1/Lt. John W. McClane, navigator, 44th BG

'Children from six to 12 who liked candy and chewing gum were there to greet them with chants of "Any gum chum?" and, "I've got a sister mister." They seemed to know what day rations were issued. The girls were there too, the steadies, waiting for their particular date. Those airmen who were not meeting anybody disappeared into the blackout, some heading for private homes with rations they had begged, borrowed or obtained by bribery, stealth or other means for a dinner and evening in a warm family gathering.
Allan Healy, 467th BG

'It was about 10 p.m when Irene and I left the movie theatre, and started walking towards her home. Just then the air raid sounded, so we altered our route, detoured into the Castle gardens to obtain a bit of shelter. Apparently, the German raiders were approaching Norwich, and soon the anti-aircraft guns were filling the dark sky with flak. What goes up must also come down, and soon we heard the sound of glass bouncing on the cobble-stone walkways and the cattle market. This was the flak returning to earth, making that unusual metal-glass sound as it hit and bounced.

'There were seats in the garden and some were covered, so we selected the covered one and tried to sit out the air raid. About 15 minutes later, the flak diminished, so we continued on toward Ber Street walking Irene home. About half way across the Cattle Market we heard the ominous sound of a dive bomber beginning his dive – and it was nearly overhead. Caught out in the open, we grabbed hands and ran toward some bombed-out buildings we knew were nearby. But just as we reached the open doorway of one building we ran straight into another couple, who, like us, were dashing for any cover. All four of us hit the doorway at the same time, and precious seconds were lost "sorting" ourselves out.

'By then it was too late, and we heard and felt the concussions of the exploding bombs – quite close. Not hearing any other bombing run, we walked over to Ber Street and saw an incendiary bomb burning near the road, and a building had recieved a glancing blow from another bomb – people appearing from the dark to examine the evidently slight damage. So with the excitement over, we walked the remaining distance to Irene's home. When she went to work the day after our "bombing" they had roped off that section of Ber Street and excavated, digging up two unexploded bombs. And just where were those bombs? Why, just on the other side of the building where we almost got to "safety" that evening!'
Sgt. Will Lundy and Irene Lundy, née Haines

'McAdams, our flight engineer, who was about 5 ft 4 in, was what we called a "little Napoleon". Once he went in a bar in Norwich and met a British line sergeant who must have weighed about 300 lb, standing alone at the bar. McAdams knocked into him and said: "Who the hell are you? Do you need the whole damn bar?" (The bar was 50 ft long.) The sergeant had just returned from two years in North Africa. He didn't even use his fist. He just swiped McAdams with his hand and knocked him 20 ft through the air. McAdams broke his arm in the fall and flew for four weeks with his arm in a cast.'
John Holden, navigator, 452nd BG

Roll Me Over in the Clover
*'Now this is number one
and the fun has just begun
Roll me over, lay me down
and do it again
Roll me over, in the clover
Roll me over, lay me down
and do it again.
Now this is number two
whatever shall I do?'*

'We would get off our convoy trucks in the centre of Norwich before starting leave time and then hurry across town to the Thorpe Station to catch a train to London. Being Americans, and in uniform, we could not go far without being stopped by girls. One night a Norwich girl, I presume, stopped a group of us and, placing herself in front of us, started 'Roll Me Over'. We were quite stunned by this until we realized that none of us had time to comply to her wishes. We merely brushed past her on our way to the train and London.

'One of my friends said: "You know, I always

regret that we never picked that girl up in Norwich.''

'To which another replied: ''Would it have been worth missing the train?''

'To which another said: ''She probably would want to marry you after one date. Who wants a wife to sing ''Roll me Over''?'

S/Sgt. Forrest S. Clark, gunner, 44th BG

'I remember the Liberty Runs into Norwich and the occasional girl that was smuggled onto the base on the return trip.'

Jim Brock, 882nd Chemical Warfare Co., Attlebridge

THE GIRLS

> *'Her mother never told her*
> *The things a young girl should know*
> *About the ways of Air Force men*
> *And how they come and go*
> *Now age has taken her beauty*
> *And sin has left its sad scar*
> *So remember your mothers and sisters*
> *Boys*
> *And let her sleep under the bar.'*

'There was a particularly shy young air gunner on our crew who seldom accompanied the rest on the wild and erotic forays into London on three-day passes. One night, as he climbed into his bunk, lo and behold, there popped out of a GI blanket one of the ravishing local beauties, ready for fun and games. With a mission in the offing for early the next morning there was little the startled crew member could do to handle the situation. As a matter of fact, he was in no position to handle anything. He held his fire like a gunner would do when confronted by so unexpected a target.

'She had come back from town in the back of one of the convoy trucks returning to the base that night. Several of the most daring of the town damsels did manage to smuggle into the base and stowaway in barracks for a wild night making the rounds of the beds. The girl was reportedly last seen dashing off into the adjoining farm fields before dawn and was never seen again.'

8th Air Force gunner

'It did not take long to meet girls. You met them at the Cottage, a pub, or the Samson & Hercules,

It did not take long to meet girls ... We learned not to judge them by their clothes, for these were shabby to us, nor by beauty – drugstore or otherwise. (the late Lt. Col. John H. Woolnough)

Every day they seemed prettier and there weren't only a few that one might marry – and did. (via Steve Adams)

called the "Muscle Palace". They were brought in truckloads to our monthly dances. They gave us a royal welcome. We learned not to judge them by their clothes, for these were shabby to us, nor by beauty – drugstore or otherwise. Every day they seemed prettier and there weren't only a few that one might marry – and did.'
Allan Healy, 467th BG

' "I've got a Yank. Have you?" the girls would say.'
S/Sgt. Forrest S. Clark, gunner, 44th BG

'I remember vividly a slender English girl who let me take her home. She told me that I was nothing but a baby, which news took me aback. No matter – she was very tender and sweet to the "baby" and I never forgot her.'
Ben Smith, radio operator, 360th BS, 303rd BG

'When you see a girl in khaki or air force blue with a bit of ribbon on her tunic – remember she didn't get it for knitting more socks than anyone else in Ipswich.'
A Short Guide to Great Britain (which was issued to every GI)

'My mother drove a "tea-wagon" for the Church Army to Hethel and Seething airfields and we acquired a weekend American "family" of home-sick armourers. They joined in everything we did, always bringing a bag full of canned fruit, ham and oranges, as their contribution to our inadequate larder ... In 1944–45, I was working at the hospital in Bury St. Edmunds, and in the evening, as a volunteer for the American Red Cross Officers' Club. I learned how to drive (illicitly and at night) on a command car, played endless table-tennis and darts, and served up "creamed chicken on toast" almost every night, which was blanched minced rabbit – none of those extremely well-fed Yanks would have knowingly eaten rabbit, so it was a deadly secret! The rabbits came unskinned from some countryman, and those skins eventually altered my life for good. Cured and softened, I made fur gloves which the Yanks bought for their girlfriends, and that money paid for my sea fare to the US in early 1946.'
22-year-old Sheila Peal

'You almost got used to British accents but you kept your own. In fact we bent English ways to ours and had the girls talking American slang and dancing jitterbug ways.'
Allan Healy, 467th BG

'Americans made love to English girls in many bizarre places and situations. I had a crew mate who made love to his girlfriend in Hyde Park in the centre of London after the "All Clear"; another made love in a shelter, another in the Under-ground, in the back of taxis, on the ground under

My mother drove a 'tea-wagon' for the Church Army ... and we acquired a weekend American 'family' of homesick armourers. (USAF Official)

the barrage balloons, in the booths of pubs, in London buses, in trains, in haystacks, in farm fields, in hay wagons, in boats on the Thames, and in the blackout, without knowing who the girl was.'

Forrest S. Clark, gunner, 44th BG

'I was dating someone from HQ who entrusted me to American serviceman Keith Vorhees for the dance at Metfield village hall. When I found Keith was a natural at the jitterbug things went from there.'
Edith, who married Keith Vorhees

'Shortly before being assigned to the 44th BG, I happened to meet a very nice girl at a local ballroom in Norwich; her name was Margaret Colman. For some reason, the chemistry was right so we hit it off well from the very first encounter. She worked in a Tea Room downtown. She told me she was 18 years old but I later learned it was 16. She was a mature-looking young lady and I was anything but a mature-looking 21-year-old; this helped our relationship. After we had dated a time or two, Margaret asked me to cycle with her to her home to meet her family. Mr Colman's name was William, his wife was reared as a Cockney in the East End of London and still, after many years, had a distinct Cockney dialect. A lovelier couple has never been born. It was obvious from the first that they approved of me. They welcomed me into their home as if I were their own son. There is no way I can explain what this meant to me during my tour of combat. To have a place where I was welcome as if I were in my own home was a benefit to which no value can be assigned.

'There was nothing extraordinary about the relationship between Margaret and myself. We were both young, it was war time and we filled each other's need for companionship. Our friendship, which could be characterized as young first love, was beyond reproach. We enjoyed walking and cycling together. Before dusk, after the evening meal, we would often take a long walk in a wooded park nearby. Sometimes, on my day off, we would bicycle to the foot of Ringland Hills, taking along my portable radio. After parking our bikes, we would ascend the top of one of the slopes. There we would lay in the grass, listening to the American Armed Forces Radio music programmes. Overhead, the 8th Air Force would be assembling, squadron after squadron, group after group, hundreds and hundreds of four-motor bombers creating a steady rumbling drone. From seeming confusion would come order. This was especially interesting to me as often I was the navigator who directed the assembly when it was my time to lead and other times when I monitored the formation in our black and yellow assembly ship, *Lemon Drop*.

'During the Blitz, Mr Colman had bought a small piece of property approximately five miles NE of Norwich. A narrow river flowed on the southern boundary; this was one of the many tributaries of the vast waterways of Norfolk County known as the Broads. Up the slope, away from the river and close to the road, stood a small cabin. When the Luftwaffe was bombing the city of Norwich, the Colman family would bicycle to this retreat. There they were safe but with concern that when they returned home at daylight, their home would be burned or destroyed by bombs. They could see the fires and hear the explosions. Searchlights, anti-aircraft shells and the burning buildings lit the sky.

'Many an afternoon, the whole family and I would cycle out to the camp. Mr and Mrs Colman had a tandem bicycle. Mr Colman, wearing his billed cap, occupied the front seat while Mrs Colman, pedalling with all her might, sat on the rear seat. Between them they made a picturesque sight. The older daughter and husband, Fred, often came along. Margaret's bicycle had a wicker basket attached to the handlebars. In it she invariably carried her dog, a small short-haired terrier. I rode the bike that I kept at the Red Cross in Norwich. Mr Colman almost had a fit when I told him I bought it for £50 ($25.00) from an airman who had completed his tour of duty. In today's coin, it would be like giving over $1,000. I did have at least two of the three attributes the English credited to all Americans: I was overpaid and I was over there. Money meant nothing to me.

'A decision was made for all of us to take a train ride to the vacation resort coastal city of Great Yarmouth, located 20 miles east of Norwich, adjacent to the North Sea. I insisted that I buy the tickets. I approached the ticket window asking the agent for six tickets to Great Yarmouth. He gave me a set of tickets which I paid for. When I got back with the family, they almost had a fit; the agent had given me second class tickets. I thought nothing of it but I was quickly informed that Officers only travel first class. I insisted it made no difference to me, but Mr Colman and the others were more insistent than ever. They finally convinced me that it would be an insult to the Officer corps and an embarrassment to them if I did not exchange them for first class. After complying with

their requests, we boarded the train for a most pleasant ride and wonderful day at the seashore and on the boardwalk. Of course, none of us went swimming.

'One of the many nice customs I enjoyed in England was that a person could not travel far in any city without coming to a "fish and chips" stand. For a nominal charge, the vendor dispensed a very tasty, as well as nutritious "quick food". The chips were potatoes ... cooked in the fish grease. On this outing to Great Yarmouth, we ate our fill of fish and chips out of newspaper, as well as other foods.

'One evening, I left the Colman house knowing that they planned to spend the following day at the river camp. I informed them that I had an early morning practice flight and to be on the look out for my plane to overfly the camp. The next morning, I told pilots Peritti and Palmer what I wanted. They agreed that if I'd lead them to the site, they would fly low over the camp. As soon as I pointed out the exact building along the river bank, the pilots revved the motors, getting them out of sync' so they made a loud noise. I could see Margaret and the rest of the family standing in the yard, waving at us. Then, Peritti did his thing: he banked to the right in order to re-cross the river, then turned back towards the cabin, which stood perhaps 100 yd up a slope from the river. Rather tall trees were about the building, but the campsite was in plain view amongst the trees.

'*Lili Marlene* headed straight towards the camp with the family still out in front, waving at us. We

I rode the bike that I kept at the Red Cross in Norwich ... Mr Colman almost had a fit when I told him I bought it for £50 ($25.00) from an airman who had completed his tour of duty. In today's coin, it would be like giving over $1,000. (USAF Official)

were diving straight at the cabin and the trees, but at the last conceivable instant, Peretti and Palmer pulled up just in time. I saw the Colman family throw themselves on the ground as they were sure it was all over for them. Because we had other things to do, no second pass was made, much to my relief. We returned to the base in the early afternoon. As soon as I could, I caught the truck to town and cycled to the Colman house, arriving about supper time. Their eyes were still as big as saucers. We had given them either the biggest thrill in their lives or the worst fright, to this day I'm not sure which. The buzz job dominated the conversation for the rest of the evening.

'There was a mutual love and respect between the Colman family and myself. I was happy when my combat tour was complete but sad also knowing I would soon be transferred to the ZOI. My last visit with the family was in the middle of October 1944. They nor I had any doubt that we would meet again after the war. At the same time I was leaving England, my brother-in-law, Claude Boydston, arrived. He was the pilot of a B-17 Flying Fortress crew and the husband of my second-oldest sister. I wrote to him to ask if he would visit Margaret and the Colman family. He did visit several times while he was with his bomb

group. He told me later that he really enjoyed the Colmans, but felt a little foolish taking Margaret to the movies, as he did once or twice, being as she was so much younger than he. I appreciated what he did.'
John McClane Jr., navigator, 44th BG

'I met Lilian Algar at the Officers' Club dance at Watton in June 1944. Later, I asked Col. Grey for permission to marry her. He refused! He said: "You have the right to know it's because 90 per cent of overseas marriages in World War One failed. I might hurt 10 per cent, but I'm helping 90 per cent!" I was lamenting to one of my friends at mess when the Judge Advocate, who was sitting there, heard me. He said: "He can't do that. For an enlisted man, yes, but not for an officer – you have the right to petition a higher office." My petition went through channels to Gen. Spaatz, but he was in America on R & R so it went up to Eisenhower at SHEAF. I received a reply which said: "You have permission to marry Lilian Algar – no-one else."'
1/Lt. Byron Pollitt, B-17 pilot, 652nd BS, 25th BG

'My left waist gunner met an English girl at the railway station in London by chance one night. They formed a steadfast love relationship; so much so that she resolved to come to the US when the war was over. Jack always spoke so lovingly of her, but years later when I mentioned her to him he shrugged off the question. I suspect that his case was indicative of thousands of American GIs who had passionate affairs with English women, only to have to break them off in the post war years.'
8th Air Force sergeant

'I met Hilary at a dancehall just off the Haymarket, not far from Rainbow Corner. At first we were afraid of each other. She was very shy and not sure of Americans as many English girls were at the time. She walked me back to my Red Cross club, would kiss and then beg one of my American cigarettes if I had any. She also insisted on eating fish and chips as a late night snack. Hilary clung to me. She always wore a raincoat, or a slicker as they say, and wool sweater against the dampness of the London nights. I recall taking a taxi or two with Hilary and making rather passionate foreplay in the cab while we raced through the blackout. I had one of those overseas caps that kept falling off and she took it from me, clamping it on her head and pulling one edge of it down over one eye. Once, she said to me: "Do you want me to show you

I met Hilary at a dancehall just off the Haymarket not far from Rainbow Corner. (Author's collection)

around?"
'I was puzzled by this and replied, "Around where?"
"Around my old neighbourhood," she replied.
"Okay," I said, rather casually.
'We got into a taxi. I didn't know where I was going but the night held promises far in excess of my poor anticipations. I had visions of some romantic hideaway in Southwark. I was young; the night pregnant with promises and Hilary snuggled against my olive drab tunic. I could see her face in the moonlight; a complexion that shone in the darkness like the silver path of the moonlight on the Thames. She became very passionate in the taxi, flinging her body hard against mine and kissing me so vigorously that I lost my cap. She started undoing my jacket and shirt. I took this as a sign that some sexual adventure was about to begin and this increased my anticipations. As was the custom of English girls, she called me "love" over and over again.
'As a consequence of her lusty approach and her constant embraces, my arousal was reaching breaking point and I asked the cab driver to stop so we could get out. However, she persisted in going to a place she had designated to the driver. All this while my passion was mounting more and more and I had visions of the most lusty kind.
'We had gone through an air raid warning earlier in the evening, but by this time there was a strange

peace over the city of London. There had been nightly raids on the city for several days. It was such a bright moon that night the bombers could easily be seen by the ground batteries.

'By this time the cab had gone through the blacked out streets to the vicinity of the Elephant and Castle. I imagined a secluded hideaway of a lover's nest where we could complete our love-making in privacy. For many nights in wartime London I had been forced to sleep in a Red Cross Club in a large barracks-type room with cots among many men. Now I had visions of sharing a bed with Hilary.

'We finally stopped and Hilary gave the signal for the driver to let us out. We found ourselves in the middle of one of those old eighteenth century squares or parks surrounded by row houses. It was past midnight by now and the moonlight filtered through the trees and spangled the grass in the park. Hilary and I sat on a park bench and the first wisps of the famous London fog began to drift across the moon and creep over the grass. There was a long silence as we merely sat. Then, breaking the silence, she spoke.

"I used to live here," said Hilary, pointing to a gap in the buildings now filled with rubble. "It was bombed out in the Blitz."

'She began to sob. As the tears filled her eyes, I kissed her.

'We sat there until the first faint twinges of dawn showed in the eastern sky. I couldn't leave her so we spent the night in that park, huddled together in the damp fog of a London dawn.'
8th Air Force sergeant

'Went to a bar and was introduced to English beer and girls. Ten o' clock soon arrived when the bars had to close and proceeded back to the base while the sun was still shining. It took a long time to get used to the sun in the northern latitudes and the English double summer time clock schedule. Both Fergie and I were proposed to during this first outing. English girls were desperate to go to America.'
Col. Robert H. Tays, pilot, 392nd BG, Wendling

*You are their love, their life, their all,
And for your mother they would fall.
They'll love you dearly, 'till death do part,
If you leave them, you'll break their heart.*

*And then they leave you broken-hearted,
The camp has moved, your love departed,
You wait for mail that doesn't come,*

Then you realize you're awfully dumb.

*In a different town, in a different place,
To a different girl, with a different face,
"I love you darling, please be mine"
It's the same old Yank with the same old line.'*

The GIs, *by a WAAF at Shipdham*

"SOMEWHERE IN ENGLAND"

*Dear old England's not the same,
We dreaded invasion, well it came,
But it's not the beastly Hun,
The G.D. Yankee Army's come.'*

The GIs, *by a WAAF at Shipdham*

Somewhere in England ... (Author's collection)

'England gave compensation for the life of combat and work. We lived in the cold of its Winter. The peace and beauty of its Spring and Summer were salted with the bitterness of war. Its people were our friends, though to some they were too like us to be considered foreign and their tolerance of bad plumbing, cold, and what was thought was a lack of progress did not too much endear them to us.'
Allan Healy 467th BG

'The English people were the friendliest I ever met. They were always ready with a cup of tea. We also had parties for the kids. They always preferred Milky Way candy bars. We used to load up on them but when they were gone, they would take any kind. They would repay us by putting on stage plays. They were all about the history of England.'
Rocky Starek, gunner, 712th BS, 448th BG

'Our narrow roads were busy with convoys of supplies and there were many young and so-friendly Yanks who stopped to ask the way. They were very good to the children and we were invited to the camp for special occasions for a party.'
Patricia Everson, Seething schoolgirl

'The Air Ministry had built our base. Its plan was far different from that of American bases. There were no serried rows of bleak buildings with grass and trees scraped from the ground and everything barren, efficient, and a scar on the landscape. Rackheath had benefited from the necessities of camouflage. Nissen huts were grouped under tall trees at the edge of woods and in and under them. Roads passed under rows of fruit trees. The farm croft and byre were left untouched. One site was far down by the rhododendron drive, another across the Jersey pasture where the ornamental sheep and tame deer grazed. You walked through bluebell carpeted wood in spring from Site One to the Operations Block, and past straw ricks from there to the Briefing Building. A hedgerow lined the land of a civilian-travelled road right through the base, where, on Sundays, the children stood

There were many young and so-friendly Yanks who stopped to ask the way ... (Mrs Muriel Colborn)

I was fond of taking long walks and bicycle rides in the countryside. I loved this verdant country. (Col. William B. Cameron, 44th BG)

Somehow, I had the feeling that I had been here in another life . . . I knew it ultimately from my books. So I bicycled constantly – over hill and down dale. (Col. William B. Cameron, 44th BG)

Our first engineer . . . and right waist gunner . . . bought an old English motorcycle which we used to ride around the base. (Col. William B. Cameron, 44th BG)

and asked, "Any gum chum?" ... We were impressed by England's state of siege. The wrecked homes and buildings of Norwich showed the ruthless hand of the German bombing that we were about to return to them a thousandfold. Every crossroad had its tank barriers and pillboxes ready for use. We saw how grimly the British citizen was prepared to defend his homeland.'
Allan Healy, 467th BG

'I visited a lot in nearby towns and villages. Kimbolton was nearby and Thrapston too. These picturesque villages with thatchroofed cottages were a delight to me. I was fond of the dignified, sturdy villagers, who were very friendly and hospitable once I learned a few "ice-breakers". Molesworth was in a lovely section of England, on the perimeter of what is usually referred to as the Midlands. The countryside was unbelievably green and rolling. Many stately groves of trees ringed the base and I was fond of taking long walks and bicycle rides in the countryside. I loved this verdant country. Somehow, I had the feeling that I had been here in another life. I knew that my roots were here – that my people had all come from England in earlier times. Anyone with a passion for English literature could not help but be in love with this lovely pastoral land, the matrix of English literature. Beginning with "Mother Goose," this land had shaped my life from childhood on – I knew it ultimately from my books. So I bicycled constantly – over hill and down dale, rejoicing in the lush greenery of Huntingdonshire.
'The war seemed far away.'
Ben Smith, radio operator, 303rd BG

'There was smoke coming from the 'plane and after we stopped rolling I grabbed a fire extinguisher and ran to see if I could help, although it was a minor fire. The right wing was resting on the porch of a house and although the crew were out, the LIFE photographer, who was on board, was having a field day. He ran around the 'plane and the house and after three circles I finally stopped him and asked what he was doing. He said he was going to take some pictures but he was so excited, he never took any until I calmed him down.'
Howard E. Hernan, gunner, 303rd BG

'Our first engineer-top turret gunner, William Cook, and right waist gunner, Marvin Taylor, bought an old English motorcycle which we used to ride around the base. However, some of the local citizens complained that we were using too

much petrol so we had to get rid of it. We laughed about this as we used more petrol cleaning our uniforms than we ever did in the motorcycle.'
Elvin O. Cross, tail gunner, 445th BG

'The air base was completely mingled with farm, field and spinney. Pheasants crowed near the barrack sites and rabbits came out in the late evenings about the operations Block. It was a lovely spot, even to homesick Americans ... We smelled the perfume of English hedgerows and saw woods blanketed in bluebells. Poppies grew in profusion on the sides of the air raid shelters and along the roadways. The massed bloom of many-coloured rhododendron was magnificent along one complete driveway into the field.'
Allan Healy 467th BG

'Starving bees raided our Mess Halls for sweets as their hives had been robbed.'
Maj. Newton L. Mclaughlin, Special Services Officer, 448th BG

'"Buncher 12" was socked in so we landed at RAF station Boscombe Down and were put up at a nearby British Army training base. At any rate, before we left for Tidworth, the RAF fed us at their fabulous Mess. Women waited on table and there were white tablecloths. Later, we watched the RAF men bring down their ensign and noticed they didn't seem to mind that it touched the ground. Then saw one of the new gas turbine-powered aircraft taxiing along the flight line – odd to see an aircraft without a propeller. It certainly made a lot of horrible whining sounds.'
Abe Dolim, 94th BG

'The combat crews were kept separate from the rest of the base personnel and we lived primarily in the NE corner of the Molesworth base in small nissen huts with 12 men to a hut, making two crews. Most generally, right next door lived eight officers which formed the rest of the two crews. We had a little coke stove, but toilet facilities were a little lacking. We had a couple of flush toilets but no facilities to take a shower, so we rigged up a couple of barrels with a charcoal stove underneath to get a little warm water. A dirty body at high altitude was so much harder to keep warm and it always surprised me that better washing facilities for the combat crews were never provided.'
Howard E. Hernan, gunner, 303rd BG

'Suddenly, out of the sky loomed a B-17 in a dive

of about 45°. The sentry at our bomb dump heard it and ran from his post, only seconds before it crashed into the dump. It had on board two 2,000-lb bombs which exploded with a hell of a roar, throwing some debris all the way across the field. The tannoys crackled out, "Every man for himself. Get off the base!" Men, some of them naked, ran for their lives across snow-covered fields while for the next hour and a half great clouds of smoke and debris cascaded onto the surrounding countryside. Bertie Piper, a farmer near the base, saw an American running for all he was worth, pushing a GI bicycle by the handlebars. Bertie shouted: 'Why don't you get on it bor?' Without stopping, the perspiring "Yank" called back: "I ain't got time, I ain't got time!"

'Unfortunately, many of the men had taken the warnings to get off the base very literally indeed and local police had to comb the district telling personnel the danger had passed. George, the landlord of the Billingford Horseshoes, had never had it so good ... !'
Bill Carleton, 351st BS Engineering Officer

'Our 'planes were returning to base early with their bombs due to cloud cover over the continent. The cloud also covered the British Isles. One of our aircraft broke out of the clouds, heading directly for the control tower. To avoid crashing into it he banked to the right and crashed into two of our pyramidal tents which housed our maintenance crews. Fortunately, God was with us because these 10 men were at squadron headquarters for pay formation as it was the last day of the month. The only occupant in the tent was a black cat by the name of Jack, who evidently escaped injury but did not return for two weeks!

'The 'plane itself belly landed, slid across the little public road that ran next to our tents and stopped in the field. The 'plane was on fire but it was possible for all of the crewmen to escape with no serious injury. The 'plane burned for possibly 20 or 30 minutes and then the bombs exploded. Although that area of the base had been evacuated, we were not able to get the airplanes out and three other aircraft were so badly damaged they had to be destroyed. One engine from the disabled 'plane was literally blown 300 ft into the air and it landed on top of another.

'At the time of the explosion there was another minor miracle. An American serviceman was driving a couple of English Red Cross girls onto the base. He was refused entry due to the evacuation and on his own decided to ignore the orders of the

MPs and drive on the public road which actually ran right next to the burning airplane. He had to stop his weapons carrier to push a propeller and debris off the road so he could continue. While he was bending over to perform this function, the bombs exploded and blew him into a ditch filled with water. It also blew the roof off the carrier but the two girls escaped injury, although there was evidence of shrapnel strikes all over the vehicle. An explosion of this nature has a mushroom effect and evidently they were so close to the explosion that they were in the little umbrella where the concussion passed over them, and they were fortunate enough not to have been struck by the flying shrapnel and debris.'
Bill Carleton, 351st BS Engineering Officer

'We were on a general inspection and Maj. Gen. Partridge and his staff had arrived in the tower to observe the 'planes coming back from a daylight mission. At the time we were parking seven airplanes in the dispersal points adjacent to the tower. The ball turret gunner from one of the 'planes which had landed was removing his guns when one of the .50 calibres began to fire. He should have stayed in his turret but he backed away and the one gun firing caused the turret to revolve. It spun around and killed him.

'It continued to fire off ammunition and made two complete revolutions, spraying the entire countryside with .50 calibre bullets. The story goes that on the first pass, when the bullets struck the tower, everyone "hit the deck". That is, with the exception of the General. His comment was: "What the hell is going on here?" He immediately got his answer as the turret made the second revolution, whereupon he joined the others on the floor. Sgt. Lemon had the heel shot off his shoe and Sgt. Pickard had his sheepskin jacket creased. Two of the airplanes caught fire and I personally hauled one out to the centre of the field and let it burn. The only other casualty was Lt. "Shiverin" John, a skinny hillbilly from Tennessee who was our fire marshal. In the excitement, he had put a ladder against the airplane and then had run up the ladder so fast, it fell over backwards, whereupon he broke his shoulder. Unfortunately, his fire department refused to get closer to the airplanes than the length of the hose, which was some distance away, and they could not really tell when to turn on and when to turn off and in so doing, they blew Maj. Robert Rosenthal off the wing and covered him with white foam so he looked like Santa Claus. Luckily, he was not hurt and we escaped what

could have been a very serious tragedy.'
Bill Carleton, 351st BS Engineering Officer

' "Crash alarm, Red bandits, take cover." Our air raid shelter was only about 50 yd away, but no-one rushed outside to freeze in the cold, enemy or no enemy. Inside hut 28 we were welcoming a new crew. Soon we heard the unforgettable rapid beat of unsynchronized twin-engined enemy intruders. I told the newcomers the enemy was overhead and if he followed the usual procedure he would cut his engines and glide into position as soon as he identified his target. Several bombs exploded some distance from Bury. The new crew felt we were "putting them on". Suddenly, the raider cut his engines and seconds later all hell let loose as the sound of hostile cannon fire destroyed the absolute quiet of the station. The rookie navigator, sitting on the bed across from me, clad only in his underwear and flying boots, darted out the door. An hour later, he returned from the air raid shelter looking somewhat blue.'
Abe Dolim, radio operator, 94th BG

'One day, two enlisted men came to my office and said they had found a crippled children's hospital named after the Swedish nightingale, Jenny Lind, and the matron informed them they were short on rations. Our men wanted to arrange to share their rations with the children. When this was presented at a staff meeting, Col. Westover sent a chaplain and a surgeon with me to visit the hospital and asked us to report back to him. We found conditions as represented and the colonel approved our sending them powdered eggs and milk. The men also dropped their candy rations in a box placed in the PX marked for the children.
Maj. Newton L. Mclaughlin, Special Services Officer, 448th BG

'Most prominent memory of your courageous people, your great air crews, and their supports, your ATS, WLA and so many who inspired this Yank, is the family of Mr Tom Betts of Mergate Hall Farm near Hethel, who adopted me and in spite of my American strangeness, treated me as one of their own. And since I worked a night schedule, on base, I became a part-time daytime farmer as the Betts' place was only five minutes' bike ride away. Although awkward at farm chores, believe me, I did try to earn my keep.'
Martin H. Schreck

'One of the Circus pilots . . . was Walter Stewart, a

big, ebullient blond from Utah ... Before the war Stewart had been a Mormon missionary in England. When he returned there in uniform, he resumed his rapport with English crowds by speaking at War Bond rallies. One day, after selling a fortune in British Bonds at King's Lynn, Norfolk, he was introduced to two members of the audience who had asked to meet him. Stewart shook hands with Queen Mary and her 15-year-old grand daughter, Princess Elizabeth. He put the girl at ease with a chat on literature. "I've just finished The Robe," he said. "I'll bet you'd like it." The future queen averred she would. "I'll lend you a copy," said Stewart. "Where are you putting up?" "Sandringham," said Elizabeth.

'The next day, Stewart borrowed Col. Timberlake's Cub, *Fearless Fosdick*, flew low over the palace lawn, and dropped the book. When he got back, Timberlake was waiting with a teletype from the Air Ministry. "HM Government takes a dim view of aircraft dropping objects on Sandringham Palace," said the CO. "A servant took your number." Stewart received a series of reprimands, although the admonitory officers had a hard time keeping straight faces.'
Lt. Walter Stewart, pilot of Utah Man, *93rd BG, in* 'Ploesti', *by James Dugan & Carroll Stewart.*

'The one nice thing I remember would happen as we were circling, waiting our turn to land. We flew very low over a schoolhouse and the children would always be out waving to us. Evidently, it was a ritual the teacher allowed the children to enjoy and of course we looked forward to them being there waving us home.'
Lloyd W. Hughes, gunner, 453rd BG, Berlin, June 1944

YULETIDE

'Beer, Beer for old Pappy Wayne,
You bring the whisky, and I'll bring champagne
Send the 'N' crews out for gin,
Don't let a sober flyer in.
We never stagger, we never fall,
We sober up on wood alcohol,
While our drunken 'S' crews are staggering,
Back to the bar for more.'

'On Christmas Day our base served dinner to the London children billeted in our neighbourhood

On Christmas Day our base served dinner to the London children billeted in our neighbourhood. (Maj. Newton L. McLaughlin)

and many of our men were guests in English homes.'
Maj. Newton L. Mclaughlin, Special Services Officer, 448th BG

'I think it must have been Christmas Eve of 1944, snow on the ground, frosty, and we all walked down Thunder Lane to midnight service at Thorpe St. Andrew. Two of the GIs were of Welsh extraction and had wonderful singing voices, and we all sang carols all the way down and back, finishing up with "The Old Rugged Cross".'
22-year-old Sheila Peal

'The US chaplain from Horsham St. Faith brought a group of incredibly handsome young men to sing at Silver Road Baptist Church. I still remember the face of the one who sang the solo, 'The Old Rugged Cross'.

'After the service, we had a cup of tea with the airmen and I learned one was called "Spam". Because I didn't understand his accent, I never found out why! But Chappie told my mother, a young widow then, that he would arrange for me and my sister to spend Christmas Day at the airbase, while she relaxed at a friend's house.

'It was a very cold morning when the jeep arrived, and the ice crunched under our feet. How smart Chappie's uniform seemed, with its brilliant badges and bars. He took us to his office on camp and let us play with the typewriter and the kittens

which slept in a box under his desk. Later, we saw a Disney film and walked along endless corridors of glittering Christmas cards and lifesaver sweets that hung as trimmings over our heads. Chappie cut strings of them down to give to us. The long lunch tables, set for crowds of children, were decorated with foil-wrapped chocolate bars laid end to end down the centre. A GI scooped some up and put them in my lap. We were served with turkey and cranberry sauce ("They put jam on their meat," I told my mother that night). Then there was pumpkin pie – a marvellous new taste.'
Norwich girl, Ann K. Spredbury

'I took a happy but sad photo of Christmas Day in our barracks at Hethel. We were to win a bottle of Scotch for the best decorated barracks. The Christmas tree was cut from the countryside as was the holly to decorate it. Some of the tinsel was picked up on a two-day pass to London by Art Marsh. Marsh also had an idea for the coloured balls to hang on the tree. He rounded up all the pro-kits (rubbers) he could, got some multi-coloured paints from the line, and recruited a few windy boys to blow them up and paint. It worked for about two of every five. By the time we had enough to decorate the tree we all had rainbow-coloured spots on our faces caused by "blowouts" from rough brush bristles. I wonder how they "stood up" under their primary uses? All but five men (my crew) in the picture were lost in the next two missions. A very lonely place with so many empty beds to stare at.'
Russ D. Hayes, 389th BG, Little Gramper *crew*

'I was on my first visit to Norwich, I was there with my buddy, Fred Bumch, when we were walking through the market and a man approached us and asked us if we would like to share Christmas Dinner with a British family.'
Charles H. Mills, 458th BG

I took a happy but sad photo of Christmas Day in our barracks at Hethel ... All but five men (my crew) in the picture were lost in the next two missions. (Russ D. Hayes)

'Christmas Eve finally arrived, dressed in white. Even as the 453rd was going all out against Hitler's Fortress through the medium of the air, those who had remained at home were going out in a different manner. The 453rd played host to more than 1,250 British children ranging in age from four to 14. They were gathered from the neighbouring villages and towns. Many were orphans or evacuees from the London Blitz.

'The party had been in the making since 1 November. Some of the personnel conceived the idea of making toys for the children of Paris, so many of whom had never experienced the spirit and thrills of a child's Christmas. The idea spread like wildfire to and among the neighbouring children who began to donate their own toys or make new ones. Rag dolls, wooden toys and myriads of Christmas cards were enthusiastically donated by these youngsters for their small French allies.

Judith McDavid, 11-year-old orphan of the Blitz, christened the ship Liberty Run. (Frank Thomas)

'Wheels began to grind. The American Red Cross chose more than 300 French children to receive the gifts on Christmas Day at the ARC Club at Rainbow Corner in Paris. The Group received permission to fly the gifts to Paris. An all French-speaking crew was chosen to ferry them over. T/Sgt. Reuben Brockway was chosen to portray the part of Santa Claus, uniform and all, but minus the paunch.

'A nameless Lib', veteran of 74 missions without an abortion, was chosen to act as Santa's reindeer and sleigh. Personnel on the base contributed their PX rations to fill the stockings of the little guests. The Aero Club was all bedecked, even to the Christmas tree. Decorations consisted of silver cones and balls made of chaff. Coloured chains were made of red and silver strips of paper. Lights were added. Everything was set.

'The children began to arrive in GI trucks and were placed in three groups according to age. Those from four to seven gathered at the Aero Club where they were entertained. Here, too, they received their stockings filled with candy and toys

The traditional turkey was served for Christmas dinner with all the trimmings. (Author's Collection)

from Santa himself and were served ice cream and coke to their heart's content. Those aged seven to 11 were taken out to the perimeter and shown through the planes. Then came the big show.

'The procession walked to the hardstand where a huge platform had been erected alongside one of the ships. It was this ship that was to carry the gifts of these youngsters to their little French friends. With Sgt. Al Klauber of the 734th Squadron acting as "em cee" and Santa receiving the gifts, Judith

All good things must come to an end and so did Christmas. (Author's Collection)

McDavid, 11-year-old orphan of the Blitz, christened the ship *Liberty Run*.

'Fully loaded, the ship attempted to take off but slipped off the runway as the engines were revved up. Fortunately, the ship was not damaged but take-off was postponed 'till morning. Meanwhile, those aged 11 to 14 had been taken to the base theatre where they were entertained by Corporal Sissenstein of Special Services and quite an amateur magician. He kept them laughing and held their interest with his feats of magic and sleight of hand. Joined later by those who had witnessed the christening of the 'plane, the entire group were shown animated cartoons and a comic feature. Then they returned to the Aero Club where they, too, received gifts and filled themselves with candy, ice cream and cakes. After the last child had been fed, they were returned to their homes. It is safe to say that many will long remember the Yankee hospitality shown them on this Christmas Eve by the personnel of the 453rd BG.

'As night fell, the Aero Club was thrown open to all regardless of rank. Officers and GIs celebrated Christmas Eve in true American style. At the base chapel, Chaplain Healy led the Midnight Mass as many observed Christmas Eve in the ETO as they had observed it at home. Still others celebrated by drowning their sorrows, if they had any, in mild 'n' bitters plus a surprising amount of wine, Scotch and rye.

'After a final check-up, *Liberty Run* was ready. At 10:15 the engines were revved up and the ship raced down the runway and into the air. Two hours and 15 minutes later, at 12:30, the 'plane touched down. The precious boxes were eagerly unloaded and disbursed by the Red Cross hostesses and Field Attendant. At Rainbow Corner in Paris, the gifts were handed to the children by Santa. Without a doubt, *Liberty Run*'s mission was a grand success. The French children who received the gifts experienced something new even as those who had given them and ferried them across the Channel.

'Back at Ole Buck, the Group was stood down. Needless to say, the Officers' Club and Non-Com Club did a bang-up business as practically everyone took advantage of the situation. The traditional turkey was served for Christmas dinner with all the trimmings. Many of the personnel invited their lady friends to a real Yankee dinner. This consisted of tomato juice, fresh fruit, turkey, giblet dressing, vegetables, hot parkerhouse rolls and butter. All good things must come to an end and so did Christmas. Fortunately, for many who had taken their celebrating a bit too seriously, December 26 stood the group down. New Year's Eve found the group doing business with Hitler, the only kind of business he knew. Nevertheless, once the day's business was over, the personnel turned to ringing out the old and bringing in the new in true American style. With a dance at the Aero Club, open house at the Non-Com Club and plenty to cheer with at the Officers' Club's new Snack Bar and bar, the men soon got into the proper spirits. As many rung in their second New Year in the ETO, there was a fervent toast that there would be no more.'

Gen. Andrew S. Low, 'The Story of the 453rd Bombardment Group (Heavy)'

RELIGION

'jesusgodpleasenojesusgodpleasenojesusgodpleaseno'

What you said when he was dying in your arms, 'Yank' magazine, 1945

'We were called out to a very early briefing. When we entered the briefing room the Chaplains were very visible. This made us uneasy and we thought it must be something big.'

Larry Goldstein, radio operator, 388th BG

'The crews begin to gather and soon the Catholic Chaplain is giving the prayer to all of us Protestants.'

Lt. Robert L. Ferrell, 20-year-old lead navigator, 458th BG

'As briefings break up I have seen groups of crewmen off in a corner kneeling while the rest of us head for the flight line. Once I inquired and was told that the Catholics flying the mission were going to confession and receiving communion. We have no Catholics on our crew. Ken and I passed this scene once and I paused to watch.

"What's going on there?" I asked him.

"They are getting the last rites," he said.

T/Sgt. Robert T. Marshall, radio operator, 15 October 1944

'While going over the maps, perhaps talking to the bombardier, I became cognizant of someone trying to get my attention. Just as I looked up, I caught a full slash of water in my face. It was the

Group Chaplain asking God to look after us as we began our combat tour. Later, I was to know why there are no atheists in combat. On many missions, I had good reason myself to pray for God to spare us just this one more time. I will never understand why God answered this prayer for some and so many others were required to give their all.'

1/Lt. John W. McClane Jr., navigator, 44th BG

'To further acquaint him with flying, one of our Chaplains requested permission to go along on one of the test flights. This was granted but unfortunately, engine trouble developed. Emergency procedure was immediately utilized which included the opening of the bomb bay doors for emergency bail out. The Chaplain, who was in the cockpit, asked how his parachute worked. He was told to put his hand on the red handle, jump, count three and pull the handle. With that, the crew went back to the emergency at hand. Suddenly, the co-pilot said: "My God, there's a 'chute!" A quick check indicated that, sure enough, they were short one man. The Chaplain had gone. The crew radioed the tower for a jeep to pick up the errant cleric and returned to base to report on the Chaplain lost on a flight over England.'

Bill Carleton, 100th BG Engineering Officer

'Out over the North Sea we were flying the tightest and the best formation anyone ever saw, and this was just the beginning! Then, up near the border of Denmark, we were led into a great cloud mass. Really pea-soup! There was a great flash ahead of us as the lead element of our squadron collided. We were leading the second element. Our left wingman came sliding over the top of us, just missing us. Pilot said: "I don't know what to do!" A second or two later he said, "I'm going to stay on this heading in a slow climb." We came out on top just under 30,000 ft! Suddenly, the ball gunner called out: "A Ju 88 just popped out right below us!" Then he cried: "My GOD! My guns are frozen up!"

'I was right waist gunner and I gritted my teeth, expecting the slugs from that Ju 88 to come right up my rear-end! Maybe he was having his problems too; whatever, the '88 levelled off and flew away!

'Thanks GOD!'

John A. Miller, 100th BG, 3 March 1944, Berlin

'After the mission briefing, Father Gerald Beck, our Catholic Group Chaplain at Hethel, would distribute communion to the combat crews. It was

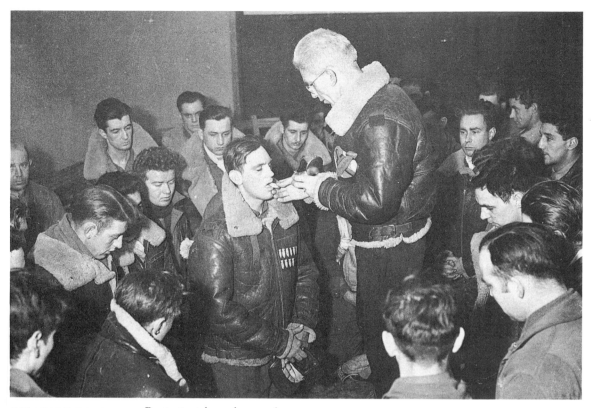

After the mission briefing, Father Gerald Beck, our Catholic Group Chaplain at Hethel, would distribute communion to the combat crews. (USAF Official)

not uncommon to see a Protestant boy also receive as a feeling of more spiritual insurance. Many, many times, I have seen Father Beck driving his jeep at top speed from B-24 to B-24, making sure that no one was denied communion before take-off. One time in North Africa, he was inside the Liberator administering the sacrament at take-off time and was an Observer for that mission. He loved it. Father Beck was probably the most influential driving force behind the men of the 389th BG. He defended his boys, regardless of their guilt. He played poker with his boys; officers and enlisted men alike. (Win it from the officers and loan it to the enlisted men.) Shooting craps was his meat. He would shout as he threw the dice: "For the Chaplain!" He played baseball with GIs 20 years his junior. He would drink beer with them in town (removing his Chaplain's cross and replacing it with a Field Artillery insignia to get the full benefit of a night with the boys).

'Saviour of many. Enemy of none.'
Russ D. Hayes, gunner, 389th BG

'This mission was the first time I can remember praying out loud for God to let me live through the battle. I asked him to let me survive the day. I promised I'd do anything he asked of me if only he would spare me.'
Lt. John W. McClane Jr., navigator, 44th BG, describing his third mission, to Berlin on 29 April 1944

'An almost hopeless feeling welled up inside of me. It occurred to me that only God could see me through it safely. In desperation I silently bargained with God: "Lord, if you'll bring me through this alive, I'll serve you for the rest of my life." This hasty communication brought much relief from the almost unbearable anxiety.'
2/Lt. Robert W. Browne, pilot, 487th BG

'Something strange happened on 26 September 1944. A Bible prophecy, uncannily accurate, foretold the safe return of seven crewmen of Flying Fortress, *Heavenly Body*, after ditching in the English Channel. Before the Fortress took off from Horham early that morning to bomb Bremen the radio operator, S/Sgt. Gilbert Woerner, inserted a £1 note at random between the pages of his pocket bible for safe keeping. When he returned, he saw that the book had been opened at Revelation VIII, 1-4, an allegorical description of the experience the seven crew mates had just undergone.

'*Heavenly Body* left its formation over Germany with one engine out. Over the Channel two other engines failed and the bomber crashed on the water, breaking into three. The pilot and co-pilot were trapped in one section, which sank quickly beneath 20 ft waves. The other seven crewmen either huddled in their rubber dinghy or clung to its sides. Chapter VIII of Revelation reads: "And I saw the seven angels that stood before God."

'While the airmen were buffeted by waves and drenched by spray, they looked up to see a British Air Sea Rescue plane circling overhead, radioing their position to rescue craft . . . Revelation: "and another angel came." The crewmen waited anxiously for help. Some 30 minutes passed . . . "There was silence in heaven about the space of half an hour."

'Finally, they saw a rescue launch speeding towards them. As it approached, the circling aircraft dropped smoke flares to direct it to the survivors . . . "And the smoke of the incense, which came with the prayers of the saints, ascended up before God out of the angel's hand . . . "'
Newspaper report

'Believe me, I am not ashamed to say that I was scared today and never prayed harder to come through.'
Larry Goldstein, radio operator, 388th BG

'Chaplain Duhl and Father Sharbaugh were always at the briefings. On every mission the crews had the opportunity, which many took, to have a word with their Chaplain and the comfort of prayer. This, more than anything else, gave those of us that didn't fly but who watched the men go out, a truer realization of the fact that death rode with them, and it gave us a conviction that everything we could do to protect the fliers in careful preparation and training would be done to prevent every loss that work and care could make possible. To their fliers, and to their people at home, this devout ministration was a stengthening thing.'
Allan Healy 467th BG

'George Triantifillous (The Greek) was in his ball turret no doubt, praying as the flak was doing

everything but flying the airplane. Planes were falling and burning all over the sky and the worst was yet to come. The airplane commander was having a problem with a ship that cut across his formation causing the pilot to curse the wayward pilot with every known cuss-word he could shout on the intercom.

'Suddenly, a voice on the radio from the ball turret, hardly audible, said: "Don't listen to him Lord, he don't mean it."'
Russ D. Hayes, gunner, 389th BG

'When we arrived at Hethel, Chaplain Widen, the Protestant Chaplain, was already there, having come over from the USA with the 389th ground echelon. He and Father Beck really hit it off good and told Pappy we could do anything we liked to make the place into more like a church. Father Beck immediately turned this little chore over to me. Fortunately, I have always been pretty good at scrounging up stuff and I had an excellent partner in Rocco Moreo, a radio operator on one of the crews. All I had to do was ask and he delivered everything from extra blue blackout curtains, paint, a services board that I painted in blue, black and gold.

We even talked Lt. Zuna at the motor pool out of a jeep that we never returned. After painting the chapel part of the building a more pleasing shade of light green, it was decided I should paint a crucifix on the wall behind the altar. This I did in February/March 1944. When I finished the painting I asked Father Beck if it was OK. He said it was fine except I didn't put the feet together as they should be, but not to worry about it because nobody would notice. Boy, was he wrong about that. However, it was well received even though it gave the chapel a definite Catholic appearance.

The Chaplain's office became more like a club than anything else. The place was full most of the time with mostly men from the various combat crews that treated it like a second home. I painted the map of Europe on the office wall so we could discuss the various missions as they came up. The combat Mess was just in back of the chapel, so coffee and occasional steaks were to be had courtesy of Tiny the Mess Sergeant.'
Charles 'Bud' Doyle, 389th BG

'Long missions, eight hours or longer, were extremely tiring and mentally fatiguing. I recall a long, deep mission into southern Germany, flak most of the way, some bad weather and the loss of several aircraft and crews. This was somewhere

NO SINGING IN THIS PUB!

WILD IRISH ROSE

between my 25th and 30th mission. We came home exhausted, and something happened to me after landing. War, death, and destruction just didn't make any sense to me anymore. That evening, instead of singing and whooping it up at the bar as was my custom, I chose a table off in the corner to be by myself. My friend, Father McDonough, came over with a drink, having noticed the change. I told him my problem and asked for help. He was silent for some time, contemplating the drinks and my problem.

'Then he looked me square in the eye and said: "Tays, all of the major religions of the world have as their primary mission to teach man to live in peace and harmony with his fellow man. When I do not do my job as a man of the cloth, then you will have to do your job as a soldier."

'His wisdom shocked me into reality and has held me on a meaningful course ever since. Thanks, Father McDonough, wherever you are.'
Col. Robert H Tays, pilot, 392nd BG

'Thursday December 21, 1944. No mission today – cloudy, rain and fog. It is really terrible, cold, raw

That evening, instead of singing and whooping it up at the bar as was my custom, I chose a table off in the corner to be by myself. My friend, Father McDonough, came over with a drink having noticed the change. (Rackheath Memories)

weather. Gave three sex morality lectures this morning – 420 men. This is the last of the series which has been going on this past week. Gave seven talks on Tuesday to over 1,100 men. All officers and men on the Base must attend at least one a year. A regulation for all service men. It's a peculiar setup. The doctor speaks first. He explains how to use a prophylactic to avoid VD. Then I explain the sex moral law, stressing obligations to God, church, country, self and others, especially the family, a wife, or a sweetheart. All this in order to avoid future regrets and remorse. One Squadron CO told me some of his men, after attending, cancelled their London passes. That's encouraging.'
Father Joe Collins, Chaplain, 94th BG

Chapel 'a la nissen'. (Rackheath Memories)

LONDON

Have you ever sat in Trafalgar Square
Beneath the morning sun, in the morning air?
Have you looked at the lions 'neath Nelson's feet
And watched the traffic pass by in the street?
Have you seen the people taking their time
While Big Ben sounds out its hourly chime?
I'm sitting here now and it thrills me to see
A preview of peace. How good it will be!

Pfc Sidney Jrueger, 'Stars & Stripes'

'We went on a two-day pass to London and we arrived in town late in the evening. When we woke up in the morning we read in the papers that American air forces had heavy losses on the raid the day before. It made us relieved that we were safe in London while our friends may have gone down or were PoWs.'
Larry Goldstein, radio operator, 388th BG

'We caught the train to London and bivouacked at the Strand Palace on the famous Strand, near Trafalgar Square. [Depending on resources, crews could stay at the Columbia Club Red Cross Hostel in Marble Arch for 10 shillings a night, or the Regent Palace Hotel in Piccadilly for £1 a night.] The staid English management took the bawdy Yanks in their stride, never lost their cool and were totally hospitable, although I'm sure they must have been sorely provoked on occasion.'
Ben Smith, radio operator, 360th BS, 303rd BG

Listen Buddy!
Nothing bores me so terrific'ly
As being given so damned specific'ly
A wordy story-play by play
Of your latest visit down London way.
So Shaddup!

'Stars & Stripes'

'We dressed in our OD's and ventured out into the night. Even in the blackout, throngs of people were surging up and down the street. Wartime London was a melting pot for the armed services of every nationality and their uniforms were colourful, often picturesque. In the United Kingdom women were drafted into the services, so most decent girls were in uniform. Only prostitutes and elderly ladies were in street dress.'
Ben Smith, radio operator, 360th BS, 303rd BG

'I remember seeing Winston Churchill, the great Prime Minister, drive by when I was on leave in London one weekend in 1944. His bulldog look was no sham; his defiant rhetoric and adamant stance rallied his people to do their part to help earn ultimate allied victory when, early in the war, it looked like England was doomed to annihilation, as she faced the Nazi war machine alone after the fall of France.'
Douglas D. Walker, 'Carpetbaggers'

'The conviviality of wartime is unimaginable if one hasn't actually experienced it. People who had not seen each other five minutes ago became comrades. Romantic attachments were formed on the spot, sometimes with no more than a searching look. Complete strangers drank out of the same bottle with no thought of disease. Virtuous girls quickly availed themselves of the chance of dinner

Virtuous girls quickly availed themselves of the chance of dinner and dancing and a one-night stand with boys who would be dead within the week. (452nd BG)

and dancing and a one-night stand with boys who would be dead within the week. Australians, Canadians and Yanks prowled the city together, denigrating their English cousins and declaring their undying friendship. Language was no barrier; the bottle was the universal language bestowing upon Pole, Norwegian, Free French and Yank alike; perfect understanding and instant communication . . .

'The great dance halls of London were fantastic fun places. My favourite two were Covent Garden and the Hammersmith Palace. They featured American-style swing bands; damn good ones, too. The peculiar Limeys had some strange dance-hall behaviour. There was no freelance movement. All of the English danced in a circular direction, swooping and dipping with great sweeping strides – exactly like a giant carousel. I got dizzy just watching. It was insane to try and dance upstream. We got clobbered if we did. These orderly people would line up to go into the gates of Hell. To them it made sense for all to dance in the same direction.

'The boys came stag and the girls did, too. Most often it was the girl who broke with the boy. Everyone was very polite about it; there were no scenes. If the girl wanted to dance with a boy, she came up and broke and the other girl gracefully bowed out for a while, although she would be back in a short time if she liked him. I was much in demand as I could do the shuffling, graceful Lindy-Hop of the Southern Negroes and the girls loved it. The boys from Brooklyn and the Bronx did a frenetic hopping-about step that was also very popular but they marvelled at my hang-loose Southern version of the Jitterbug.'
Ben Smith, radio operator, 360th BS, 303rd BG

*'I didn't want to join the Air Force;
I didn't want my bollocks shot away.
I'd rather hang around
Piccadilly Underground
Living on the earnings of a high-born lady'*

'Whenever we were in London or on leave anywhere and some member of the crew had a date, before he took off to meet his date we would join in singing to him, "Roll me over, lay me down and do it again. . . ."

'On a few instances I recall some crowd in a pub singing and the girls joining in the verses.
Forrest S. Clark, gunner, 67th BS, 44th BG

'We went from one pub to the other drinking Gin

and Guinness, a standard affectation of the English but a pretty neat drink withal. One thing's sure, it would get the job done. Imagine the improbable combination of gin and beer (Guinness Stout) – boiler makers, English style.

'I loved the uproarious good humour of the Cockneys. These people are a breed set apart, quite unlike the other English I had met. Hitler had not been able to break these people's spirit. They thrived on adversity. We had a grand time together, but inevitably time would run out on us. Of all sad words of tongue or pen, saddest were these: "Time please Lideys and Gentuhlmen!" Oh, how we dreaded to hear the familiar closing words.

'To awake with splitting head and a full load of remorse – was it worth it? Hell yes; we were soon at it again. In and out of bars, cafes, theatres, peep shows and dance halls. Fish and chips, delicious and served in newspaper right on a street corner –

I can taste them now! Piccadilly was all of this. Nude girly shows they had long before the US. My favourite was the "Windmill". The star of the show was named Dixie. To be legal there was an odd requirement: once the girl had peeled down to the buff, she had to remain completely motionless.'

Ben Smith, radio operator, 360th BS, 303rd BG

'I took a trip to London,
To look around the town;
When I got to Piccadilly
The sun was going down.
I've never seen such darkness,
The night was black as pitch,
When suddenly in front of me,
I thought I saw a witch.

I could not see her figure,
I could not see her face,
But if I ever meet her
I'll know her any place.
I couldn't tell if she was blonde
Or a dark brunette,
But gosh oh gee, did she give me
A thrill I won't forget.

Of all sad words of tongue or pen, saddest were these: 'Time please Lideys and Gentuhlmen!' Oh, how we dreaded to hear the familiar closing words. (Rackheath Memories)

In and out of bars, cafes, theatres, peep shows and dance halls. Fish and chips, delicious and served in newspaper right on a street corner ... Piccadilly was all of this. (Col. William B. Cameron, 44th BG)

They sing of "Dirty Gerie"
And Ma'moiselle in French,
But give me a Commando
In a foxhole or a trench.
And in the thick of battle
You'll find me happy there,
But say chums, be sure she comes
From Piccadilly Square.

Give me a Commando ... from Piccadilly Square. (Rackheath Memories)

Now when my children ask me,
'Please tell us, daddy dear,
What did you do to win the war?'
I'll answer with a sneer:
'Your daddy was a hero;
His best he always fought.
With bravery he gave to
the Commandos his support.'

'Oh it was Lilly from Piccadilly,
You know the one I mean.
I'll spend each pay day, that's my hey day
With Lilly, my black-out Queen.'

Mickey Balsam

'Something moralistic about my make-up made me eschew the favours of the army of prostitutes that thronged Piccadilly. I never liked the idea of buying sex; however, they didn't lack for customers simply because I was squeamish. They were ignored by the "Bobbies" who wisely knew that this had to go on in a war. These "Ladies of the Night" were in every doorway with a cigarette lighted so you would know they were there. They never left the doorway; when they got a customer, the trick was turned on the spot — in a standing position. They could turn five tricks that way while turning one in an hotel room. Our lads called them

"Piccadilly Commandos", a name that stuck.'
Ben Smith, radio operator, 360th BS, 303rd BG

'The economic impact of much loose money in the hands of visitors from other shores caused a sharp decrease in morals, and the "Piccadilly Commandos" and "Hyde Park Rangers" did brisk business after dark. Their prices ranged from chocolate bars and nylons to 10 shillings in a doorway and £2.10s all night.'
8th AF crewman

'All in all, it was a never-to-be-forgotten experience and most of all, it made me love London and England and it was where I made up my mind that theatre was what I wanted to do with my life after the war, so I am grateful for the whole experience.'
Delbert Mann, Squadron Intelligence Officer, 491st BG and post-war film producer

'I took a cab to Parliament and Westminster Abbey. Later, as I meandered through the streets,

Lilly from Piccadilly ... my black-out Queen.

I heard a parade approaching. In the vanguard was a Scots regimental band, their war drums throbbing. As the kilted veterans passed me they began to skirl their pipes – the most stirring sound I have ever heard. It got my battle blood up, appealing to some antique strain in me that I was not aware of before. It is said the Scottish regiments marched into battle at El Alamein to the tune of their bagpipes and completely routed the Axis troops. I better understood this after hearing them that day.'
Ben Smith, radio operator, 360th BS, 303rd BG

'The Tower of London particularly impressed me as well as the place nearby where one of our Cameron ancestors, Dr A. Archibald Cameron, was beheaded because he supported Bonnie Prince Charlie during the rebellion.'
Col. William Cameron, 44th BG, Shipdham

'We were based at Rattlesden, near the village of Stowmarket, in what was called "Buzz Bomb Alley" as the V1s and later the V2s, cut out over London and came our way.'
Al Steller, 709th BS, 447th BG

HERE AND THERE with CARTOONS BY SGT. FERRIS PARSONS

'Life in London was very noisy as the V1 rockets were just starting. One dropped at the back of Selfridges and within minutes the dining room was cleared as officers piled into cabs to rush and see the damage. For many of them it was their first taste of being at the receiving end of what air warfare was all about. None of the bomber crews would sleep on the top floor – and who could blame them – I was not very keen myself.'
Mary Thompson

'I went to London and I was really down. All alone in a crowd. I met a good, decent, Irish girl working at Rainbow Corner and out of thousands of GI's, she liked me. (I would always see her when I made it to London. The first part of July 1944, she was killed by a "buzz bomb". All the damn luck!)'
John A. Miller, gunner, 100th BG

'Shortly before the V2 attack on London, there were about 33 missiles fired to the vicinty of Norfolk. We surmised that this target afforded a better opportunity for triangulation to determine the points of impact, since the Germans were pushed back up into Holland and Belgium at that time. In a period of 72 hours, three V2s came within a mile of the base. One was an underground burst which blew out a hole about 20 ft deep. The other two burst at varying levels above the surface, one being at an altitude of about 1-2,000 ft, the parts being easily identifiable where they lay scattered on the ground. A day or two later, the missiles began falling in the vicinity of London.'
Col. Albert J. Shower, CO 467th BG

'The parents of an old pen-pal have invited the American flyer to visit with them in the London suburbs. Their son, whom he has written to for several years, is in training at an RAF gunnery school in the Midlands. The middle-aged couple own their cottage, which is located in an area subject to a goodly amount of bombing by enemy V-type weapons. They proudly show the American their steel bed with an overhead frame designed to withstand a caved-in roof. At dinner that evening, the flyer realizes that the British couple have used up their entire meat ration for that week – a whole can of SPAM!'
Abe Dolim, navigator, 94th BG

'We arrived at Liverpool Street Station without mishap and decided to take the "tube" downtown. This was a mistake, as none of us had learned to speak the language and it was practically impossible to communicate with the natives. We lost Junior on the "tube" and didn't see him 'till we returned to the base.'
Bill Carleton, 351st BS Engineering Officer, 100th BG

'We three ended up at one of those bottle clubs called the "Miami" Club. We paid $45 for two bottles of whisky (labelled 'Scotch') and the big fat owner of the club, who said that he had been to the United States, did us all the highly doubtful honour of joining our table and trying to drink up all of the whisky he had sold us out of the bigness of his heart. We were sitting there drinking and talking about combat – the more we thought about combat the more we drank. From then on I don't remember too much. I remember two WAAF's and after that it seems that Turnip got tangled up with the cigarette girl; and a faint memory of my getting involved with the oriental dancer in the floor show.'
Bill Griswold, pilot, 100th BG

'I was bone-weary after my sight-seeing tour, but not so much that I was incapable of rejuvenation. I soaked in a tub of hot water, dressed, and went back to the flesh pots of Piccadilly – it was our last night in London and I didn't intend to spend it abed.'
Ben Smith Jr., radio operator, 360th BS, 303rd BG

'I asked her if she had a friend who'd like a good time.

"Depends on what you mean by a good time", she answered.

"Well you know, kinda like, sort of . . ." I stammered.

"Do you mean a party?" she said.

"Yeah, a party. That would be fun."

"What kind of party do you want? An ordinary one, a good one or a super?" she asked.

'She must have heard our money jangling in our pockets cause she said: "I'll need money for food and drinks and all that goes with them".

"Name it baby", I said. "What do you need?"

"£25 each should pay for a roaring good party. That should do it."

'We dug into our pockets and each of us brought out £25. She stuffed it down her cleavage and told us to sit down on some steps nearby and wait while she went for her friend.

"Don't leave this spot or I'll never find you", she warned.

"I'll be back in two sec's", she said as she hurried away.

'We sat down on the steps she pointed to and blissfully awaited the return of two young chicks. We sat there for 10 minutes before a red light came on in our brains. Jumping up, we looked at each other woefully and dashed off in the direction our young maiden had gone. It was too late. Our £50 had vanished into the night. We went to bed in the Columbia Red Cross that night each £25 wiser.'
44th BG crewman

'We were permitted a two-day pass every two or three weeks and found the Imperial Hotel at Russell Square to be very hospitable. We could usually get accommodations for the five of us enlisted men in a comfortable room and the Imperial had a steam bath facility that was great for revitalising after a couple of weeks of sweating, working and splashing around with gun-cleaning solvents, etc. with no really satisfactory shower facilities. On this particular two-day pass I could not depart the base with my crew due to a duty assignment, so I requested they reserve a bed for my later arrival. When I got to the Imperial I found a single room adjoining my crews' room awaiting me. After a good night's rest I dressed and went next door to see what our plans would be for that day. To my surprise, I found their door ajar, clothing scattered about the floor and four gunners sound asleep! It became clear they had been burglarized. All their money and valuables had been expertly removed. Access had been gained by scaling a wall several floors above street level, entering an open window and exiting through the door and out via the fire escape. The Imperial management was notified. They expressed sympathy but fortunately I had enough money to get us all back to base.
T/Sgt. Frank M Mead Jr., Flight Engineer/ Gunner, 837th BS, 487th BG

'I had a three-day pass to London and was staying at the Reindeer Red Cross Club on Clifford Street. My accommodation was a cot set up in the hallway on the third floor. It was late in the evening and I had just gotten into bed when the air raid sirens sounded. As it happened, an elderly char woman was mopping the floor near the stairway. I hurriedly got dressed and headed for the stairs. Now I could hear a buzz bomb coming – a sound never to be forgotten! I fully expected the cleaning lady to bolt down the stairs ahead of me, but she only leaned on her mop and listened. I made up my mind not to appear panicky in front of this brave lady, so I too stopped and listened.

'The devilish V1 sound came ever closer, until it appeared to be directly overhead. At this point the lady resumed her mopping. I kept listening and soon the pulsing sound stopped and there was a terrific explosion in the distance. I learned later that a bus had been struck and demolished at Kennington Oval. When the all-clear sounded I went back to bed, marvelling at the savoir faire of that calm old lady!'
George M. Collar, 445th BG

'I was sleeping in the early morning and all appeared peaceful and quiet. Suddenly, there was a shattering explosion followed by two or three more in quick succession. Plaster fell from the ceiling onto my bed and the entire building shook, swayed and appeared to crack. My room-mate, a British airman, was standing before the mirror shaving when the explosion came.

"What was that?" I cried to him.

"Oh that, that's just one of those Jerry bombs.

The devilish V1 sound came ever closer, until it appeared to be directly overhead. (Jim Tootell, 446th BG)

Don't pay any attention to them," he replied as he continued to shave without missing a stroke.'
Forrest S. Clark, gunner, 44th BG

'The next night the air-raid sirens sounded. We were in the hotel bar at the time and should have stayed inside. However, we went out in front. The searchlights and guns over in St James Park were all in action and had locked in on a low-flying plane. I thought at the time that it was strange that the pilot was not taking evasive action. Then I realized that the ship did not have a pilot. It was a Buzz Bomb. Suddenly, the engine stopped and then there was a big explosion.

'The next morning we went to Mass in a church that was on the far side of St James Park. During Mass the drone of a Buzz Bomb was heard and then it stopped. That is when I hit the floor. There was an explosion. When I looked over the top of the pew, the priest was still saying Mass prayers. I don't think that he missed one word.'
Norm Kiefer, 506th BS, 44th BG

' . . . I was a quarter of a mile away from a V2 that exploded near Marble Arch in London. In my opinion this is the most sinister weapon yet invented. We stopped over in London for the night on the way back to Bury and were promptly greeted by a V1 at Waterloo station. The next day, July 1st, while we were on our way to Simpson's restaurant, a V1 flew over at about 400 ft altitude doing around 400 m.p.h. Its noise was nerve-wracking (even more so than the London klaxons), reminding me somewhat of a pack of motorcycles racing by. It passed over us, its motor stopped and it began a 180° turning dive to the left, exploding a couple of blocks away. My admiration for the British people has increased a good deal since I arrived in Britain. They walk about as though the *"Vergeltungswaffen"* do not exist.'
Abe Dolim, navigator, 94th BG

'People were going about their business as usual, taxis were running, stores were open, and everything was going according to routine. However, I looked down the street and two or three buildings from where I was standing I could see that an entire block of houses had been levelled, smoke was rising from the rubble and rescue crews were pulling people out of the wreckage. Part of the buildings were still burning.

"We've been hit by one of those German V2 rockets," said a British "Bobby" standing nearby when he saw my surprise and shock. "They come

over every day now, little gifts from Hitler," he said.'
Forrest S. Clark, gunner, 44th BG

'Each night, at least once or twice, the air-raid siren would begin its mournful dirge and the "ack-ack" would start up. As searchlights plied the sky, we watched from the roof of an hotel, in our drunkenness scornful of shelter or succour. My companions were Australians or Canadians. The English always went dutifully to an air-raid shelter. It was not that they were afraid; they were cool customers under fire. It was just that they always did what they were supposed to do, exactly as they were supposed to.'
Ben Smith, radio operator, 303rd BG

'I had just returned to England after escaping through France with the aid of American and French underground agents and was in what I thought was the relative safety of London. It was a few days after Christmas 1944 and despite the war, the intense bombing of the city, a gay holiday mood appeared to prevail. I remember I had checked into a Red Cross club where British and American servicemen and women could find lodging and was catching up on many hours of lost sleep. I was a bomber crew member and was shot down after many missions with the 8th Air Force. London did show many scars of the German bombing and it was impossible not to be reminded of the damage done and lives lost in the Blitz.'
Forrest S. Clark, gunner, 44th BG

'A two-day pass or the seven-day leave that came to most once meant a trip to farther away. Everyone went to London, saw Westminster, St. Paul's, perhaps the Tower or art galleries, and all the sights an American tourist sees. One went to the theatre at 6:30 and saw the Lunts or a musical comedy, or went to the "Windmill". Most somehow found girls and sat in pubs or went to "bottle clubs". You saw the incredible gaiety and corruption that was Piccadilly in the wartime blackout. You were in a large city again with lots of people and stores and something that passed for a carnival atmosphere.'
Allan Healy, 467th BG

'Things were not always so pleasant in London as the Nazis took great pleasure in dropping bombs on the inhabitants. Usually, the Nazi bombers would come only to the outskirts of London, drop their bombs on the suburbs, and high tail it for home before the AA got too heavy. Occasionally, however, they would bomb the heart of the city. Most of our crew were in London on this occasion when the Nazis mounted a large-scale attack against the centre. It was well after dark, between 9 and 10 p.m. on a moonless night. On such nights, blacked-out London was about as "black" as any place could be. We actually had to use flashlights to see the sidewalks under our feet – small pen-light flashlights at that! If we used our regular GI flashlights, a British "Bobby" would tell us in very stern tones, "Put out the torch, Yank!"

'When I realized that the bombs were getting close to my hotel (the Red Cross Reindeer Club), I went out into the street to get a better look at the action. Searchlights were lighting up the skies and picking up many Nazi bombers. They would hold a plane in their beams until one of the AA crews shot it down, then pick up another one. The British planes were also in the melee and their tracer bullets could be seen streaking across the sky. I have often wondered how those Limeys could fly their fighter planes at night, avoiding each other and their ground gunners, while very systematically shooting down the intruders.

'Many of the bombers found their targets and dropped bombs all over downtown London. As I was viewing all this in awe and wonder, the people near me were running in various directions. Soon, a zone air raid warden happened upon me gawking up at the sky. He looked at me in exasperation and asked if I had never seen an air raid. Before I could answer "No" he took me to the nearest air raid shelter and ushered me inside. There were so many people in the shelter, calm and collected, as if they took such refuge frequently. It was then that I realized where all those people I had seen earlier were hurrying to.

'In less than an hour, the raid was over and we emerged to view the damage and be about our usual business. Several buildings in the area were damaged and a couple were burning slightly, but the London Fire Department was already busy putting out the blazes. My hotel was undamaged so I went back to the lobby where the others had gathered to exchange tales of their experiences. I was rather stunned to realize that I had been through an air raid, but thankful that I had suffered no injuries and very few inconveniences.'

1/Lt. (later Capt.) Alvin D. Skaggs, pilot, 448th BG

'February 20:
  Left for pass in London – had mighty fine time, bought battle jacket, gloves, etc. Saw an English burlesque – pretty corny gags, but good looking girls, and several naked ones too!

February 22:
  Back from London – suspect mission tomorrow – Hope not, too tired, and I'd sooner let the Russians win the war.

March 8:
  Spent today in London. Saw Westminster Abbey, Thames river, Parliament, Trafalgar Square, etc. Made a date with O'Donnell's WAC's, and had steaks! Tasted mighty fine too. (Bob O'Donnell came up with two American WAC's, both of enlisted rank. As officers we were not supposed to "fraternise" with enlisted personnel other than occasions such as a Red Cross dance. We spent the evening dancing and they invited us to come to their Mess Hall which was in the basement of a building that was part of SHAEF, we were told. These two girls were assigned to work there. When we entered this basement Mess we saw several servicemen of all ranks being fed food from home, such as steaks, corn on the cob and cherry pie. It was hard to believe a war was going on.)

March 9:
  Spent in London – more sight seeing.

March 22:
  Happy birthday Bob! (Thanks) Today our pass began and Bob and I went into Cambridge to meet Terry and Maxine.

March 23:
  Still on pass and having one whale of a good time. Weather is beautiful and "Slapsy Maxy" of the WAAF is more fun than a barrel of monkeys. Looks as though I am getting in solid. She has invited me to her home town south of London to see a castle where Henry VIII once lived with his harem.

March 24:
  Returned from pass very regretfully as it's about the best I've spent in the Army, let alone the ETO. Maxine and I have a swell time together. I think I'll see more of her – lot's more.

March 31:
  Nothing – got a letter from Maxine and her picture. At present we are alerted, and it looks like we will fly tomorrow . . .

Postscript: We got along very well and it was great to have these girls show us around London, since we saw them on subsequent passes. In fact, in line with their duty on their base they were able to deduce when we were due for another pass. One occasion Bob and I decided not to notify them we were going to London and they learned we had been there and not asked to meet them. They were upset, but neither of us wanted to get deeply involved, and it looked like things were heading in that direction ... '

Diary entries by Robert L. Miller, pilot, Son Of A Blitz, *863rd BS, 493rd BG*

'We got in at 18:30 in complete black out. We tried several hotels but they were all full and finally we got a couple of beds in the King George Club for officers. Then it was on to the Park Lane Hotel where they had an "American Bar". We met two pretty gals who took us to an underground restaurant called the "Landsdown", some 50 ft below street level, so there was no worry from bombs. We had a wonderful dinner and dancing.'

Lt. (later Capt.) Franklin H. 'Pappy' Colby, 94th BG

'One might get a room in a four- or five-storey building half destroyed by a bombing. There would be running water and a bathroom down the hall. It was not the Waldorf-Astoria but it was okay. Forget leg of lamb or roast beef. We would go into the city and scrounge up some newspaper-wrapped fish and chips. Base chow was much better, but this was all high adventure to us. Once we read a newspaper advertisement about the availability of horsemeat at a certain London restaurant. We made the trip to town just to try that horsemeat.'

T/Sgt. Norman R. Pickstone, engineer, Peoria Belle, *493rd BG*

'The bomb damage in London shocked me. At the back of St. Paul's Cathedral there were whole blocks of houses that had been reduced to complete rubble. Almost every block of standing buildings had one or two gone where a bomb had hit and the marks of explosions and fires were everywhere. I was particularly astonished at the fact that the Underground and platforms had been converted into sleeping quarters for people who had been bombed out of their homes. They slept in three-decker beds along the back wall of the platform, with no privacy, and the noise from the continually passing trains. But they seemed quite cheerful and I learned some of them had been there since the Blitz in 1940. I saw Green Park and a bit of Piccadilly, and of course uniforms and rank were all over the place. The taxis were beautifully

polished and overhead were hundreds of balloons to discourage air attack.'

Lt. (later Capt.) Franklin H. 'Pappy' Colby, 94th BG

'I thought I was sophisticated and grown up. Then one night I found myself lost at least 10 miles from the centre of London with no buses running. I stopped in a pub in Islington and sought transportation of some sort. No results. I struck up a conversation with a fatherly gentleman who, after a beer, offered to take me home and let me sleep on the couch. Next morning it was "You must have breakfast and then we will put you on the bus."

'Next weekend I was back with a bag full of whatever goodies I could get my hands on. I was told: "We will not let you go back to the Red Cross – you stay for dinner and stay with us. There is always enough for one more". (These were people of little material wealth but a working class family with seven children age four and up.) After a few weeks and many good times, I was told that I was not just another Yank but a member of the family. I was given a key to the house so that I might come and go. The Air Force provided many essentials – food, clothing, shelter – but I had found the missing ingredient, the love of a family.'

Dan Jacobs

'Relations with the Britons saw an occasional difference of opinion, often comical differences in lifestyles. Once, members of the crew did witness that rare clash between the GI and the Tommy. While in a London pub, a British soldier made a crude ethnic joke that a Yank took exception to. It turned out a real riot. On another occasion in London, Lew, Jack and Gene were discussing the relative differences between the British and American peoples. Lew said that if one treated the British with kindness that they would reciprocate. Gene, however, said that he believed the American people to be much friendlier. Lew then saw a sweet little old lady coming up the street. Lew said that this was an opportunity to demonstrate English kindness. He approached the elderly lady and said: "Good morning, madam, how are you this fine day?"

'To this the lady replied: "Mind your own business Yank!"

'Gene was roaring with laughter. Lew was left wondering how he had been so lucky to have chosen this particular old lady from the crowd.'

T/Sgt. Norman R. Pickstone, engineer, Peoria Belle, *493rd BG*

'Sooner or later, American military had to get back to their bases and to do so they had to take railways. They will all recall the hot steaming tea in mugs and the soggy buns served up by volunteers at every railway station.'
Forrest S. Clark, gunner, 44th BG

The station clock with staggering hands and callous face,
says twenty-five-to-nine.
A cigarette, a cup of tea, a bun,
and my train goes at ten

'Steel Cathedrals', D. Van Den Bogaerde

'Every time one departed from Liverpool Street station, one never knew if it was the last time or not. Many an airman departing was killed in action before his next leave or pass. So for this reason and others, the station took on a highly charged significance to airmen. Trains departing that station served the East Anglia region of England, where the majority of the American air bases were located. Once, I shared a compartment with a young British soldier and his girl. They made love all the way to Cambridge where he got off. It was the custom in those times to travel with curtains drawn on the compartments so as not to emit light in the blackout. It was unusual for the English to show so much affection in public.'
Forrest S. Clark, gunner, 44th BG

'Once, returning from a three-day pass in London, I sat next to a lovely young lady from Ipswich. I was the only American in the train compartment. As I tried to get acquainted with the young lady the other passengers were acting very "British" as if not noticing us. Just before reaching Ipswich station, I worked up enough courage to ask the young lady for her address and if I might call on her. She said "yes" but I searched frantically and could not find a pen or pencil with which to write down her address. Without a word, but with just a trace of a smile, three passengers all at the same time, reached into pockets and purses and offered me a pen.'
Elvin O. Cross, tail gunner, 445th BG

'I had a fellow crew member, Sgt. Jack Harmon, who upon returning from leave in London would say: "They tell me I had a good time." He could walk into a dance and in five minutes have dates with several girls. After the leave and we got back to base, he couldn't remember any of them.'
Forrest S. Clark, gunner, 44th BG

'About every two weeks we were given a three-day pass to do as we pleased and relieve the tension of combat. London town was our destination on almost every occasion. Good old London. Wartime London was a dark and forbidding place with little to cheer you up until you found the interesting places behind darkened doors and blackout curtains.

'Staying at the Jules Club operated by the Red Cross for four shillings per night, we had a good base of operation to see London – one block from Piccadilly Circus and some of the best hotels and bars in town.

'The day started with a continental breakfast in our hotel followed by a massage in the barber shop, then to the ticket desk for a stage performance for that evening. The Palladium was our favourite. Tickets were followed by an hour of reading the newspapers to see how the war was going. Lunch at the Brass Brasserie consisted of cold lobster tail, potato salad, and that good hard bread. The drinking for the day started here with a pint of something. Whitbread's dark ale was my favourite. Visiting famous places took up most of the afternoon. Piccadilly Hotel was a must for High Tea at four o'clock, then to the evening theatre performance starting at six. Intermissions between acts were drinking and snacking time. Interruptions by air raid alerts provided the same goodies, except we took them outside to watch aerial combat show. Most of the people went to the safe bomb shelters, but Fergie and I thrilled at the action of searchlights, flak, night fighters, bombs and all the reaction teams the brave British used to report the death and destruction.

'Dinner at the private Exhibition Club came with drinking, dancing and carousing until well into the night came after the show. Being a private club, it could stay open until 2:00 a.m. with continuous entertainment on three floors.'
Col. Robert H. Tays, pilot, 392nd BG, 1945

'A time in London and about Piccadilly, the best you could find in female companionship, and you caught the 8:00 train from Liverpool Street Station to come back to complete your tour and really sweat the last ones out.'
Allan Healy, 467th BG

THE TOUR

*'We took a tour, tour, cripes we took a tour
In the Ruhr, In the Ruhr
We took a tour, tour, cripes we took a tour
In the valley of the Ruhr'*

'I flew a tour of missions with the 709th – all lead crew missions - and it was a real 60!'
Al Steller, 709th BS, 447th BG.

'Some fool stood up and asked what were the odds. The lecturer responded thusly: "On an average, mission after mission flying against the Nazi Fortress of Europe, the 8th Air Force lost four out of every 100 planes, i.e. 4 per cent." Of course, some would be "milk runs" with no loss, but others would be a disaster due to very aggressive enemy action. Still, on average we could expect a 4 per cent attrition rate. This being the case, he reasoned, a crew that flies 25 missions has

We took a tour, tour, cripes we took a tour/In the Ruhr, In the Ruhr. (452nd BG)

a 100 per cent chance of being shot down on their last mission. A great quiet fell over the room. For many, including myself, this was the first time it had dawned on us that we were not playing for marbles. Someone could get hurt. Up to now we were just big boys playing with expensive toys, not a care in the world nor a thought of danger. This was a sobering thought. How can anyone expect to survive such odds? I estimated later that one-third would.'
Lt. John W. McClane Jr., navigator, 44th BG

'I met plenty of boys in London who completed an entire tour without seeing a single enemy fighter.'
Griswold Smith, pilot, 100th BG

'When we took off on the Russian shuttle raid the limit was 30 missions. When we returned I had 32 missions. Thank God I had made it! Then they gave me this stuff that it had been raised while we were gone and that I had to do 35. I said, "No way" as they would pro-rate it like when it was raised from 25 to 30. I was called into Group Operations and the officer I talked to said I would have to fly three more missions. I objected. He said: "It's Bennett's order and you know how he is."

'It looked like either the Krauts or Bennett was going to get me for sure. I flew three more missions and Townsend had a couple more to go. They went down on their last mission. During my time in the Air Force I missed going down with five different crews and sure death with three of them! I was the only one from Townsend's crew to complete his missions and return to the States.'
John A. Miller, gunner, 100th BG

'I was now an old combat veteran; and though only 21 years old, I had seen enough for a lifetime. I had literally grown up in the war. More of my friends were dead than alive. A seemingly endless procession of crews had come and gone out of our squadron. Only a handful of them had completed a tour of operations. I had seen them come and go, but always on my mind was the spectre of Lt. Long's crew, who went down on their final sortie. The same thing happened to Lt. Holdcroft's crew. I was getting closer and closer to the day when my tour would be complete. Now that it looked like I had a chance to finish, I began to sweat it out. I had finished 25 missions and had collected my DFC. Before I had completed the required 30 missions, the brass said we were going to fly unlimited missions (as did our friends, the RAF).

This was so disastrous to morale that they finally relented. I actually had to fly 31 and was given credit for four I didn't fly. I don't know how they figured it; it made no sense to me.'
Ben Smith Jr., radio operator, 303rd BG

'Many of the combat hardened veterans of the original group were still around, and although most of them had finished their missions, a lot of them wanted to stick around the ETO in some capacity, rather than be re-assigned back to the States.'
George M. Collar, 445th BG

'I was Squadron Intelligence Officer, having completed my tour of flying which I did from May 29 '44 to September '44 with the 467th at Rackheath. Did 35 missions, some rough, some "easy"; places like Munich (three times), Hamburg, Keil, Brunswick, Lubeck, etc. Never to "Big B," thank God. Flew on D-Day over the beaches.'
Delbert Mann, Squadron Intelligence Officer, 491st BG and post-war film producer

'I already had five missions to my credit. "Only 30 to go," I thought to myself.'
2/Lt. Robert W. Browne, pilot, 487th BG

'When I first started flying, the Major, CO of the 326th, told me that if you could survive seven missions, there was a good chance of surviving 25. The loss rate between 7 to 25 was low. Unfortunately, he was shot down on his sixth.'
Bill Rose, pilot, 326th BS, 92nd BG

'In the men's room, Turnip was in there talking with a captain who had just finished a "tour" in P-51s. Wilk' blustered in and was introduced to the captain by Turnip, who also told him that they were on the same crew. In the course of the conversation the number of missions that each had completed came up. The captain said that he had just finished a "tour" in fighters and Wilk', not wanting to look like a beginner and heavily fortified with our $45 whisky, turned to Turnip and, with a wise look, said: "How many is it now, Turnip, 23 or 24?" Turnip replied with an innocent look that he had just told the captain that we had finished our second mission. Wilk' suddenly remembered that he had important business on the dance floor.' *Bill Griswold, pilot, 100th BG*

'There was one crew that had just about completed their tour. However, the pilot had an abnormal number of aborts. Consequently, there was much conversation and insinuations that these aborts were more of pilot doing rather than mechanical failures. In order to prove that this was not the case, the pilot volunteered to fly an additional five missions. He was shot down on his 26th mission.'
Leonard W. Herman, 95th BG

'We went overseas as a crew of 10, on the *Queen Mary*. We were with a group of 30 that trained in the states. Of the 30 crews, only about five survived intact to finish 25.'
Larry Goldstein, radio operator, 388th BG

'I had it figured that the quicker I could get my missions, the quicker I could come back as a fighter pilot. Instead of being a clay pigeon, it would be nice to dish it out for a change.'
Joe Wroblewski, pilot, 351st BG

'We had two frustrated short bomber pilots on base. They thought the Army had made a real mistake. They should have been made fighter pilots. So, they went to a neighbouring base that had P-38s, checked out, and proceeded to give us one of the best buzz jobs I have ever seen. They came in very low over the cabbage patch next to the Officers' Club, cabbages rolling all over the place, pulled up to go over the club, dropped down again, knocked about three feet off of the top of a 15-ft telephone pole, and with parts and pieces trailing, pulled up to about 1,000 ft, and bailed out. Within minutes, he was at the bar, parachute under one arm and drink in the other. He had to pay for the 'plane. What a show!'
Col. Robert H. Tays, pilot, 392nd BG

'The mission count at this point was 20. We started thinking about it but did not say it out loud; "Can we as a crew make it through 25?" No-one talked about it, but I'm sure we all thought about it.'
Larry Goldstein, radio operator, 388th BG

'Our last mission to this city was a nightmare. I'm sure that all my fellow crewmembers felt the same as I did: "Will we survive this one, will we come home to our own beds?" It seemed from past experiences that every time the Eighth went to Brunswick it was a bloodbath.'
Larry Goldstein, radio operator, 388th BG

'At this point we as a crew figured that the next

three missions to bring us to the magic number of 25, would, by the law of averages, be simple, light missions. How wrong we were.'
Larry Goldstein, radio operator, 388th BG

Tuesday July 11: 'A combat tour is now officially 35 missions. Our crew was approached about volunteering for a second combat tour with the group. I elected to take the 30-day rest and recuperation leave and return to fly combat. To refuse means to fly eight more missions and I've had my fill. My home is in Honolulu, Hawaii, and

What we didn't realize was that we were war-weary. My weight going into combat was about 160 lb but I was now down to 140 lb. (Bill Rose)

I calculate what with slow convoys and Patton on his way to Paris – the war in Europe may be over before I have to return ...

'I gambled and lost – the Army Air Force gave me an A-4 air travel priority and Patton slowed down after he got to Paris ... It was good to be back among my comrades. People back home did not comprehend air warfare.'
Abe Dolim, navigator, 94th BG

'All the way I kept rejoicing that my promotion had never come through. Since I was a captain and my tour was over, I could go home. When we got to England the White Cliffs never looked so good. When we passed London I told it goodbye. I was on my way home. When we got back over Thorpe Abbotts, Jack Kidd was at the flying control tower. When we came onto radio I heard his voice. I called out to him.

"Jack," I said excitedly, "I got in an extra mission. I am sorry but now I have 25. I will have to go home."

His voice came back clearly, "No you won't, MAJOR!"'
Harry Crosby, navigator, 100th BG

' "Son-of-a-bitch and this is my 25th mission!" Eyes turned toward the speaker and there were expressions of sympathy and condolence, until a baby-faced pilot spoke: "What the hell are you crying about? This is my first!" '
Col. Budd J. Peaslee, CO, 384th BG

'The pace had so quickened by the summer of 1944 that some airmen could complete their tour of 30 missions in as little as two months. Everyone was getting fatigued, both the flying crews and the ground personnel.'
1/Lt. John W. McClane Jr., lead navigator, 68th BS, 44th BG

'Everybody wanted to see our crew make it. We waited for a milk run to complete our tour. On 19 March we went to Frankfurt and we made it. As we entered the flight pattern over Podington, we broke away to buzz the field. There was a definite pattern for this. We went 90° to the landing runway and right at the tower where we pulled up, went around and landed. Of course we had to be last in the formation to do this and have no wounded on board. It was a great day and we duly buzzed the tower. Then we partied until our papers came through. What we didn't realize was that we were war-weary. My weight going into

combat was about 160 lb, but I was now down to 140 lbs.'
Bill Rose, pilot, 92nd BG

'One more to go. God be good to me on the next one!'
Larry Goldstein, radio operator, 388th BG

'I was probably too scared to realize how dangerous it had been. Nevertheless, it was 25 and home. We walked away from the plane and said our own individual prayers of thanks.'
Larry Goldstein, radio operator, 388th BG

'My last mission was a whingding. Nobody seems to give a damn whether or not we hit the target anymore. What in blazes is tonnage worth if it does not hurt the enemy? Group is sore because we loused up their paper war – I'm glad. To hell with them – tonight I will celebrate by getting plastered and forgetting the whole bloody war.'
Abe Dolim, radio operator, 94th BG

'After tomorrow's,' he chuckled, 'I'll only have to finish up 10 more.'
Arch Whitehouse writing in 'True Magazine' about Capt. John B. McCormick, 389th BG pilot, killed the following day

'Two days later, my photograph was taken for the group records. One look at it and I saw the same look that I have seen so many times on others. A sort of weariness is apparent but most of all the expression is one of emptiness, features completely drained of emotion. I have lost 15 lb since I started combat flying, but none of my shirts fit me around the neck – it has expanded almost one inch within the last year. My nerves are not what they should be; I've become tense, irritable and unfit to fly or live with.'
Abe Dolim, radio operator, 94th BG

'I got tired sitting around and decided to take another trip with the boys. I led the 359th Squadron, which flew low. We bombed by squadrons from an altitude of 12,000 ft. Naturally, the flak was very heavy and accurate. We hit a barrage just inside France and Lt. Hungerford's ship was hit by a burst that disintegrated the tail surface and must have killed the tail gunner. He was right in front of me. His ship went into a steep vertical climb, stalled out at the top, dropped off on one wing and went into a dive which developed into a flat spin. 'Chutes came out and it is presumed that

A sort of weariness is apparent but most of all the expression is one of emptiness, features completely drained of emotion. I have lost 15 lb since I started combat flying but none of my shirts fit me around the neck – it has expanded almost one inch within the last year. (Abe Dolim)

most of the crew got out.'
Claude Campbell, pilot, 303rd BG, who, having completed his tour, had the feeling that the mission to the V1 site at Meillard on 14 January 1944 would be a 'milk-run'!

'And there's many an airman just finished his tour,
And many a twerp signing on-
They'll be no promotions this side of the ocean
So cheer up my lads and bless 'em all!'

'Maybe I made a mistake in coming home after the first tour, but at the same time if I had continued flying I might not have made it. So everything worked out real well, coming home, having a rest, do something new and then go back with a fresh crew, ready to go again. People said: "Gee, you're out of combat; why do you want to go back to it?" I just never had the feeling that I was going to be killed.'

Bill Rose, pilot Sky Scrapper, 327th BS, 92nd BG 1945

BIG WEEK

'Cold, distant stars flickered at us from a frosty sky as we entered the briefing building. Like on so many mornings in England, the sky was clear, but a few stray clouds drifting in from the North Sea gave promise of an instrument assembly above 10/10ths clouds by take-off time. In one respect, not yet apparent to us, this morning was different from the others. Our raid today was the beginning of a week which was to mark the biggest air battles of the European war, a week of "all out" conflict between the USAAF and the Luftwaffe. Before the next six days were past, hundreds of American bodies would lie scattered across the continent; other hundreds would be in German prison camps and scores of our bombers would lie, bits of crumpled wreckage in their own craters. But hundreds upon hundreds of Jerry fighters would drop from the flaming skies to rest in ruin as complete as that of many of the factories from which they came — the hoarded power of the Luftwaffe, built up during the winter, shattered into a fraction of what it was on this morning of 20 February 1944.'

Lowell H. Watts, pilot, 388th BG, Posen

BIG-B

*'From Bremen to Bordeaux
From Berlin to Oslo
Wherever those heavies go.'*

'On 6 March, as we lay comfortably in our beds at four in the morning, there was a call for briefing. It was a great thrill and some satisfaction to all of us to just turn over and go back to sleep.'

Larry Goldstein, radio operator, 388th BG

Suddenly, we were told to circle Berlin again. We had already survived the flak. We almost decided to abort.(Thorpe Abbotts Memorial Museum)

'At 12:15, flying at 23,000 ft in the vicinity of Dummer Lake, two more B-17s went down. Dean Radtke's ship was one and Lautenschlager's was the other. Stryjeski grabbed a "walk-around" bottle of oxygen and fought an inferno in the bomb bay. The bombs were dropped and the crew prepared to bail out. Lautenschlager gave the order to bail out and, last to leave, just cleared the tail as the ship blew up. Stryjeski's heroic day came to an end watching the ground come up. His parachute did not open. They had not yet reached Berlin.'
John A. Miller, gunner, 100th BG, 6th March 1944, Berlin

'We got to Berlin and could see our checkpoints on the river. We were around 24,000 ft and ready. Suddenly, we were told to circle Berlin again. We had already survived the flak. We almost decided to abort. We made a very sharp turn out of the area and headed for the secondary target. We were scared. We did not want any more flying over Berlin.'
Ray Newmark, bombardier, 388th BG Shack Rabbits, *shot down, 6 March 1944*

'During the trip to the target, the most impressive sight was our glimpse of Berlin. As we passed by, we all vocally pitied the poor devils who drew it as their target for the day. There was the usual cloud of flak to wade through, and there's no rougher job. We saw a few B-24s go down as their turn came.'
Harry Crosby, 100th BG

'When an airplane went down, you had to shut out the fact that it took 10 men with it. In the Berlin raid this became most difficult because so many were lost. The crew from our own barracks was flying off the right wing of our airplane. Suddenly, during one of the fighter passes, their entire wing was on fire. In the next instant, there was nothing there.'
Lt. Robert J. Shoens, pilot, 100th BG

'A real rough one.'
S/Sgt. Robert J. Starzynski, gunner, 306th BG, first mission, to Berlin, 6 March 1944

'John J. Kovacs was a radioman in the 349th Squadron. He had a very good friend who was a M/Sgt. in Group Communications. This M/Sgt. came around to our hut quite often to visit with Kovacs. John would always let the M/Sgt. know

We saw a few B-24s go down as their turn came. (Bill Robertie)

when he was going to fly a mission as they had an arrangement that if Kovacs was shot down, he would get a message off to the M/Sgt. before he bailed out. Kovacs flew the 6 March '44 Berlin mission and did not return. The next day, the M/Sgt. came to our hut. "Did John send a message?" we asked. The Sarge's eyes grew misty as he answered.

'Yes, he sent, "On fire, going down over Zui ..."

That was the end of the message. "Oh-h-h," we understood. Obviously, John was trying to send, "On fire, going down over Zuider Zee." It is also obvious that his B-17 blew up before he could finish his message and bail out. Trying to fulfil his promise to his good friend probably cost John his life.'

John A. Miller, gunner, 100th BG

'Heartiest congratulations on first U.S. bombing of Berlin. It is more than a year since they were attacked in daylight but now they have no safety there by day or night. All Germany learns the same lesson.'

Air Chief Marshal of the RAF, Arthur Harris on the first American bombing of Berlin on 6 March 1944

'I took the last train, returning from my pass on 8 March. When I checked in with "Irish," the night CQ, he said: "My God, what are you doing out?"

'I said, "48-hour pass to London, why?"

"You're flying, that's why."

'Whew, I ran over and took a cold shower, got dressed, grabbed a bike and headed for briefing. Too late for chow, too late for briefing also. I changed and made it out to the hardstand, just in time to take off. After we had formed up and left the English coast, I introduced myself on the intercom (this was a new crew, Townsend's, on their first mission) and told them I'd just got back

Suddenly, during one of the fighter passes, their entire wing was on fire. In the next instant, there was nothing there. (USAF Official)

from London. I asked them what was the target for the day.

Back came the answer, "Berlin!"

I felt sick.'

John A. Miller, 100th BG, 9 March 1944

'Promptly, at 09:15 hours the lead plane took off. Taxiing behind a line of Fortresses that one after the other soared into the grey sky, the pilot, Capt. Douglas H. Buskey, swung our 'plane onto the runway as the B-17 before us started on its way into the "wild blue yonder." The four 1,200-hp Wright Cyclone engines roared and our heavy bomb-laden plane shuddered as Buskey pushed the throttles forward. Bobbing gently, it rolled down the runway with increasing speed, the ride becoming smooth as the massive bulk lifted gracefully above the Huntingdonshire farmland. Climbing steadily, one by one, each of the 18 'planes slipped into its designated place of the group formation; six in the lead squadron and six each in the high and low squadrons. Wide-eyed, my heart racing from excitement, or was it apprehension from the realization that I'd soon be departing the friendly shores of Britain, I was awed at the magnificent sight of the vast air armada stretching for miles in precise formations against the frosty blue sky. The palms of my hands were moist when we headed over the English Channel and I noted in my log, Altitude, 20,000 ft, time, 11:06 a.m., ground speed, 170 kts.

'Scattered flak greeted us at the Dutch coast a few miles north of Imuiden. Happily though, the fighter 'planes we saw were identified as our "little friends," P-51 Mustangs. On we droned, due east and the Dummer Lake in western Germany loomed ahead. Suddenly, black splotches darkened the sky around us a few miles north of the lake. FLAK! The concussion from exploding shells rocked the plane. Fragments of flying steel tore through its aluminium skin. The oil line of number one engine was cut and, gushing like a geyser, the oil covered the cowling and adjoining wing surface, quickly congealing on the metal in the −30°C temperature.

'Promptly, Buskey feathered number one engine as he called over the intercom, "Number two engine's only pulling half power." We were flying on two-and-a-half engines!

'Fortunately, none of the crew was hit. We learned upon our return to Kimbolton that flak had damaged the vital induction pipe of the turbo-supercharger, reducing the engine's thrust.

"Pilot to navigator, what's the estimated flying time to the target?" Consulting my map and log, I applied pertinent data to my E-6B computer and made a calculation.

"Navigator to pilot," I replied. "It's approximately two hours' flying time at our present ground speed."

'The 'plane rocked gently. "Bandits at 2 o'clock high," the engineer called. Warily, I watched the two Me 109s, as yet out of gunfire range, while I manned the right nose gun. Flying high and ahead of us, suddenly they peeled off into a screaming dive, the front edge of their wings, from which the tips of machine gun barrels protruded, lighting up like firecrackers when they fired. In a flash they were way below us and out of range. Lucky! All the Fortresses in the formation continued droning determinedly toward Berlin. If any of them had been hit by the Me 109 gunfire, none had gotten it fatally this time.

"Pilot to crew. Despite the flak damage to two engines the plane's flying well. We'll continue to the target in formation instead of dropping out and trying to get back to England alone. It could be tough going."

'Breathing heavily from the excitement of my first major encounter with flak and fighters, I slid onto the seat by the navigator's worktable to make

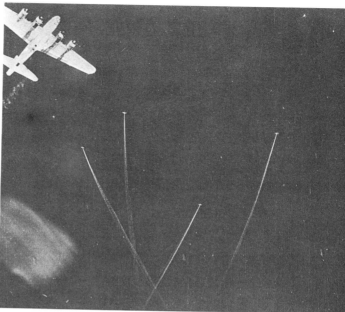

Happily though, the fighter planes we saw were identified as our 'little friends', P-51 Mustangs. (USAF Official)

entries in the log. Peering through the window over the worktable I saw twin-engined P-38 fighters engaging enemy fighters, keeping them away from the bomber formations. A reassuring sight. High above the peaceful-looking German countryside we flew, in tight formation. Our course to the IP took us far enough south of Berlin to avoid the formidable anti-aircraft defences. A lump rose in my throat when we turned onto the IP for the 13-mile run to the target. Five miles above the ball-bearing factory, the Germans had the sky enveloped in a murderous box barrage of flak and the air was filled with black puffs of exploding shells and unseen fragments of deadly steel.

'The formation flew in a straight and unwavering line to the target. There was no turning back, no evasive action. The lead bombardiers were busily aiming their Norden bombsights on the target and the lethal loads of bombs would drop automatically from the bomb bays when the cross hairs in the exquisite bombsight centered on the buildings far below. At that moment, bombardiers in other 'planes of the group would release their bombs by flipping a toggle switch and the destructive explosives would hurtle toward the doomed factory.

'Ahead of us, 'planes in precise group formation

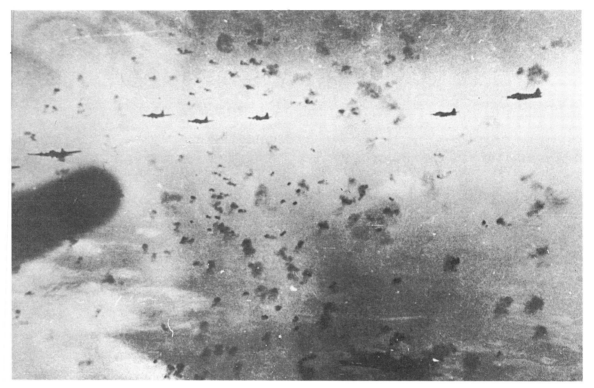

Five miles above the ball-bearing factory the Germans had the sky enveloped in a murderous box barrage of flak and the air was filled with black puffs of exploding shells and unseen fragments of deadly steel. (Gordon & Connie Richards)

entered the pall of smoke from bursting flak. Suddenly, a brilliant ball of orange lit up the sky. Hit by flak, a bomber exploded! No 'chutes were seen. Off to the right, one of the splendid aircraft, out of control, spun lazily to its destruction. It reminded me of a seedpod drifting from a tree. One, two, three 'chutes emerged from the plane as it disappeared into a cottony cloud. Sweat from my brow trickled into my eyes.

'The 'plane rocked from the concussion of bursting shells as we entered the envelope of fire.

"Bomb Bay doors open," the engineer called.

"Bombs Away!" cried the bombardier.

'The plane lifted perceptibly when the tons of bombs dropped from her belly. Ahead of us, bombers emerging from the flak barrage in ragged formation were attempting to close up for maximum protection against the Luftwaffe fighters circling above us as we pulled away from the target area, the 'plane perforated by flak but the fliers unscathed.

'Buskey said: "We've got to get the bomb bay doors closed quickly. There's too much drag and with only two-and-a-half engines, I may not be able to keep up with the formation."

'Closing the massive bomb bay doors was no easy job. The engineer had to crank them shut since the electrical system was out that powered the motor that normally closed them. In a cramped space 25,000 ft above Germany, temperature way below freezing, wearing a weighty fleece-lined flight suit, gloves, flak vest and helmet, an oxygen mask with the hose dangling like an elephant's trunk and hooked into the life support system, wires from his throat mike' and earphones to contend with, plus a parachute strapped on his back, all helped to make it an interminable task.

"Pilot to crew. Someone help the engineer close the doors."

"Yes, Sir," the right waist gunner volunteered.

'This meant he had to disconnect from the 'plane's oxygen system and hook onto a walk-around bottle that provided about eight minutes of the life-giving element, a routine anytime a crewman left his position to go elsewhere in the 'plane. The walk-around bottle was an aluminium cylinder six inches or eight inches in diameter and about 30

The medics removed the dead body of the right waist gunner and took him away. (USAF Official)

inches long that had to be carried. Really cumbersome. To get to the engineer and help him, in his bulky flight gear, the waist gunner had to shuffle through the radio operator's compartment, then into the bomb bay, balancing precariously on a narrow catwalk, squeeze between V-shaped bomb racks, the bomb bay doors below him only partly closed, until he reached the engineer's station behind the cockpit.

'Buskey continued to do a magnificent job of flying the disabled aircraft and managed somehow to stay in formation. The engineer, Sgt. George Thomas, was slowly and laboriously cranking the bomb bay doors closed. Those of us on the guns were warily watching the enemy fighters in the distance, who, fortunately, didn't attack.

'Sgt George Thomas said: "Engineer to pilot. I see the waist gunner on the catwalk. He's stuck between the bomb racks. He can't move."

'Sgt. Louis J. Kyler, the radio operator, closest to the helpless waist gunner, attempted to extricate him but his oxygen bottle fell through the partly opened doors and he had to go back to his

position and hook into the 'plane's oxygen system. Pte. Willis Volkeming, the left waist gunner, on his 12th mission, the only experienced combat crewman aboard, came forward and tried unsuccessfully to rescue his buddy who had fainted from lack of oxygen. Somehow he had freed himself, but unfortunately he had toppled off the catwalk and dropped part of the way through the bomb bay doors that were nearly closed.

'The radio operator came back again and tried once more to save his pal, but to no avail. He had to go back to his position for much needed oxygen. "Radio operator to pilot. We can't get the waist gunner out of the bomb bay. He's unconscious. You'll have to hit the deck if he's to live."

"Pilot to crew," Buskey called, his voice faltering. "If I leave the formation and try to go it alone at 10,000 ft or lower, where we don't need oxygen, we may not make it back to England. German fighters will jump us. It means losing one with the hope that the rest of us will get back."

'The waning winter sun of late afternoon shone warmly through the transparent nose of the battle-scarred B-17 as we approached our airbase. The red flare fired from the 'plane by the engineer alerted the ground personnel that we had a casualty aboard and the tower gave the pilot priority to land. The 'plane dropped smoothly to the concrete runway and the tyres screeching on touchdown sounded like a whining protest against the terrible ordeal the 'plane and its crew had endured.

'Buskey taxied the splendid Fortress to its dispersal area. The medics removed the dead body of the right waist gunner and took him away. I dropped to the ground from the 'plane's nose hatch. Sombre and weary after more than eight hours in the plane I realized the hardening of a naive airman to combat in the crucible of war had begun.'

Lt. Franklin L. Betz, navigator, 379th BG, 9 March 1944, Berlin

---

'The crews of the 45th Combat Wing delivered a punishing blow today to the morale of all Germany. In successfully putting bombs on the enemy's capital and his vital plants, they furthered the war effort more than any of us can adequately evaluate. At the present writing, the major part of the hurt to the Third Division forces fell on the gallant crews of the 96th, 388th and 452nd BGs. The spirit and fight these units displayed made it easier on the other wings who wanted to share the brunt of the battle with them. Convey to all officers and men who participated, my deep admiration for the courage and determination with which they pushed the air attack into the heart of the enemy's territory and blasted Berlin.'

Curtis E. LeMay, Third Division Commander. Daily Bulletin, No. 69, 9 March 1944

'Altogether, we started out for Berlin seven times. Twice our co-pilot went nuts and tried to crash us into the sea. These times the crew fought him off the wheel and we aborted. After the second time he didn't return to our crew. He wasn't a coward; he just couldn't go back to Berlin.'

John A. Miller, gunner, 100th BG

'I started for Berlin three times but we had to abort the mission each time due to engine failure.'

Ralph L. Nasch, co-pilot, 92nd BG

'This mission was another long haul into and out of Germany. Our crew in the *High Tailed Lady* had made it before. All went well until we approached the turning point toward the IP west of Berlin. We were flying at 24,000 ft when suddenly, an accurate burst of flak hit our ship. The co-pilot was seriously wounded, one engine quit, the intercom only functioned sporadically

and all the control cables on the port side except the rudder, were severed. This caused us to bank to starboard at about 30°. We dropped from formation, apparently unseen, lost altitude and turned toward Berlin. At only 12,000 ft over Berlin a second flak burst smashed part of the Plexiglas nose, stopped a second engine, ruptured the oxygen system and started a fire in the bomb bay. Twelve 500-pounders stuck there would neither jettison or toggle. Several crewmembers were hit by shrapnel. Our pilot gave us the alternative of bailing out or staying while he attempted to ride the *Lady* down to a crashlanding in Poland. As we gazed directly down at the "Tiergarten" no-one had the nerve to jump! The fire in the bomb bay was finally extinguished and we managed to jettison our bombs into a lake below. Thankfully, we were alone. No German fighters appeared. As we crossed the Oder river at only a few thousand feet, our Russian allies fired on us but no hits were sustained. Our pilot did a magnificent job of approach to what appeared to be a level field enclosed on three sides by woods. We had no flaps, gear, air speed indicator and many other vital instruments, but all the crew survived the crash landing.'

Paul M. Montague, armourer-ball turret gunner, 487th BG

'At briefing, when they were pulling the curtain back from the map on which our route to the target was always marked with a red ribbon, it looked as if the ribbon was never going to stop. This was always a dramatic moment because no-one ever knew where the mission was going until the lights were turned off and the curtain withdrawn. When the curtain was half way drawn you could hear "Berlin" whispered all over the room. My heart quickened a little.'

Griswold Smith, pilot, 100th BG

'Germany announced the raid as soon as we hit the IP, 18 minutes at least from the target. There was little flak going in but plenty over the target. Their aiming point seemed to be in the lower boxes and we were in the higher box, so we didn't get touched. The mission was planned for PFF but we could see the target quite clearly. Plans seemed to change at the last minute and we made a 360° turn near Berlin and went in 30 minutes late. We dropped three 1000-lb demolition bombs and six 500-lb incendiaries and they hit near a river bridge in the centre of the capital. Each 'plane dropped three tons right on the target. The place must

really have taken a beating: three divisions of ten wings bombed different sections and I saw only one 'plane go down, right over the target. It was in flames and broke up after a direct flak hit. There must have been 600 'planes and even more fighters. I couldn't see how the city could be standing that night.'
Perry Rudd, pilot, 457th BG, 29 April 1944

'It was my seventh Berlin mission and the Germans now had about 1,200 88 mm guns around Berlin. The flak seemed to be more accurate and the barrages more effective than some months ago.'
Abe Dolim, navigator, 94th BG

'We unloaded our delayed-action GPs and incendiaries over the Charlottenburg district while heavy flak from the 900-odd 88 mm cannon around Berlin gave us the most accurate and sustained fire we had encountered to date. We watched one of our bombers drop out of formation and head for the deck. As we turned away from the target, we saw many brightly blazing pin points of fire in the heavily built-up residential area below.

'The demolition bombs used were fused to explode from one to 72 hours' after impact. These, coupled with the incendiaries, created the maximum hazardous situation for the enemy fire-fighting and "UXB" demolition crews. The 500-lb incendiary canisters were designed to disintegrate after dropping about 1,000 ft and spew out approximately 200 $2\frac{1}{2}$ lb thermite bombs which literally rained death on the enemy. Some thermite bombs had anti-personnel fragmentation devices to discourage countermeasures. They exploded in contact with water and could only be put out by smothering with non-combustible material. Under no circumstances were we allowed to return and land with a load of delayed-action bombs as they were sensitive to shock which may cause them to explode prematurely. These are murderous weapons to use against civilians and there are many among us who are not proud of the day's accomplishment.'
Abe Dolim, navigator, 94th BG

'After getting up at 01:00 hrs for three straight days, each mission was scrubbed. All would have been "milk runs" or "easy" raids. Then at briefing on 19 May, when the weather finally cleared, I sat through briefing and the target was Berlin! What a way to end my tour!'
Joe Wroblewski, 351st BG

THE WESTWALL

*'The bridge attributed to Belisarius
Is blown, and we cross the stream on foot
Towards the little town'*

'A Minor Front', Robert Conquest

'There have been all sorts of rumours about an imminent invasion of the enemy coast.'
Abe Dolim, navigator, 94th BG, 5 June 1944 diary entry

'Rumour going around that the invasion has started. After supper it was confirmed by news man . . . '
John Hurd, gunner, 401st BG PoW, Krems, Stalag 17B, Tuesday 6 June 1944

'We saw RAF aircraft and gliders coming over, wave after wave. We knew we would be going in the morning and thought there would be hell to pay. We didn't sleep much that night.'
Ben Smith, radio operator, 303rd BG

'To be awakened about 04:00 hrs for a mission was pretty much routine; but to be hauled out of the sack at about 01:30 hrs to report to briefing – well, something unusual must be up, I thought as I groped sleepily for my clothes.'
Franklin L. Betz, navigator, 379th BG

'I knew when I was awakened by the orderly that morning that something unusual was afoot as it was not our day to lead. At briefing I found the answer to my question. We were not going to fly the usual large squadron and group formation but rather small groups of six planes each. Every lead navigator that could be rounded up was required for this maximum effort. The rest of my crew were held in reserve for a later raid but for this early effort, I was assigned to another crew. I'm sure they were not pleased to have a strange navigator forced on them and I did not relish flying without my crew. A strong bond of trust developed among crew members as it was a life-or-death situation on every mission.

'One thing that did please me was that I was not going to miss out on the invasion. I really wanted to be a part of the show and would have been greatly disappointed had I not been selected to

lead the flight. We were told that our 'planes had been painted with special recognition markings during the night and any 'plane in the air that day without these markings would be shot down by our fighter escort without exception. The markings were black and white stripes that completely encircled our fuselage and wings. No one could miss them even if half blind and not fully alert.
John W. McClane Jr., navigator, 44th BG

'Don't worry about the 'planes you will see overhead. They will be ours.'
Gen. Dwight D. Eisenhower, Supreme Allied Commander, SHAEF.

'We're the D-Day Dodgers out in Italy,
Drinking all the vino, always on the spree.
We didn't land with Eisenhower,
So we fear we're just a shower,
'Cos we're D-Day Dodgers, way out in Italy.'

'D-Day Dodgers', sung to the tune of 'Lili Marlene'

'Every individual keenness, every refinement of technique, and every aid to accuracy must be exploited so that the pattern of our attack is exactly as ordered, and so that there are no gross or avoidable errors to bring disaster to our troops on the ground. The necessary hazards have been accepted. They can be minimized only through exalted performance on the part of our air leaders and bombardiers. I have every confidence in you.'
Gen. Curtis E. LeMay, Commanding General, Third Division

'The atmosphere at briefing was invariably sombre. Sitting quietly on benches, dozing or languidly puffing on cigarettes that glowed eerily in the soft light of the starkly furnished rooms, there was very little talk while the fliers, officers and enlisted men waited for the CO, Col. Preston, to arrive. At 02:30 hrs, when the briefing officer announced, "This is it – this is D-Day!" a lusty cheer shattered the quiet of a moment before. Whoops, whispers and yells echoed from the grey walls. It was an

"This is it – this is D-Day!" a lusty cheer shattered the quiet of a moment before. Whoops, whispers and yells echoed from the grey walls.

unprecedented and ecstatic vocal demonstration by the fliers who had doggedly been carrying the war to Germany for many months with considerable losses of men and planes. It was the day they had awaited to share with the ground forces and together they would assault the Nazi war machine, hopefully gaining a foothold on the mainland with the ultimate goal of driving the Wehrmacht back to the Fatherland and crushing it.'
Franklin L. Betz, navigator, 379th BG

'At briefing at 10:30 we were told "this is it". There would be wave after wave of planes hitting the coast. Our target was coastal defences at Le Havre. We could not drop any bombs after 07:30 hrs, the time the invasion was to start, for the danger of hitting our own troops.
Henry Tarcza, 95th BG

'We heard Eisenhower's inspirational message to the departing troops. At least it was supposed to inspire. I remember thinking that Churchill could have done it with a lot more class.'
Ben Smith, navigator, 303rd BG

'The red streamers on the map ran from every airbase in England and crossed the Channel, converging on one tiny spot near Cherbourg. The briefing colonel pointed toward that area with what happened to be an old billiard cue and said: "Yes gentlemen, this is the day you've been waiting for and this is the spot that has been selected." It was a relatively short briefing because the navigators had already been given separate instructions. Before unlocking the exit doors the briefing officer smiled and said: "Good luck gentlemen and give 'em Hell!"

'As we crossed the Channel at the beach head we saw many landing barges up on the beach. I had never seen so many boats before in my life. There were many gliders on the ground near the beach. Our target was well hit and there were few bursts of flak. After the bomb run, we started across the Channel and were flying at 1,000 ft. We passed over 13 ships in a convoy on their return to England for more troops and supplies. We passed over a harbour in southern England which was crowded with boats of every type.'
Henry Tarcza, 95th BG

'Take off was at 03:00 hrs. We were told in no uncertain terms that we were to fly a fixed and preset course to and from the target area. Once we broke the coast of England and passed over the

SUPREME HEADQUARTERS
ALLIED EXPEDITIONARY FORCE

Soldiers, Sailors and Airmen of the Allied Expeditionary Force!

You are about to embark upon the Great Crusade, toward which we have striven these many months. The eyes of the world are upon you. The hopes and prayers of liberty-loving people everywhere march with you. In company with our brave Allies and brothers-in-arms on other Fronts, you will bring about the destruction of the German war machine, the elimination of Nazi tyranny over the oppressed peoples of Europe, and security for ourselves in a free world.

Your task will not be an easy one. Your enemy is well trained, well equipped and battle-hardened. He will fight savagely.

But this is the year 1944! Much has happened since the Nazi triumphs of 1940-41. The United Nations have inflicted upon the Germans great defeats, in open battle, man-to-man. Our air offensive has seriously reduced their strength in the air and their capacity to wage war on the ground. Our Home Fronts have given us an overwhelming superiority in weapons and munitions of war, and placed at our disposal great reserves of trained fighting men. The tide has turned! The free men of the world are marching together to Victory!

I have full confidence in your courage, devotion to duty and skill in battle. We will accept nothing less than full Victory!

Good Luck! And let us all beseech the blessing of Almighty God upon this great and noble undertaking.

Dwight D Eisenhower

We heard Eisenhower's inspirational message to the departing troops. At least it was supposed to inspire. (USAF Official)

Channel, there could be no alteration in course for any reason whatsoever that would be tolerated. We were told that British fighters had instructions that any 'plane flying outside of the narrow prescribed corridor or any 'plane aborting and flying the wrong direction would be shot down without exception. The point was made so clear that I believed it 100 per cent and so did everyone else.'
John W. McClane Jr., navigator, 44th BG

'The target was really flaming and smoking as we dropped our bombs and closed the bomb bay doors. Smoke reached as high as 5,000 ft. On the way back to the coast we saw many targets which had been bombed. They were burning and smoking and smoke reached as high as 10,000 ft.'
Henry Tarcza, 95th BG

'The flak was extremely heavy at the target and we were bounced around by the flak bursts. Holes were appearing everywhere. Just before bomb release my pilot, who was concerned about damage, asked all of us to access the situation. At that moment I saw fuel in a large stream coming from No.2 turbo. "Feather No.2 quick," I yelled anxiously. My heart was pounding. It was done. The pilot then asked why, because his instruments had given no hint of danger. We made it back to Horham but our B-17 was out of action for two days for repairs. One of the spars had received a direct hit. As we left the ship on the taxiway with a flat tyre, I picked up my 'chute and found it riddled with holes.'
Henry Tarcza, 95th BG

'All was going well. We were climbing on course through very dense clouds. There was no reason to suspect danger as every 'plane had its prescribed course to fly until we broke into the clear. I was busy at my desk doing dead reckoning. Visibility was at best only 50 to 100 ft through the haze of clouds. Suddenly, a low and confusing shout of voices filled my earphones and about the same time I felt the tail of our aircraft go down sharply, perhaps as much as 30, then almost as rapidly level out again. The babble of voices continued until the pilot calmed them down enough to find out what had happened. The men in the rear were almost in shock. They could hardly speak but finally, the story came out. A British bomber had hit the right twin rudder of our 'plane. The waist gunners had seen it coming before the collision and assumed it was going to hit us broadside. We collided at right angles, the British bomber came from the north while we were going west . . .

'The clouds had cleared and we had a full view of the water. Our target was the shoreline of the western landing site near the town of Isigny. As we got closer to the French coast, the invasion fleet came into full view. I could see hundreds and hundreds of ships. The smoke of the guns from the battleships, cruisers and destroyers was very clearly visible to me. I could see hundreds of landing craft making large circles as they assembled to prepare for a run to the beaches. We passed directly over the fleet. I suppose I could say that I have personally seen with my very own eyes, the largest number of ships ever assembled in the history of mankind.'
John W. McClane Jr., navigator, 44th BG

'The lead 'plane roared down the runway, lifting gracefully into the grey light of the early morning. The remaining Fortresses, lined up like dancers in a conga line, swung onto the runway in turn and followed. Aboard No.003 my heart raced from the excitement of knowing that I was involved in an undertaking that, if successful, would be a major turning point of the war.

'The fluffy layer of clouds below hampered visibility but there were some breaks in them and I could see the choppy dark waters of the English Channel. Droning steadily toward the continent, I gasped when a huge opening in the clouds revealed ships and boats of all sizes dotting the water as far as I could see. Hundreds – no, there must be thousands, I thought. Although no one type of ship could be identified from nearly three miles high, I was to learn later practically the whole spectrum of powered vessels from battleships to motor launches made up the invasion fleet.

'Landing ships carrying thousands of troops, tanks, guns, vehicles and ammunition, were positioning for the daring dash to the Normandy beaches. Barrage balloons swayed lazily above the ships to which they were attached by stout cables.

'More holes appeared in the clouds and the awesome spectacle continued to unfold. I arose from my seat in the navigator's cramped work area in the left rear of the B-17G's nose to get a better view from the right waist window. Fascinated, I saw puffs of white smoke snort from the huge guns of battleships and cruisers aimed toward the mainland, and a moment later massive explosions could be seen a short distance inland where the shells landed, kicking up a fountain of dirt and debris that, I reflected, must be a mixture of steel and stones, flesh and bones when the targets were hit.'
Franklin Betz, 379th BG

'Obviously, the long-planned invasion had remained a well guarded secret. We encountered no German aircraft in the target area and enemy gunfire was very light and inaccurate.'
Henry Tarcza, 95th BG

'We were plenty tired after getting no sleep the night before, having been forced to land at a B-26 base following a raid on Paliseau on 5 June. We had flown back to Glatton that night and were unable to get to bed at all before being awakened for the raid on the Cherbourg peninsula. We flew over our target at 16,400 ft and dropped 38 100-lb demolition bombs through overcast. The landing troops hit the beach 14 minutes after we dropped our bombs. There were reports that

Later, massive explosions could be seen a short distance inland where the shells landed, kicking up a fountain of dirt and debris that, I reflected, must be a mixture of steel and stones, flesh and bones when the targets were hit. **Front row, L-R: Frank J. Bagdon, flt engineer; Frank Marsh, tail gunner; Al Tenenzaph, radio; Al Smith, waist gunner; Otis Creighton, waist gunner; John Snyder, ball. Standing, L-R: John L. Swanner Jr, pilot; John East, co-pilot; Frank L. Betz, navigator; Walter G. Collings, bombardier. (Frank L. Betz)**

and disrupt the enemy's fighting capabilities far below. I noted in my log: time, 07:07 hrs; altitude, 14,750 ft; temperature $-6°C$; indicated airspeed, 150 kts; magnetic heading, 344.

'The briefing officer was right. "There would be meagre flak, if any at all," he had said.

'There was none. The German guns were busily exchanging fire with the mighty invasion fleet massed in the Bay of the Seine and stretching for miles into the Channel.'
Perry Rudd, 457th BG

some of our bombs were still exploding as the boys went in.'
Perry Rudd, pilot, 457th BG

'The cloud cover required a blind bombing technique using radar. According to my log we were close to the target; gun positions near Arromanches roughly midway between the Cherbourg peninsula and Le Havre.

'The bomb bay doors of the planes in our formation opened.

'"Bombs Away!" the bombardier cried over the intercom.

'The bombs dropped from the bellies of the bombers, disappearing in the clouds to devastate

'We flew two missions on D-Day and did not see a single German fighter or even a burst of flak. Amazing! I could see a battleship out in the Channel; I believe it was the *Texas*, firing at shore targets. There was a solid mass of ships offshore and we could see the beach head landing craft and others streaking in with their precious burdens. At least we knew we had made a beach head.'
Ben Smith, radio operator, 303rd BG

'Coming back across the Channel, we could see more ships than you could count. It really was a sight to see the invasion fleet at a port in England ready to set out. They must have been part of the second wave to go over. The boys wanted to go in

low for a look but they made us stay up.'
Perry Rudd, 457th BG

'The return to Kimbolton was uneventful and was indeed a "milk run" from the standpoint of no enemy fighter attacks and no flak. We touched down at 09:26 hrs and I could sense an air of excitement on the base when I dropped to the ground from the plane after the pilot parked it in the dispersal area.

"How was it lieutenant?" the crew chief in charge of keeping the magnificent Fortress flying, an intense look on his leathery face weathered by the winds of his native Texas, asked.

"What I saw through the breaks in clouds was an unforgettable sight," I replied.

'There was no time to say anything more. A truck pulled up to take the crew to interrogation after which we had to get ready for the afternoon flight, my 30th mission. B-17s continued to peel off from the formation and land as the sun shone brightly through the cloud covering that was breaking up. It was a good omen.

'It is doubtful if any of us will ever again in our

The bomb bay doors of the 'planes in our formation opened. 'Bombs Away!' the bombardier cried over the intercom. (USAF Official)

lifetime, participate in a historic undertaking of this magnitude. So far nobody has.'
Henry Tarcza, 95th BG

"MILK RUN"

*They were over the Channel bound for Calais
The crew knew for sure it was judgement day
No fighters, no flak, came up from the ground
but the brave crew's hearts began to pound.'*

'A "milk-run!" The briefing officer described our mission and our route and it really sounded sweet. We would start our run over the water and only be over land a few minutes. "There are only about

eight guns there that will be able to reach you,'' he said. Wow! This was really Great! We wondered how the ''Bloody Hundredth'' happened to get such a soft mission.'
John A. Miller, gunner, 100th BG

'Supposed milk run mission.
The Germans threw a box formation of 10 fighters high and 10 wide. We were flying in the diamond slot in the high element of the 452nd. Our P-51 escorts, which were above us (we were flying at 38,000 ft), on sighting the German fighters jettisoned their belly gas' tanks; one of which went and put a hole four feet in diameter through our left aileron. There was flak and Lutz, the ball turret gunner, who could not wear his heavy B4 sheepskin jacket in the turret because of the cramped conditions, would leave his outer uniform thrown inside the 'plane.

'This crazy sergeant was tracking a German fighter and he put about 175 .50 calibre shells through our tail assembly. A good many shells shredded Lutz's flying jacket. We also sustained two 20 mm cannon holes in the waist area. On the return to Deopham, Lutz was amazed to see his B4 jacket in shreds. He saved it and only wore it on rare occasions, I assume to impress the girls. He was later issued a replacement. We lost quite heavily on that mission.'
John A. Holden, navigator, 452nd BG

'The excitement of my first mission over enemy territory crowded out almost all thoughts except an expectation of seeing fiery Messerschmitt fighters flashing past with cannons blazing. But all my expectations were in vain. Nothing exciting happened. No fiery fighters, no flashing cannon, no exploding anti-aircraft shells nearby. Frankly, I was disappointed. At approximately 15:00 hrs I was swinging my B-17 about the circular concrete hard-stand and the big ship halted in its sharp arc. As the engines were being cut, I could already see my crew chief, Sgt. Jim Haley, racing down the taxi strip in a jeep, heading towards our Fort'. I believe he got his jeep training at LeMans! The jeep stopped just short of the No.1 engine propeller arc, just as the props were coming to rest and Jim was coming to meet me as I swung down through the bomber's forward escape door, seven feet to the concrete below.

"Boy," I yelled at him, "If all my missions are like this "milk-run," I've got it made."

'Jim was a veteran. He had already wet-nursed six Fortress crews, efficiently keeping their ships running smoother than any in the group. I detected a rather incredulous look on Jim's face. He said "Lieutenant, let me show you something." Then he methodically guided me on a tour around the Fort'. Before we were finished, he had shown me no less than 27 jagged shrapnel holes in my ship, all from enemy anti-aircraft fire!

'Jim added, "It's the ones you don't see that get you."' '
Lt. Bob Browne, pilot, 487th BG

'It looked like the beginning of a ''milk run'' but I was getting scared. It was too easy.'
Cliff Hatcher, co-pilot Kac's Flak Shack, *94th BG*

' ''I'll see you at briefing,'' I said.
"You'll love this. It will be a milk run."
The next morning, sleep-stiff, I walked across the mud and found Bill McShane. It was Bill who had actually aroused me but I didn't remember getting up. I asked him where I could get some flying equipment. "What for?" Bill asked.
"I'm going along with Mac."
"You are not!" Bill said. "Don't be a fool. Have you ever been on oxygen at 27,000 ft?"
"Well, no."
"Alright. Wait until you've done a couple of test flights and try it out. You don't want to go up and pass out on these kids do you?"
"Well, no. I just thought. I've done a lot of flying, but not that altitude stuff. I guess I'm a rhubarb merchant, eh?" I grinned.
"There's no rhubarb where these guys go. You stay home today."
'So I didn't go with Mac. He was keenly disappointed. He even brought S/Sgt. Gerald E. Murphy of South Bend, Indiana, over to try to kid me back on. Murphy was McCormick's gunner-radio man. When Mac wasn't looking, Murphy said sotto voce: "Maybe you're getting out of something. I wish I could stay home today. I don't feel too good. I've got a cold."
"Mac says it will be a milk run," I suggested.
'Murphy adjusted his parachute straps and said: "Maybe, but I don't think there's any such thing. There ain't any milk runs, any more."
Arch Whitehouse, writing in 'True Magazine' about the last flight of the Vagabond King, *389th BG*

COMBAT

'Off we go into the wild sky yonder,
Keep your wings level and true.
If you'd live to be a grey-haired wonder,
Keep your nose out of the blue.
Flying men, guarding our nation's borders,
Will be there, followed by more
In echelon, we carry on,
For, nothing can stop the US Air Corps.'

The US Air Corps Song

'Combat is pretty good, if you make it back. Especially the money. But the raids are very tiresome as the oxygen and the cold temperature really tire you out. A lot of my good friends have gone down. At first it bothers you, but now I don't mind it so much. To think I used to be afraid of the dark and I wouldn't even ride the roller coaster. But I can say with the truth that I'd rather face fighters than flak. At fighters you can shoot back; but flak you can't. You just have to ride through it and hope for the best. Another I sweat out is my heated suit. This damn war is getting tough. You have to beg to go on a mission as our pilot took another crew into Sweden. So we are just spares now. Hoping to stay together. The fellows are fighting over my cap as I leave it behind when I go on a raid. When you don't make it back they divide up anything they wouldn't send home to your next of kin. We receive a bar of candy and a package of gum. I am now in a different squadron which gives you two Mars bars and a package of gum.'
Mission diary, S/Sgt. John W. Butler, gunner 389th & 93rd BGs

Eight different pilots
17 different planes
Four aborts
13 raids to Germany
Nine raids to France
Three raids to Italy
60 tons of bombs dropped
139 hours, 25 minutes of combat time.
S/Sgt. John W. Butler, gunner 389th & 93rd BGs

' ... During that time I got soaked from head to foot with gas. Before I could move, one or more 20 mm shells went off under my feet, wounding me in the right foot and both legs. The blow lifted me up and hurt my back and I fell on my back on the catwalk. Then I saw a blinding flash and I was on fire from head to foot. I felt my face burning and that was all I remembered as I thought I was dying.'
Theodore J. Myers, top turret gunner, 445th BG, Kassel, 27 September 1944

'The day was as bright and crisp as I have ever seen; more like a technicolour movie than real life. There were a few small wisps of white cotton clouds interspersed through the picture but mostly

I'd rather face fighters than flak. At fighters you can shoot back. (Sam Young)

it was clear. The sun glittered back from reflections of the shiny aluminium skin of the other ships in the formation. Before we reached the IP, I could see the stretch of this great city. The streets were like a chequerboard beneath us and once in a while, an ant-like motor vehicle appeared on the streets. The movement of the scene below was unbearably slow and we seemed as though we were motionless. The black bursts of flak were also hanging ahead and right at our altitude the sky was completely peppered with the stuff. As I looked ahead I said to myself, "And we're going to have to fly through that?"

'I turned the ball turret to the right, at about three o'clock position, and I could see the lumbering hulk of a Fortress, which was probably from another squadron, about 4,000 ft below us going in the opposite direction. Its nose was pointed downward with its right wing toward my left. Its right outboard engine was engulfed in red-orange flames streaking back about 10 feet. There was no doubt that the plane was going down.

'I watched the scene transfixed and uttered silently to the crew of the plane, although really to myself, "Get out, Get out!" As I watched, one, two, three and then four small white blossoms appeared behind the craft. Some had made it out. I changed my gaze to one of the small white

I could see strips of aluminium skin peeled back from the right wing. When we landed we found we had taken what must have been a 105 mm anti-aircraft shell through the wing. It left a hole that a man could put his head through. (Francis X. Sheehan, 448th BG)

parachutes in the air with something hanging below; an airman, another American. As I watched, small black puffs appeared around him as he slowly floated downward. The Germans were shooting at him with anti-aircraft fire. They could have used the 88 mm ammunition better by going after the rest of us still flying.

'As we proceeded over Berlin the ship lurched and twisted from impacts, but we kept going and finally unloaded our bombs onto a railroad station in the heart of the city. Once away from the city, the flight back was uneventful. When I turned my turret to about two o'clock, I could see strips of aluminium skin peeled back from the right wing. When we landed we found we had taken what must have been a 105 mm anti-aircraft shell through the wing. It left a hole that a man could put his head through near the inboard end of the Tokyo gas' tank. There were hundreds of smaller holes throughout the main body, wings and tail sections but no-one was hit. I had learned what accurate and intense flak was.'
William C. Stewart, 92nd BG

'I heard the groups in front of us calling for P-51s as they were being hit by Me 109s. Baugh was the first on our crew to see an enemy fighter. He reported them attacking and shooting down a straggler. The first pass was made from seven o'clock low, up through "C" Squadron and then on to us. This Me 109 put a couple of slugs into us. One went through the nose and almost got Wilk' and "Turnip." When this happened, Wilk' said he looked at "Turnip" and could see it dawn on "Turnip's" face that this was the "real

McCoy." "Turnip" started unlatching the nose guns and firing like hell. Wilk' said that he started shooting at our P-51 escort and "Turnip" maintained he was "keeping the area clear". The fighter went past us and turned back down at us. Wilk' and Szalwinski were pouring .50s into him from their two turrets and O'Leary got a few from the waist. I think he was diving directly for us, but he came just in front and knocked the left horizontal stabilizer off Lt Martin's ship in front of us. That Me 109 diving into the formation spurting flames all over presented such a vivid picture that I shall never forget it. When he hit Martin's ship there must have been some sort of explosion as the nose and cockpit of our ship were filled with black smoke and dust. The Me 109's wing flew off and went over my wing, knocking Lt. Joe King's ship in the "horizontal diamond" (both Martin and King managed to make it back to England and they were each awarded the DFC. Wilk' and our crew got credit for that Me 109).

'Another Me 109 came in from five o'clock high. Everyone said he was coming directly at us, but our gunners put out so much lead that he diverted and crashed into a ship in the lead squadron. We saw both ships explode. The reason we got so many fighter attacks directed at us was because we were the top ship and the corner ship in the group and therefore around us was the least possible concentration of friendly fire. Ordinarily, fighters made their passes in a dive to get greater speed. The enemy fighters stayed with us for about an hour.

'We were at 15,000 ft as no flak was expected. However, there was plenty of accurate flak at the target. I never thought I would be glad to see flak, but I was this day because it meant the fighters wouldn't "come in". We started out with 10 ships in our squadron and on "bombs away" there were six ships. We were glad to return from this one. There were so many holes in the nose that Wilk' nearly froze sitting up there on the way home.'
Griswold Smith, pilot, 100th BG

'After this mission the mental and physical strain was so much that I was too tired to keep up the log of my missions. Missions were coming every day with no rest in between. I would return from a mission and the pilots' truck would be waiting to carry me to the mission critique. From there I would stagger over to the Mess Hall and gorge myself. After that I would waddle over to my barrack and fall in bed until the alert sergeant woke me the next morning for briefing. Following that

schedule I didn't have much time to write notes on my missions. I planned to catch up on them in a couple of days while they were still fresh in my mind, but somehow I never got around to it.'
Griswold Smith, pilot, 100th BG

'Get a load of those guys, high in the skies,
Winging to victory,
Up and at 'em in the fight for,
People like you and me . . . '

People Like You and Me

By Mack Gordon and Harry Warren. c 1942 by Bregman, Vocco & Conn Inc. Copyright renewed 1969. All rights reserved. Used by permission

'The bombing was carried out at extremely low altitudes and our targets were secondary rail junctions and marshalling yards in smaller cities not previously bombed. Just east of Ansbach, our target, we passed an enemy airfield and I counted 10 Me 109s and other types on the field. We were only 5,500 ft above the ground but they did not fire at us. This was the first time that I felt the concussion of our own bombs and also the first time I saw boxcars tumble through the air. I felt we were unnecessarily exposed to light flak which can be murderous at low altitudes and slow speeds. I feel uneasy when a boxcar attains almost as much altitude as our bomber.'
Abe Dolim, navigator, 94th BG

'We finally got through after what seemed an eternity. We found ourselves flying in formation with only one other 'plane and that was all in flames. If it had exploded we would have gone up with it. I was so scared I couldn't even tell the pilot to get the hell out of here. Finally, "Pops," the top turret gunner, screamed over the interphone to "get his bloody arse out of it or we would never see Polebrook again." He shouted many other choice words over the interphone but our pilot did what "Pops" said and broke off.
S/Sgt. Adolph J. Smetana, tail gunner, 351st BG

'One of the '109s exploded just above our squadron as the rest of the enemy formation passed over us. Breitbach, in the tail, reported the same enemy squadron attacked the group behind us from 12 o'clock level, and that about 10 B-17s were in trouble. Our combined .50s created a tremendous earsplitting, reverberating racket and the entire bomber seemed to vibrate. The stench of exploded cartridges filled our nose compartment. The floor

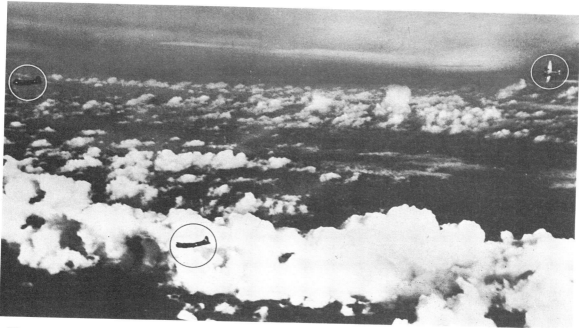

The same enemy squadron attacked the group behind us from 12 o'clock level and that meant about 10 B-17s were in trouble. (USAF Official)

of our navigator-bombardier compartment was covered with empty .50 calibre casings, and in moving about I felt like I had roller skates on my fur-lined boots.'
Abe Dolim, navigator, 94th BG

'Out of the corner of my eye I saw "cripples" heading for Sweden, but mostly my eyes were focused on the flying coffin in front of us. It finally went out of control and started down. Tears welled up in my eyes and I prayed that nine spots would come out of that plane. One who didn't was our usual waist gunner who had been with us since we had been grouped together at Ardmore AFB, Oklahoma. It was his very first mission in action.'
S/Sgt. Adolph J. Smetana, tail gunner, 351st BG

'Gen Doolittle had said missions were now getting shorter and easier! We were under constant fighter attack for four-and-a-half hours, but we weren't so bad off as the Luftwaffe attacked us from the tail position. They would sit out of range of our gunners and lob rockets at our formation. I had a ringside seat of the 45th Wing who were right in front of us. B-17s, P-51s, '110s and '109s were going down all over the place. I heard that the

452nd really took a beating. While all this was going on, all that was running through my mind was Doolittle telling us missions were getting shorter and easier. Well we finally got back and after debriefing and cleaning up, I went to the officers' club and proceeded to get gloriously drunk.'
Mike Wysoki, 94th BG

'I was still only 22 years' old but felt "much, much older".'
Abe Dolim, navigator, 94th BG

'All the way back until we hit warmer altitude I had to keep exchanging his mask, as he kept turning blue. The blood froze and he could not breathe. But we got him back alive.'
Earl Zimmerman, radio operator, 389th BG

'Warga did release our bombs. If I live to be 100 years old I'll still be able to close my eyes and see it again. He picked out a German farmhouse in the middle of nowhere. The bombs started "walking" across the barn yard, through the barn and into the house, coming out the other side of the yard. No one on the ground could have survived this completely unexpected disaster. When questioned at interrogation why he picked this target, his reply was: "What's the difference in destroying a farm house or a city house?"'
Lt. John W. McClane Jr., navigator, 44th BG

'This was my 20th mission and it was to Zwickau, Germany (12 April 1944). We took off loaded with 4,200 lb of fragmentation bombs. We entered the coast of France at Dieppe and as we made our way over France we had not encountered any flak or enemy fighters. The weather started closing in and we were ordered by radio to abort the mission and return to base. We made a long swinging turn and dropped to 15,000 ft to get under the cloud formation. Our fighter escort was very high and above the clouds. From nine o'clock several formations of 'planes appeared in "V" formation. There were five "V" formations of about 20 'planes each. They started firing at us and flying through our formation which consisted of nine 'planes only, since we had been separated from the rest of the group when we dropped through the cloud formation.

'By the time I had been lowered down in the ball turret the 'plane on our left wing was already on fire. I saw the tail turret shot completely off, with the gunner reaching his arm back as if to get his parachute. They lowered the landing gear and the German fighters made no more attacks at them. Those that were able, bailed out.

'I saw one B-24 blow up just under us. The enemy fighters attacked for about 45 minutes. By the time it was over we had lost five B-24s. Our tail gunner shot down three Me 109s; one after another and they blew up right over us. The ball turret got one Me 109 just under us, causing the 'plane to bounce like a ball. The top turret, nose turret and left waist each got one Me 109. The enemy fighters would line up about 20 in a line and fly into us and just keep coming, then another 20 would line up and do the same; over and over. We fired most of the ammunition we had on board our ship. There was a little ammunition left in the right waist and ball turret guns as these guns finally jammed. The tail turret gunner's guns melted and he had no ammunition left. It was the same at the other gun positions. When my ball turret guns jammed I thought we had just about had it, so I opened my turret door, planning on getting my parachute and getting ready to bail out. As I opened my door I could see the rear of the 'plane and the tail gunner must have had the same idea. We hesitated as our eyes met and explained our situation on the intercom to each other. Then he said: "Why don't we try flashing our trouble lights (small lights on the end of our extension cord to help see when making repairs) off and on and maybe the fighters will think it's our guns flashing." It was crazy, but we did it.

'Enemy 20 mm shells were bursting all around us. One 20 mm went up between the right and left waist gunners and exploded in the ceiling. One hit the column on top of the ball turret. One cut our hydraulic lines in two and exploded in our hydraulic reservoir. In general, the ship was full of holes and looked as if someone had used a can opener on it. We were just sitting there, waiting to be shot down as there was nothing more we could do, when out of nowhere came the prettiest P-38s and scattered enemy fighters everywhere. After the P-38s took care of the enemy fighters they escorted the four of us B-24s left, back to our base in England and peeled off and tipped their wings. We had no hydraulic system left and no brakes so we had to crank the landing gear down. We hit the runway at about 100 m.p.h. and as many of us that were able ran to the tail end of the ship as far as we could so that the tail would drag on its tail skid and slow us down. We slowed it down some but still ran off the runway. Our ship was full of holes and had to be completely overhauled before it would fly again. We all felt lucky to be back, and that for some reason God had been with us on this mission.'

Elvin O. Cross. 445th BG ball turret gunner

'After landing, the whole crew gathered around the 'plane congratulating and slapping each other on the back. This was a happy day for us. But we all knew it was only by God's Will that we made it through without an injury among us. There is no way I can express in words the relief we felt. The strain of combat had taken its toll and it would be a full year before most of us would recover from this nightmare.'

1/Lt. John W. McClane Jr., 68th BS navigator, 44th BG on completion of their 30th and final mission, on Tuesday 26th September 1944.

KNIGHTS OF THE SKY

Many a pilot who flew the pursuits
Has winged his way into heaven
But I know that the boy who was leading the flight
Was a kid in a P-47

As missions grew long through death laden skies

Our bombers had little to fear
We had the best escort acclaimed by us all
"T" was a squadron of Thunderbolts near

Many a bomber knocked out of the fight
Forever their praises will sing
For while limping home through treacherous sky
They had "white noses" under each wing

How well I remember that beautiful sight
Wispy contrails high in the heavens
And how we all welcomed the tail gunner's words
'Here come the P-47s'

'There was plenty of company joining us. Focke Wulf 190s were in formation on the left and Bf 109s off the right wing. "Mac" McCabe in the top turret kept yelling through his oxygen mask to dip the wing so he could hit them with his .50s. Not knowing what else to do, Howell and I were just trying to keep the ship flying. We had been through this before and somehow fate had brought us through. In the past, we had outlasted German fighters until they turned back over the North Sea, but now we were practically standing still in a 100 m.p.h. headwind on a 285 heading with lots of German soil still underneath. There must have been two Jerries sitting off our tail end pumping a steady flow of cannon and .30 calibre

**Our escort of P-51s departed to chase bogies.
(352nd FG Assn)**

bullets into us. I heard several .30s zing into the cockpit and bounce off the armour plate seats. Mixed in with these .30s were some incendiary bullets which made a good mixture with the intense gasoline fumes, and pretty soon we had a roaring furnace in the bomb bay.
Maj. Jim O'Brien, 44th BG

'I was flying as tail turret gunner on the 24 February mission to Gotha, Germany. We had been having engine trouble from the time we had crossed the Channel. Shortly before reaching the target, our number two engine, which had been leaking oil, began to smoke badly and we had to feather it. We were still able to keep our position in the formation until engine number three started acting up and and we could get very little power out of her. We saw some fighter 'planes coming in and thought they were ours, so we fired the colours of the day and dropped out of formation and down to the cloud cover. The fighters turned out to be German. When we fell out of formation with engine number two still smoking, the rest of the group thought we had been shot down. Evidently, so did the enemy fighters as they did not follow us down. We were able to make it back to our base flying at low altitude. A couple of times single enemy fighters came up to check us out, but for some reason did not attack. We felt lucky to get back to our base.'
Elvin O. Cross, 445th BG tail gunner

'We received reports that the Luftwaffe was up in force. Near Coblenz, our escort of P-51s departed to chase "bogies". Some minutes later, Lt. Maybank spotted a small formation of unidentified fighters at three o'clock level. I stood up to be close to my .50s and as I squinted out toward 2 o'clock, I was shocked to see about six jet-black FW 190s flying right through the high squadron,

I only needed to change aim to shoot again. Then this one stood in bright flames ... I was so surprised and fascinated that I flew alongside my victim and stared at the metre-high flames which were pouring out of this Liberator. (Ernst Schröeder)

attacking from 12 o'clock level. The group closed up – no-one seemed to be hurt. About 10 minutes later, 10 more black FWs attacked the lead squadron from 12 o'clock level, some of them fish-tailing to rake their targets. Kelch, Long and I fired as they went by at three o'clock. One of the Focke Wulfs rammed the number six aircraft in the lead squadron and both exploded. Two more B-17s dropped out of formation. One began a shallow trailing dive with all 10 men bailing out. The other maintained speed with the group about 500 ft below the lead squadron and dropped its landing gear to communicate air surrender. After some minutes, it retracted its landing gear and rejoined the group, which was then about 20 miles south-east of Frankfurt.

'At our altitude of 19,000 ft there were some stratus layers, ideal for the enemy, and as I scanned at 11 o'clock level, I spotted a large formation of fighters approaching from 2,000 yd, heading for our low squadron. I got on intercom and notified the crew – Me 109s, about 30 of them in three flights. We opened fire at about 1,200 yd and I picked the far left '109 in the lead flight. Two of the '109s were shot out of formation before they approached 500 yd. A string of cannon shells, so close I heard their sharp cracks, exploded just in front of our nose. I fired about 60 rounds at my '109 until he passed by our number one engine, forcing me to quit. It was closing fast from about 100 yd when I yelled at Wehrfritz to get him. He poured .50s into the Messerschmitt at point-blank range. Apparently, the enemy pilot was not firing at this point or he would have raked us. His aircraft stalled after passing us and our tail gunner saw it go down and crash – the pilot did not bail out.'
Abe Dolim, navigator, 94th BG, Zwickau

'When we approached the bombers in a closed formation, suddenly some of these large aircraft started to catch on fire, some even blew up. This led us to believe that other German fighter formations had attacked the Americans before us. But then it was very quickly our turn. My squadron Leader and I had had a test gyro-sight installed in our aircraft. With the aid of this sighting mechanism I was able to down two B-24s within seconds. The [first] aircraft turned on its side and plunged. Also, the neighbouring machine was already smoking from a previous attack. Both left engines were burning. I only needed to change aim to shoot again. Then this one stood in bright flames. The new aiming device was functioning astonishingly. I was so surprised and fascinated that I flew along

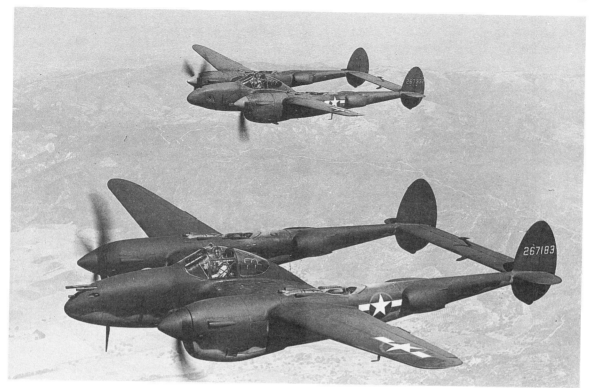

A formation of P-38s slanted overhead adding to my feeling of security. (Lockheed California)

side my victim and stared at the metre-high flames which were pouring out of this Liberator all the way back beyond the elevator. Then this great machine clumsily laid itself over on its back and went down.'
Ernst Schröeder, pilot, II.Sturm/JG 300

'The scene was innocuous enough. Nothing about it even hinted of danger. A formation of P-38s slanted overhead adding to my feeling of security. It seemed that we had been flying for hours without incident. We chatted a little on the inter-com until Chick told us to shut up.'
Ben Smith, radio operator, 303rd BG

> 'With Focke Wulfs high at six o'clock
> With Messerschmitts at 10
> With Focke Wulfs diving through the top
> To climb and dive again
> Another boring in at 12
> With neon leading edge
> Nine men can be oblivious
> But one of 10 must hedge'

'After passing each other, we both turned our aircraft around and headed at each other with blazing guns. During the first approach, I received two hits in the tail unit. During the second approach, my guns failed. Evidently, I had used up all my ammunition when firing at the two bombers, or my guns were jamming – I do no longer know exactly what happened. We made about four or five more frontal passes at each other, but all that was left for me to do, in order not to get hit again, was to take evasive action. After the last frontal approach of the American I finally "hugged" the ground and was lucky enough to escape – most likely because of the camouflage paint job of my aircraft.'
Ernst Schröeder, pilot, II.Sturm/JG 300

'The German fighter groups were called "Jagd-gruppen" and the most famous of these gruppen was the IV/JG 3 stationed in the vicinity of Brunswick. They were called the *Battling Bastards of Brunswick*. In three missions to Brunswick, we got to meet some of these boys first-hand.'
1/Lt. John W. McClane Jr., navigator, 44th BG

'I told "Greenhouse" Squadron to drop tanks and we turned into the '190s. They broke formation and scattered, some of them rolling, some split-essing, but the majority broke right and then went into a Lufberry. I got my sights on a '190 and started firing, observing strikes on the fuselage and tail. He broke left and then went into a spin. I broke left and continued turning, finding myself in a Lufberry with eight or 10 FW 190s. I started a tight climbing spiral, the '190s following, but I was able to outclimb them. My flight was broken on initial attack by enemy aircraft flying through us.'

Col. Irwin H. Dregne, 357th FG, 14 January 1945

'A '190 came up from underneath and I fired a burst at him. His right wheel fell down and he stalled. I overran him and pulled up to make another pass. The '190 was going into a spin with the right wheel still down and it looked to me like the pilot fell out. I saw two 'chutes. Two '190s came in on my tail and I turned so sharp that I spun in. I recovered at 10,000 ft and several '109s shot at me as they came down. I climbed up to about 30,000 ft but saw no more enemy aircraft.'

Lt. Col. William C. Clark, 357th FG, 14 January 1945

'The enemy aircraft seemed to hesitate in making an intitial attack [on the bombers]; they made several orbits as though they were sizing the situation up. This was to our advantage. While they were "debating", I placed my squadron in the proper position and at the same time headed towards the enemy aircraft, hoping to break up the gaggle before they could attack the bombers. They did start an attack before I could get to them, but we interfered slightly and engaged the Krauts in individual dog fights. I caught one Me 109 which slipped through and started towards the bombers. I got on his tail but was out of firing range. The pilot displayed a little judgement by looking around, then he put his ship in a 90° vertical dive from 32,000 ft. I followed him down.

'At about every 5,000 ft during the descent he would roll and do some very violent manoeuvres. I just did a tight spiral around him. At 8,000 ft he made a very tight pull-out and levelled off. Evidently, the pilot thought he had lost me for he began flying straight and level. Maybe he didn't realize the speed of the .50 calibre bullet and decided to take time out for a decision. I made a little tighter pull-out and started firing at 200 yd, closing to 50 yd. I got strikes all over the left side of the fuselage and left wing. Just before I released the trigger, about four feet of the left wing ripped

off. The pilot did not get out as his ship went into the ground, making a big explosion. The pilot had been very fair, but he had made the usual mistake which prevents fair pilots from becoming good pilots.'

Extract from report by Maj. John B. England, 357th FG, 14 January 1945.(England finished the war with a score of 17$\frac{1}{2}$ victories but was killed in a flying accident in France on 17 November 1954.)

'I turned on my gun switches and pulled my nose up and fired at the Me 262 before rejoining my flight. The '262 disappeared from sight. Maxwell got on the tail of some 25 to 30 FW 190s and a Lufberry to the left began. Two '190s got on my tail and one fired at me. I closed to about 100 ft and set him on fire and then shot the other down in flames. I bounced a third '190 and he dived and came up into a loop. At the top of it he kicked it into a hammer-head to make a head-on pass. He was going fairly slow and gave me a perfect target. I fired until he burst into flames.'

1/Lt. Raymond M. Bank, 357th FG, 14 January 1945

'As deputy command pilot, I frequently changed off flying formation with the airplane commander to keep occupied and not have to watch the Jerries press their blazing gun attacks. The interphone was alive with excited calls of enemy action. Head-on passes and tail attacks; in singles and in "gaggles"; rockets, 20 mm cannon, and even some cables were thrown at us. Seven of our B-24s were shot down. Many of us were shot up, but it was not all one-sided. The gunners of the 22 airplanes that returned accounted for 16 German fighters.'

Col. Myron Keilman, 392nd BG

'There was a long line of Me 109s, in no particular formation, except a sort of long column containing six to 10 abreast. To my right and above were several Jerries doing snaps, rolls and spins. I called my wingman, Lt. William W. Gruber, and told him that when they finally got through passing by we would tack onto their rear and start shooting. It seemed an endless procession but finally they passed by and I tacked onto their tail end. The last four Me 109s then broke into us. We started a honey of a Lufberry which went about six turns. I finally cut the butter and got a short burst into one of them. I was going straight down when I fired from about 100 yd, seeing many strikes right into the pilot through the top of his canopy. The plane went out of control and crashed into the ground.

The pilot, who I am sure was dead from my bullets, did not bail out. I reefed upwards and went after another Me 109 who was at the tail end. He flicked over and started down. I followed and opened fire from about 700 yd, but I saw no strikes. He hit the ground and exploded. The pilot did not get out. Shortly thereafter, Duncan shot down his second FW 190. This time the pilot did not get out of the exploding fighter.'
Lt. John L. Sublett, 357th FG, 14 January 1945

'I closed to about 400 yd on a FW190 at the rear of a gaggle, firing a good burst and getting strikes all over his fuselage. I believe the pilot was killed. I went back up to the bombers, looked around for a couple of minutes and saw a formation of about 40 to 50 FW 190s coming up about 1,000 yd behind. There were a couple of P-51s near and they broke with me. We met the enemy planes head-on. They didn't fire, but we did.'
Capt. Leonard 'Kit' Carson, 357th FG, 14 January 1945

'You gave the Hun the most humiliating beating he has ever taken in the air. Extend my personal admiration and congratulations to each member of your command, both ground and air, for a superb victory.'
Gen. Jimmy Doolittle in a message to Col. Dregne, CO, 357th FG, for his group's shooting down a record 60½ enemy aircraft, 14 January 1945

'A belligerent spirit and the desire to kill must be imbued in all replacement pilots. Lack of aggressive spirit and desire to destroy the enemy will result in hesitancy and indecision which are fatal in combat.'
Lt. Col. Donald R. Renwick, Dean of 'Clobber College' and ex-65th FG P-51 pilot

'The jets usually made their attacks in two's and three's from six o'clock low or level, because from that angle they looked like P-51s with wing tip tanks and the gunners were afraid to shoot until they got in real close. They would coast in on a formation from the rear with their jets off, open fire, turn on their jets and vanish with terrific speed. They were armed with 30 mm cannon. They made several passes at us from six o'clock low. I distinctly remember two ships going down in flames. I believe a couple of others were crippled and knocked out of formation; one or two aborted earlier.'
Griswold Smith, pilot, 100th BG

'Our conventional fighters, the P-51 and the P-47, didn't have a chance of catching a jet in the air. When they shot one down it was because they were lucky enough to sneak up on one with his jets off and shoot him down before he knew what had happened, or if they came out of a cloud directly on top of one. Ordinarily, they would see one floating around with jets off and would start chasing him. He would sit around 'til they were almost in range, then he would turn on his jets and make them look like they were sitting still.'
Griswold Smith, pilot, 100th BG

'On 10 April 1945, while approaching the target, Brandenburg–Briest airfield, we were caught alone, out of formation with engine trouble, by four Me 262 jet aircraft. We suffered severe damage during the attacks, but God and the skilful performance of our crew got us out of Germany to a good landing at St Tronde, Belgium, without the loss of a man!'
T/Sgt. Frank M Mead Jr., Flt. Engineer/Gunner, 837th BS, 487th BG

> *'Oh pity the poor co-pilot*
> *His wavering glance belies*
> *He gazes at the instruments*
> *With fighters in his eyes'*

'As I look back on the experiences during the second half of 1943 and early 1944, when we had no, or very little, fighter escort, I can only believe that someone was looking out for me as well as being mighty lucky. I can't deny that I was scared at times. Luckily, I was as young as I was at that time (23 years' old) with no responsibilities like a family, etc.'
Dick Perry, co-pilot, 390th BG

'We had more and more Spitfires, P-38s, P-47s and P-51s escorting us. But not as often as we would have liked.'
Henry A. DeKeyser, 576th BS, 392nd BG

'The attack was not preceded by the normal queuing up, or assembling, of the fighters out to the right, front and above or out high to the left front. Normally, the German fighters came in, in a single large mass, directly from the front – as though vectored into position under radar control. In all probability they made a direct head-on approach from a distance of some 15 to 20 miles. The first we saw of them, they were among us and already firing their guns. They made only a single

We had more and more Spitfires, P-38s, P-47s and P-51s escorting us. But not as often as we would have liked. (Col. William B. Cameron)

pass at the lead wing and then went on through the lead wing, maintaining an upright position, thus abandoning, for at least this one time, their practice of attacking inverted and then pulling out in an earthward dive.'
Col.(later Gen.) Maurice 'Mo' Preston, CO, 379th BG, leader, 1st Bomb Division strike to Schweinfurt, 13 April 1944

'Frequently they closed to spitting distance.'
Lt. Anthony Arcaro, pilot, Eagle's Wrath

'Our tail gunner, Ruben Montanez, yelled: "I see fighters, I see flak." Then the entire 'plane began to shudder and shake with the guns in the rear of the plane firing simultaneously, and from the impact of 20 mm and 30 mm enemy shells. As our 'plane continued to shake, my co-pilot pointed out his side window at B-24s in the other squadrons going down on fire, and enemy fighters exploding.'
William R. Dewey, pilot, 701st BS, 445th BG

'2 November 1944, 3 miles high, North of Erfurt, escorting B-17s. As the '109s tumbled from above, lancing through the rear box of B-17s in a

perfect bounce, Yorkshire Yellow Flight reverse course. "109s below, let's go!" Winging over into his dive, Lt. Vanden Heuvel follows an enemy, then loses it in overcast; his report continuing, 'We came out under the overcast. A FW 190 turned on Lt. Czapala and myself. Lt. Mitchell closed in on him and registered numerous hits – the FW 190 hit the ground and burned. I became separated and as I was turning around I saw a FW 190 making a steep turn head on into me. I fired a short burst, saw no hits, but the '190 did a snap out of the steep turn he was in. As we were about 100 ft off the deck at the time he did not recover, hit the ground upside down and burned. I claim one FW 190 destroyed.
66 rounds expended.
Aircraft P-51D E9-D 44-14217'
The combat diary of 1/Lt George R. Vanden Heuvel, 376th FS, 361st FG

'We weren't long into the airspace over Belgium when all hell broke loose. The yellow-nosed Abbeville Kids of Goering's crack group and the German Air Force rose to the occasion to exhibit their usual aggressiveness with upwards of 400 aircraft. In our area there were only six P-51s. Not much help with such odds. I watched as a '51 and '109 collided head-on.'
Wilbur Richardson, gunner, 94th BG

'It was a solid overcast over enemy territory, so we didn't see much of anything on the ground. Flak was fairly heavy but not too accurate. On the way back the crew members watched about six Me 109s sneaking around the tops of clouds, looking for stragglers. They found a B-24 Liberator and, like vultures, they kept firing until it blew up. During all this, one of our P-47s shot down a Me 109. We had very good fighter cover most of the time by P-38s, P-47s and Spitfires. The mission lasted $8\frac{1}{2}$ hours and we could see the Swiss Alps in the distance on our way back.'
Joe Wroblewski, pilot, 351st BG

'The bombs were smack "on target", but the battle wasn't over. No sooner had the wing left the target's flak than we were accosted by German fighters again. Strung out in-trail and with some 'planes slowed down from flak damage, our three squadrons became vulnerable to vicious attacks. For the next hour and more, Messerschmitt, Focke Wulf and Junkers fighters worked us over until our fighters could fend them off.'
Col. Myron Keilman, 392nd BG

The bombs were smack 'on target' but the battle wasn't over. (Jim Tootell)

'Any bomber that fell out of formation was a dead duck. I watched a B-17 off to our right by itself. An Me 110 got on its tail and really poured tracers into the bomber. It caught fire and as the flames licked around the tail I could see the tail-gunner still firing back at the Jerry. Finally, the bomber climbed straight up and fell off into a spin, burning and breaking up. One yellow nosed Me 109 came in between us and our wing man with his guns blazing. He must have put a few holes in our tail, but no-one was hurt. Our waist gunner fell back away from his gun for a second when he saw this 'plane so close and when he did start shooting again he shot through our tail and through the B-17 flying next to us. The enemy fighters kept falling and exploding all around us, but still they kept coming in without giving us a breathing spell. They tried real hard to break up our formation but we hung together for dear life. All I could hear over the intercom was, "Fighter coming in at five o'clock, one at seven o'clock, another at nine o'clock low. Fighter coming in at 10 o'clock level!" It was almost useless to call them out. There were so many coming in from every direction.

'At about this time many thoughts began to go through my mind. My parachute was just behind my seat and the temptation to snap it on and get the hell out of it was very strong. But then I thought about the other crew members. I don't doubt that they were just as scared as I was, but at least they could shoot back. I thought about my training that led to our present situation and about looking forward to being in combat. But that was before all this. Right then I would have settled for being just a potato peeler, mess cook or whatever, washing kettles for the duration.

'Somehow, one of our P-51s got separated from his group and he tagged along with us. We were very grateful because he fought as long as his fuel permitted, chasing the enemy until his ammunition was gone. Then he just dived after the fighters to divert them from the B-17s. Watching this one fighter escort bolstered our confidence for survival and we all admired his guts to hang in there with us. Later we learned his name was Maj. Howard. He got back to base safely.'
Joe Wroblewski, pilot, 351st BG, 11th January 1944

'On 18 September Field Order 577 Frantic 7 Dash One was started. The 95th, 100th and 390th BGs were to be escorted to Warsaw by the 4th, 355th and 361st FGs. Rendevous was to be 11:45 hrs at Koszalin on the Baltic Coast; the actual meet was between Stettin and Torun. Heavy flak damage was received by the B-17s near Stettin, but 107 of them made it to Warsaw and dropped food and medical supplies. Unfortunately, most of the supplies fell into the Germans hands. One of the damaged B-17s was escorted to land at Brzese; the remaining B-17s made it to Poltava and Mirgorod. Our fighter base was Piryatin, where we were all landed by 15:20 hrs.

'On 19 September most of the fighters left Piryatin to rendevous with the B-17s at 13:30 hrs near Horodenka, Poland and crossed over Czechoslovakia, Romania and Hungary and bombed their target near Brod, Yugoslavia. There was much heavy flak but we all made it to Italy, landing at Foggia at 16:00 hrs. After a short rest we left Foggia at 09:59 hrs on 22 September to rendevous with the B-17s near Marseilles at 13:25 hrs. All 355th aircraft were down at Steeple Morden by 17:00 hrs. This was the most awe-inspiring mission I ever took part in.'
Capt. Pete Hardiman, P-51 pilot, 354th FS, 355th FG

'A B-24 that had been lagging behind at seven o'clock drew in close at five o'clock, just as a German came through. The fighter smashed head-on into the big one right at the nose turret and both 'planes exploded in a ball of flame. Then it was all over. Just like that. But back through the formations behind us the Germans barrelled with reckless abandon. Airplanes were going down in every direction, the cripples, staggering out of formation, clinging to life – then blowing up or fluttering down out of sight.'
Keith Schuyler, pilot 44th BG, author of 'Elusive Horizons'

'They came in five abreast, wing tip to wing tip, held their guns open and dived through our flight of B-17s. It was like shooting clay pigeons. They couldn't miss – and didn't. I picked out one FW 190 and gave him half-a-dozen short bursts. He came in under our ship with the cowling billowing black smoke. I followed him through and he started to barrel roll. Then I couldn't see the fighter for black smoke. While my turret was facing forward I saw our lead ship go up in flame like a Roman rocket. Someone parachuted out and pulled the rip cord. He was all on fire. His 'chute opened and fire went up the shroud lines like a fuse. The ship had a full bomb load. It started down, then blew up.'
94th BG gunner. Bohlen, Germany 7 October 1944

'The Mustang was the sweetest airplane, one step below Angel's wings – not that I wanted to get them!'
1/Lt. Bruce Spengler, Buzzin' Cousin P-51 pilot, 83rd FS, 78th FG

'We always knew when the 78th would be flying an escort mission for the bombers because we could hear the B-17s of the 91st BG being pre-flighted a few miles away at Bassingbourn.'
S/Sgt. Bob Fitzgerald, crew chief for Willie Hegman's P-47 Busy Bee, 82nd FS, 78th FG

'The sight that impressed me most was when a flight of P-38 twin-tailed fighters would show up to escort us. The effect of this sight would send our internal communication system in a high pitch of approval and gratitude by all the crew. The P-38s were no better than the P-47 or P-51s and maybe not as effective, but it was still a beautiful sight.'
1/Lt. John W. McClane Jr., navigator, 44th BG

'I was a fast guy, yes, there's no question. But, you are forced to take over more and more responsibilities. So, one day you missed your best carefree years. That's truly a disadvantage.'
Generalmajor Adolf Galland

PROPAGANDA

'The first casualty when war comes is truth.'

Hiram Johnson, US Senate, 1917

'Welcome to England, crew of the *Blonde Venus*. Our Luftwaffe fighter boys will be eager to meet with you in the sky when you fly your first mission tomorrow. We will be waiting for you and so will our incredible flak guns manned by your Germanic cousins. We will teach you to side with the Anglo-Saxons in this war against your kin.'
'Lord Haw Haw' (William Joyce, the British traitor)

'On the way up we listened in on Radio Berlin and heard the charming voice of "Sally" of whom we were to hear a lot more later. She invited all Americans up to Stalag Luft, where the beds were soft and the sheets are clean and she'd be there. The food was also good, she said. When she had finished, her friend, a renegade American newspaperman, speaking to his "fellow Americans", attacked the "Plutocratic-Juder-Bolshevik Presi-

dent of the US." When that jerk was finished we switched to the BBC, where a charming female voice, sounding veddy-veddy British, announced a programme of choice swing music, which was very enjoyable. All good things must come to an end and her programme did. Then the BBC reporter came through with a very depressing report about the 68 US bombers which failed to return after a raid on Berlin. Gulp! And we're on our way to the 8th Air Force. Yipe!'
Philip H. Meistrich, 453rd BG

'In the radio room, I tuned into BBC in London. The announcer spoke of an allied success. "The Paris radio announces that the French capital has been liberated, with the German commander ordering his men to cease fighting immediately. General Dietrich Von Cholitz, Chief of the Nazi garrison of about 10,000 men, signed the unconditional surrender order today in the presence of French Brig. Gen. Jacques-Philippe Le Clerc and a US Corps Commander in the Montparasse railway station."

'I quickly switched to intercom. "Hey it's official. They took Paris this morning."

"Whee," came the reply.

'From the crew's reaction you'd think the war was over.'
Richard Bing, radio operator, 561st BS, 388th BG

'As we waited for our chance for take-off, I tuned to Radio Bremen which spoke in English. Here we were waiting to take-off for a raid over Germany and Radio Bremen was saying "American bombers are on their runways in England now, waiting to attack north-west Germany."

'How did they know?'
Larry Goldstein, radio operator, 388th BG

'I am now in the habit of tuning in the German Air Raid warning Service. Their announcers are women who call out their messages hysterically – "Achtung. Amerikanischer Grossbomber Wegen nach Osnabruch, Hanover, Braunschweg und Berlin."

'They know exactly what we are up to.'
Abe Dolim, radio operator, 94th BG

'Many of us had radios in our huts. We could hear the BBC and its renderings of American jazz, nature talks, or the news of Monty and his men. Often we listened to Calais One or the Luxembourg station with its German propaganda. A soft, feminine voice would try to make us homesick and they would play "Home on the Range" and then sweetly tell us that we would never see America again. We would hear the programmes interrupted as "Feindliche Flugzeugen" flew over the Reichs gebiet and the stations went off the air as the RAF passed. The best was American Forces Network on the Road to Berlin, which was all that radio should be and no soap to be sold.'
Allan Healy, 467th BG

'On the continent, particularly after Luxembourg was taken, there were many American Morale Operations broadcasts from Radio Luxembourg, the most powerful radio on the continent, into Germany.'
William J. Casey, Head of OSS

'Ben Weiner of the 466th has more whisky than any other club in the 2nd Division, 8th Air Force.'
'Lord Haw Haw' radio broadcast

'There was somewhere in England a radio station called the Armed Forces Radio Network. They would give out censored news, various other programmes and also had a period of time that they would play music if someone wrote in and requested such. They played some of the popular tunes at that time and our crew started sending requests so often that they finally gave us a theme song, which was "The Campbells are Coming" because we always requested the songs to be for Campbell's crew. One of the crew members had left the States with a small radio which seemed to be turned on all the time. (When we left the States we did not know that the electric in England was 220, whereas in the States it is 110, but we overcame that by putting a 100-watt bulb in the line reducing the voltage.) At any rate this radio would be tuned in to the AF Network and then after that programme was over, we would switch to "Lord Haw Haw". He would also play some popular music which I assumed they thought would make the boys lonesome or have some adverse effect on morale, which it didn't.

'I suppose they monitored the AF radio network and from it they got our crew's name, etc. He would also dedicate a song or two to us and then say they would be over to pay us a visit some night. I suppose subconsciously he got to me as after I would go to bed and sleeping I would always dream of the Germans coming over, trying to bomb our field. It was always the same dream, night after night, until I finished my missions. During these dreams I would always try to get to the top turret of the plane, but would always wake

up about the time I got there. I don't know why I should do that as the "guts" of the guns were in the armament shop and not in the turret.'
Howard E. Hernan, gunner, Lt. Claude Campbell's crew, 303rd BG

'Known as subliminal, or "message under the music" technique, it is a method of putting a hidden message through to a person's subconscious without the conscious mind being aware. Maj. Miller protested after being told that his music was going to be put to this controversial use.'
Ray Shields

'Like every American, I have an obligation, and that obligation is to lend as much support as I can to winning the war.'
Maj. Glenn Miller, American bandleader

'Alton G. Miller, Major, AF, Missing in flight as of 15 December 1944, presumed to be dead.'
AGO File, Washington DC

'There is a mass of contradictions about what happened to Glenn. Lots and lots of things don't add up and I don't think we will ever find out what happened.'
John Miller, nephew of Glenn Miller

There is a mass of contradictions about what happened to Glenn. Lots and lots of things don't add up and I don't think we will ever find out what happened. (Author's Collection)

'Sometimes I discover a German propaganda station on my commercial band. The British and American propaganda stations are there, too. I have heard German broadcasters using English with no trace of an accent. An announcer once said the Allies are making no inroads into Europe from their beach head at Normandy in their attack on Fortress Europe. That identified the station as German. The voices switch to German and that identifies them too. The German stations play what I call heavy classical music and a bit of Strauss waltzes. I read Hitler is a fan of Wagner. Can that heavy stuff be Wagner? This kind of music suffocates me.

'British and US stations don't hold me when they are broadcasting in German or French or Dutch. I don't understand these languages. I have heard a German announcer claim – in English – nothing happened today. No bombs fell. Life in the Fatherland was routine. Do his listeners know he is not counting those holes we leave daily in France, or what the British are tearing up in Germany at night?'
'The Flight From Boyhood', T/Sgt. Robert T. Marshall, radio operator-gunner, 385th BG

'My grandfather, who lived with us, had emigrated from Germany to the States when he was nine years old. He had warm, nostalgic memories of his homeland and refused to accept as fact the account of concentration camps and atrocities under the Hitler regime. He was in his eighties, but clear of head, not in the least senile and very much the patriarch in his attitudes. When the large family was gathered around the dinner table, he would argue vigorously that the wonderful German people would not tolerate such outrages, much less perpetrate them. Because of his convictions, it was a source of sorrow to him to have his eldest son, Lt. Col. George Wegner, serving with the 490th BG; one grandson, me, serving as a pilot with the 94th; and another grandson serving as a radio operator on a B-24 – all in the 8th Air Force and all intent on bombing his beloved homeland into submission! He died in August of '45, still convinced that all evidence of German culpability was vicious Allied propaganda!'
Bob Maag, pilot, 94th BG

He had been jilted by a Delores in the States and claimed Miss Delores would probably take them over the target but would not bring them back! (Col. William B. Cameron)

SUPERSTITION

Superstitious Alyosius
B-17 Flying Fortress, 100th BG

'Some men had their silk stockings, a garter, maybe a pressed flower. To a man we would vehemently deny any trace of superstition. Yet there were probably few who did not carry some symbol, of religion, love or pagan charm just to be on the safe side of sentimentality. As a "just in case" my Roman Catholic cousin in Philadelphia had impressed upon me a St Christopher medal that had a special place in my wallet. Despite all this occult frivolity, these charms and amulets came to have a special meaning about as ethereal as their supposed powers.

'It had become habit to tuck Pete inside my shirt as a regular preparation for the mission before leaving my hut. He was then promptly forgotten in the assumption that he would perform whatever mystic powers he possessed. Actually, he was just a bit of home, a symbol, and a rapidly dirtying fetish at that. So I thought. Yet it was on the trip home

from Hamm that I suddenly realized that I had forgotten to bring him along. I remember clapping my hand to my jacket as a faint chill crept up my spine. Then I remembered that I wasn't superstitious and promptly forgot about the doll. Pete didn't miss another trip.'
Keith C. Schuyler, pilot, 44th BG, author of 'Elusive Horizons'

'Gilbert "Gibby" Wandtke, the engineer, was not happy about flying in *Miss Delores*. He had been jilted by a Delores in the States and claimed *Miss Delores* would probably take them over the target but would not bring them back! *Miss Delores* was hit by flak over the target. One burst hit "Gibby" Wandtke and he fell from the top turret with shrapnel wounds.'
Capt. Bob Bishop, navigator, 44th BG

'The night before, I had a premonition this mission would be my last and so I caught up on my correspondence and sent home to my mother all the loose money I had in my billfold.'
Orlo Natvig, radio operator, 91st BG

'We were not superstitious, but we did not want to push fate so we called our 13th mission, which was on 29 December 1944 to Frankfurt, "12B". It was rather rough, too. Our roughest was the 14th and final mission, two days later, to Hamburg.'
William B. Sterrett, bombardier, 100th BG

'My first mission as pilot in command. We had a mixture of five crews. We were briefed to go to Lippstadt, Germany, getting up at 2.30 a.m. I didn't get much sleep. I flew *Shady Lady* II on her 13th mission without knowing it 'till we got back.'
1/Lt. Joe Wroblewski, pilot, 351st BG. 23 March 1944

'Lt. Weatherwax was a legendary figure in the 44th known as the "hard luck kid" and nobody wanted to fly with him because he always got shot up. Crew members from other crews would report to sick call if they thought they had to fly with Weatherwax. Once he was peppered with flak coming up through the navigator's position, but he kept flying. He turned grey at 26. He was one of the lead navigators in the group and a great guy on leaves.'
Forrest S. Clark, gunner, 44th BG

'The famous Cat on the Barrel in the parish of Old Catton near the base was stolen and taken across

The famous Cat on the Barrel in the parish of Old Catton near the base was stolen and taken across the Atlantic at least twice during the war. It became a sort of 'lucky mascot'. (Author's Collection)

the Atlantic at least twice during the war. It became a sort of "lucky mascot".'
458th BG ground crewman

'I moved my gear into a barracks and threw it onto one of the lower bunks which was conveniently near one of the two warm "pot-bellied" stoves. One of the men said: "You can take that bunk if you want but it belonged to our engineer, who got it through the head on a mission a couple of days ago." With no further words, I selected another bunk, farther away from the heat of the stove.'
William C. Stewart, gunner, 92nd BG; on arrival at Podington, January 1945

'The Fortress men called the 44th, the "jinxed outfit". Then the 492nd BG took over our misfortune and even the 100th BG was called the "Bloody Hundredth". The prize for the worst hard luck goes to the 96th BG. They had the unenviable title of having the greatest loss rate of any bomber group of the entire USAAF.'
1/Lt. John W. McClane Jr., navigator, 44th BG

'We heard about a hard luck group called the 100th, which was continually being wiped out. Daily we saw formations coming over, headed north, some with props feathered, others trailing smoke. Once I saw one with half the horizontal stabilizer shot off, keeping its place in the formation. We fervently prayed not to be sent to the 100th.'

Ben Smith, radio operator, CCRC Bovingdon, March 1944

'A lot of ships didn't find their own groups and tacked on to any one they could for protection. Everybody was yelling over VHF, trying to locate their own group. I heard one pilot tell his group that he couldn't locate them so he was going on in with another group. His commander called back and asked which group he was with. He replied that he didn't know but that they had black rudders and a "D" on the tail. Someone said: "Oh, that's the 'Bloody Hundredth.'" Then I saw a red-tailed ship leave the squadron in front of me. Needless to say, this didn't make me feel any better.'

Griswold Smith, pilot, 100th BG, Nuremburg 5 April 1945

'An hour later, my crew and I were at our positions inside *Fearless Fosdick*, as our Fort' was named. A four-foot-high vivid picture of "Lil' Abner" with a four-leaf clover, wishbone, horse shoe and a rabbit's foot, was painted on each side of the fuselage, just aft of the Plexiglas nose.'

Bob Browne, 487th BG

'The *Vagabond King* was just another Liberator daubed up in war paint. Mac had decided on her name, but to be fair, there were other names painted on beneath the gun turret outlets and the observation windows. I remember the names Rose and Pat and there were many others; names of sweethearts and wives to charm off death or danger.'

Arch Whitehouse, 'True Magazine' 1944

'I was a fatalist at the time. I did not keep a diary. After my first mission I made a conscious decision not to write about what happened each day and the only record I kept was a listing of my missions. This I religiously tabulated on a sheet of paper I kept with my writing paper and letters from home. I thought that the odds against my making it through the 35 missions, required for a complete tour, were slim and I wouldn't really want my

We heard about a hard luck group called the Hundredth, which was continually being wiped out. Daily we saw formations coming over, headed north, some with props feathered, others trailing smoke. Once I saw one with half the horizontal stabilizer shot off, keeping its place in the formation. We fervently prayed not to be sent to the 100th. (Charles Nekvasil)

family or some Army personnel reading my inner secrets, should the inevitable occur. I was superstitious to the point that I would not go out on a mission without being sure that I had recorded the last one on the sheet. For some reason, I thought that if I did not do this, some dire consequence would take place. I was 19 and I never really expected to make my 20th birthday, which was 28 May 1945.'

William C. Stewart, gunner, 92nd BG

'I think that most airmen will tell you that they aren't superstitious. Yet, when checking their daily life style, you will find certain things are done because that's "lucky" or that's good for me, or I feel more comfortable if so and so is done. I have carried a fish hook for a long time, attach no importance to it, but won't go without it. On the first mission my radio operator got hold of one sock somehow. We carried it on all missions. The sock was on the checklist.

'My tail gunner, Earl Fetterhof, had false teeth and removed them so as not to swallow them in the heat of battle. He tied them together with a shoe string and attached them to the bulkhead outside his turret. Those teeth swinging in the breeze from the bulkhead were a must before we would go.

'Lace these things with a generous amount of sincere prayer and faith in your Maker and your missions will be completed successfully.'
Col. Robert H. Tays, pilot, 392nd BG

BIG FRIENDS

'A B-17's a fine aircraft
A stratosphere bathtub no less!
It never drops bombs on the target
But 10 miles around, what a mess!

Mr. Douglas builds mighty fine aircraft
Constructed of rivets and tin.
It poops right along at 150
The ship with the head wind built in.'

A B-17's a fine Aircraft to the tune of 'I have No Use for Women'

'American heavy bombers, the latest Fortresses and Liberators, are fine flying machines, but are not suited for bombing in Europe. Their bombs and bomb loads are too small, their armour and armament are low.'
Peter Masefield, air correspondent, Sunday Times

'Without the B-17, we might have lost the war.'
Gen. Carl Spaatz

A B-17's a fine aircraft/A stratosphere bathtub no less! (Wiley Noble)

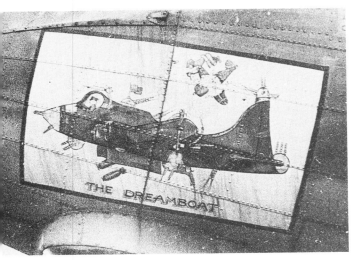

'... The Air Force kind of grew up with the B-17. It was as tough an airplane as was ever built. It did everything we asked it to do, and it did it well.'
Gen. Curtis E LeMay

'A mediocre, overrated bomber.'
B-17 navigator

'The B-17, I think, was the best combat airplane ever built.'
Gen. Ira C. Eaker

'As for the B-17, I am not ashamed to say that in 1944–45 I regarded her as a slow, flammable old lady who was really out of sorts among fast young friends and who became my potential enemy every time I flew a combat mission. Had it not been for the long range escort fighter, the Luftwaffe would have driven us from the skies over Germany.'
Abe Dolim, navigator, 94th BG

'In most aircraft, go-around procedure after a missed approach involves immediate gear retraction to cut down drag and permit climb. This was suicide in the Lib'. The 'plane would not climb with full flaps; gear and flaps were both hydraulically operated, they could not be worked simultaneously; the gear retraction cycle could not be stopped once started, and took 38 seconds to complete. The first thing my pilot told me when I joined the crew was that go-around procedure was to milk flaps up to 20 – half position (also take-off position) first, and then up gear. He was extremely emphatic about it.'
Lt. Harry C. Stubbs, 44th BG

'On Ploesti we left the target area pulling about 35/36 inches of manifold pressure and were going along at perhaps 225 m.p.h. A year or more later, 18 September 1944, on another low-level mission, to Best, Holland, we had to use about the same power settings to get 170 to 180 m.p.h.'
Col. William Cameron, pilot, 44th BG

'For a long time there were arguments whether B-24s were worse than B-17s. The "B-two dozens" were cramped and confined. Some thought they could not fly a formation as tightly as the Forts, but we proved otherwise before our tour was over.'
Allan Healy, 467th BG

'We B-17 people came along to spread culture among the B-24s. We visualized ourselves as a sort

Above: *Without the B-17, we might have lost the war. (Lockheed Aeronautical Systems Co.)*

Right: *The B-17, I think, was the best combat airplane ever built. (M/Sgt. Hugh K. Crawford, 94th BG)*

Below: *For a long time there were arguments whether B-24s were worse than B-17s. (Col. William B. Cameron)*

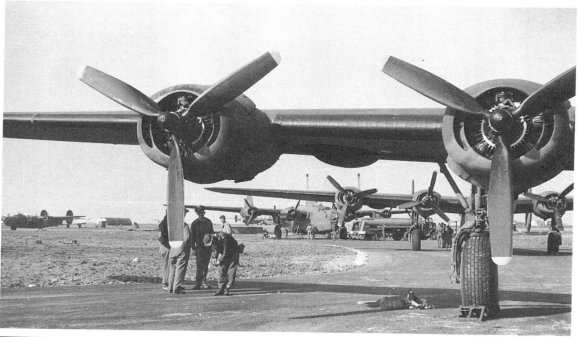

of Dr Albert Schweitzer among the natives.'
Jack Houston, navigator, 525th BS, 378th BG

PADDLEFEET

*'We're just a bunch of heathens,
And we don't give a rap,
About the groundlings point of view,
And all that sort of crap;
We want about 10,000 ships,
Of every other kind,
And then, of course, our own Air Force
And you will never mind.'*

'The paddlefeet get little recognition, but theirs is a story of devotion to duty.'
Allan Healy, 467th BG

'Lt. Melton, a pilot, referred to all non-flying personnel as "paddlefeet" and popularized the expression.'
Harold J. Johnston, 458th BG

'Many of the paddlefeet stood in the warm sunshine by the Briefing Building and were thrilled as the Liberators flew over the field in tight formation and, one by one, peeled off into the traffic pattern to circle and land . . . Exposed to the elements, the ground crew's task was miserable work. However, maintenance standards remained high. One ground crew did a 30-hour engine change in $8\frac{1}{2}$ hours in cold October.'
Allan Healy, 467th BG

'The aircraft mechanics, using any material available, whether "legal" or midnight requisition, constructed "line shacks" to protect them from the wet and the cold when not directly involved in repairs or maintenance. The quality of these shacks varied according to the skill and ingenuity of the crew. Some were so good they could have had second storeys if it were not for height restrictions there. Of course, all became fitted with some sort of heating facilities, mostly fuelled by a combination of an oil and 100 + octane aircraft gasoline mixture. Soon, cots and bedding became quite common to provide sleeping accommodations, etc. Ingenuity was often used to improve the fighting and defensive qualities of our Liberators, and, naturally, carried over into our quality of living. One group of aircraft mechanics saw the possibility of improving their living conditions by

The aircraft mechanics, using any material available, whether 'legal' or midnight requisition, constructed 'line shacks' to protect them from the wet and the cold when not directly involved in repairs or maintenance. The quality of these shacks varied according to the skill and ingenuity of the crew. (Bill Robertie)

converting an unused bomb shelter close to their work. First, they constructed a wooden cover over the entrance to shed the rain and snow, enclosed the entrance with a modified door, extended an electrical line from the sheet metal shop for lights and obtained their heat from a modified "heater".'
Will Lundy, 67th BS, 44th BG, Shipdham

'We had a 50-gal oil drum on the vent side of the shelter. We mixed 100 + octane with the motor oil for our fuel. When we ran the heater to warm the place, we also had a coil of aluminium tubing around the stove jacket. When the stove heated up, it would send little squirts of hot water up and into an old oxygen tank. That's how we got our hot water for washing and shaving! We also had electric lights, a radio and a toaster. Electricity was taken from the Sheet Metal Shop as it was our neighbour. When a 68th 'plane caught fire and burned on 7 February 1945, we had a ringside seat, but we only took a couple of looks at it 'cause we knew they had been putting bombs on it. When they exploded, it killed a guard about 500 ft from us.

'Leo Thatcher got us a couple of small kegs of beer for our shelter, and they lasted a long time. We had a nice supply of canned fruits and Spam, all courtesy of our guys who had to serve on KP.'
Sgt. Allen A. Fitch, one of the four men to occupy this unusual 'barracks' at Shipdham

'The ground crews, too, were under a lot of pressure even though the danger wasn't there. A 16-hour day was kind of easy for them. There was just no end to the work. Sometimes they might get a plane ready at two in the morning, three days in a row, each time the mission getting cancelled because of weather. So the ground crews were constantly going through setting up a plane for a mission. Every day, there was a different fuel load, different bomb load. That's what the war was for these guys. Their 'plane and the guy working with him. If their 'plane came back shot or something, they just cried tears like babies. They loved that airplane.'
Gen. Lewis Lyle, 379th BG

'Nick, our crew chief, was a solemn fellow of Polish descent who obligingly let us warm up in his shack before "start engines" time. He used 100-octane gasoline for his homemade drip pan heater. We had been very hard-pressed for fuel for our Nissen hut stove. Many of us actually had to buy our own oak wood at a nearby English sawmill, or

One group of aircraft mechanics saw the possibility of improving their living conditions by converting an unused bomb shelter close to their work. (Bill Robertie)

use the paraffin-soaked cardboard bomb rings which caused everything in our hut to smell waxy. There was a great deal of mutual respect between

Ground crews, too, were under a lot of pressure even though the danger wasn't there. A 16-hour day was kind of easy for them. There was just no end to the work. Sometimes they might get a plane ready at two in the morning, three days in a row. (Dave Mayor)

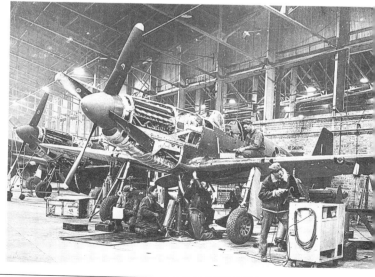

the ground crews and the combat crews. Their concern for our safety showed in their faces, their attitude and their superb workmanship.'
Abe Dolim, navigator, 94th BG

'They were cocky and they were good and they never faltered.'
Gen. Lewis Lyle, 379th BG

'The air echelon, including the maintenance crews, were a close-knit group and felt themselves a cut above the Perimeter Defence Squadron whose soldiers were actually camped in the woods on the eastern end of our line at Thorpe Abbotts. Their purpose was to protect us against marauding aircraft, but many of us were worried against the possible danger they presented to our own welfare since they were not necessarily crackshots. Some of the men were not overly impressed with their judgement. Some of the linemen undoubtedly knew that the defence crew were, from time to time, filching chickens. These were subsequently cooked over an open fire and undoubtedly were delicious. However, as to be expected, the farmer, complained to the police. Of course, our heroes knew nothing about the missing chickens, but then Scotland Yard was called in with a bloodhound. Lo and behold, that smart dog took off on a trot and led these modern-day Sherlock Holmes right to the spot where the feather and chicken

They were cocky and they were good and they never faltered. (Jake Krause [3rd right], 755th Armament section, 458th BG)

bones were buried. It was a dark day for our protectors, but a triumph for British justice.'
Bill Carleton, 351st BS Engineering Officer, 100th BG

'A lot of these guys stayed in England only a short time, maybe less than a year, but it's an important chunk of their life. They've got a lot of memories.'
Gen. Lewis Lyle, 379th BG

'As gunners on combat crews, we were supposed to check out the firing mechanisms of our guns, the ammo' and the cartridge belts when we got to altitude, or at a specific point in the mission. We also had to make frequent checks to see that they were not malfunctioning. As is human nature, some gunners got edgy and anxious so they couldn't wait. One gunner got so itchy about his guns that he checked them out while still on the hardstand and dispersal areas. As a result he sent a long string of live ammo' and tracers through the woods and across a farm, narrowly missing some farm buildings, Naturally, he heard about this in no uncertain terms.'
Forrest S. Clark, gunner, 44th BG

'SNAFU' (Rackheath Memories)

'I was working at my desk when I heard a prop runaway on an aircraft overhead. The speed of an aircraft engine is determined both by the throttle and the pitch of the propeller. The flatter the pitch, the less the load and the faster it would run. When it runs away it means that it is out of control and unless quickly corrected, will disintegrate and possibly cause the airplane to crash. As soon as I heard the high pitch sound, I put the typewriter on the floor (couldn't lose our only typewriter or we wouldn't be able to make out the reports), ran out the door and jumped into the foxhole. This time I didn't have the benefit of landing on Sgt. Spangler. The noise overhead was getting closer and closer and I correctly surmised that the airplane was in a flat spin; that is, it was out of control flying in a circle. Suddenly, I heard a swoosh of air and I immediately thought that the 'plane had dropped its bombs. I was as deep in the foxhole as one can get when there was a heavy thud about 30 ft away. Meanwhile, the airplane kept getting closer and it broke out of the clouds and crashed on the airfield in front of me, coming to a stop right next to the light trailer at the end of the runway. When things quietened down, I looked out and the airplane was a P-51. Right across the road behind us was the front turret of a B-24. What had happened was that the commanding officer of another group was monitoring his squadron and the wing of his airplane had hit the front turret of a B-24, knocking it off. The colonel was able to bail out when his airplane went into the spin, but the officer in the turret was not as lucky. He landed a couple of hundred feet up the road, near our sentry.'
Bill Carleton, Engineering Officer, 100th BG

'I noticed there was no effort for the ground crews to get close to us. Anyone could tell there was mutual admiration between us, but I suspect we flying men lived in our own dream world and that the ground crews had seen too many of their "friends" not return.'
1/Lt. John W. McClane Jr., navigator, 44th BG

'Ground crews, as well as flight crews, had trained together in the States. Ground crews were usually three in number and were aided by floating mechanics, such as John Erspamer, and other ground personnel during the readying of a bomber for a combat mission. Crew chiefs took pride in the

mechanical excellence of the bombers assigned to their care. John N. Wilson, one of the top crew chiefs of the 734th Squadron, 453rd BG, Old Buckenham, and his crew, were no exception to this creed. Wilson was big, strong and dedicated to his assigned airplane. Rounding out this exceptional crew was "The Genius" (Conklin) and "Turbo" (Rigelleto). The ground crews gave their charges pride and dedication under the most adverse conditions. The flight crew's welfare was so dependent on properly functioning equipment. To cause damage to the 'plane was a sure way to be the subject of the vented wrath of the crew chief. If you have never been chewed out by a crew chief, brother, you haven't been chewed out by a professional. No one was exempt from this chewing when deserved.'

Frank Thomas, radio operator, Never Mrs, *453rd BG*

WHITEHEAD'S TOURISTS

'It was only a small place, but a bugle was blowing.
I remember the Mayor performing an intricate dance
And the boy from Dakota most gravely, most

Anyone could tell there was mutual admiration between us but I suspect we flying men lived in our own dream world and that the ground crews had seen too many of their 'friends' not return. (Col. William B. Cameron)

quietly, throwing
The flowers from his helmet toward the deserving of France.'

St Aubin D' Aubign, Paul Dehn, August 1944

'*Never Mrs* had been assigned to Lt Kaylor C. Whitehead's crew after Korsmeyer's crew had finished their tour of duty. She was named by "The Genius" (Conklin) in the ground crew and the suitable nose art was also his idea. "The Genius" named her after Korsmeyer's crew could not agree on a suitable name. Conklin suggested *Never Mrs* because she was the first 'plane of the group to pass 13 missions without an abortion. They accepted the name and made the assignment to secure suitable nose art. *Never Mrs* was to achieve $69\frac{1}{2}$ abortion-free missions accomplished on the four original engines.

'We brought the *Mrs* back in need of many and serious repairs when the group went to Dessau, Germany, on 16 August 1944. We were spared the official crew chief going over due to one thing; the entire 36 bombers from the 453rd suffered damage of equal severity. Three days elapsed before the group could join the wing in another

'The Genius' named her after Korsmeyer's crew could not agree on a suitable name.
(Frank Thomas)

mission. We were scheduled for one of those 48-hour passes on that August day. Damages suffered that day caused us to return to the base some 1½ hours late. We had left England on three engines leading the low low left element. We were able to keep up on the trip in, it was the trip home that we were unable to maintain a speed higher than 165.

'The around-the-clock repairs were also in our favour as Wilson, our crew chief, had little time to devote to reprimanding an errant crew. The 40 hours away from the base allowed a little cooling off time, also.

'August faded into September and the relationship between Whitehead's crew and Wilson's crew had settled into one of mutual respect and trust. Personal friendship also grew between ground and flight crews. The flight crew depended on the airworthiness of the *Mrs* and the ground crew accepted the fact that damage to their charge would be attributable to enemy action and not by careless action of the flight crew. We knew and never questioned the fact that the *Mrs* would be in near, if not, perfect mechanical condition at all times. Whitehead's crew had developed a desire to be assigned to the 'plane long before Col. Dowda decided we had earned the right to our own assigned plane.

'September 1944 was an unproductive month

for the 2nd Bomb Division. The weather was lousy for flying and the 453rd flew only 13 credit missions. September did little to close the gap between number one and the final mission signalling completion of a combat tour of duty with the 8th Air Force. We flew seven of the 13 credit missions that month. Along with the seven, we had three recalls, one from Berlin and one from Ulm. The mission to Ulm was a dual-purpose mission. The 15th was to bomb Munich and we were to attract some of the Luftwaffe fighters if they showed. The other reason was intelligence learned that there was considerable fuel stored in the wooded area west of Ulm. The reason for the recall was due to the movement of additional fuel into this area. We were close enough into Munich to see the flames from the bursting bombs of the 15th before taking our heading for Ulm.

'The fuel storage was hit in the next few days and a considerable amount of fuel went up in flames. This information was not gained from any official source – rather, it came from a German woman, 12 years of age at the time of this September 1944 bombing. The conversation, some 34 years later, also revealed that 30 minutes after the first bombs hit, there was no sign of the target remaining. According to this lady, there was upwards of 20 million gallons of fuel stored in the rail yards five miles out of Ulm at the time of the bomb strike. It would seem the information provided by intelligence was accurate in this case.

'The morning of 8 September gave little hint of

the adventure awaiting us before nightfall. White-head's, Parks' and Beecher's crews were to experi-ence entirely new-found areas of Europe. Whitehead and Parks were forced to land in France and Beecher ditched in the Channel. All of White-head's and Parks' crew were to return safely; however, four of Beecher's crew were killed in action. Those killed were T/Sgt. Holden, S/Sgts. Kasil, Hooper and Hooneaian.

'The excitement for that September day really began on the bomb run on the target area to Karlsruhe, Germany, The 453rd was apparently the first B-24 group on target, leading the 2nd Wing. There was just one problem – the last of the B-17s were running five minutes' late. Their run had been made 180 out of phase with our briefed run. The lateness, according to our briefed time of arrival, presented little, if any, problem for the 453rd. What did present us with serious problems was the habit of B-17s diving to pick up speed after bombs away. B-17s flew higher, if slower, than B-24s.

'When you locked in on a bomb run 2,000 ft below a group that is letting down through your formation, you have problems. All B-24s, except one, were able to dodge the interlopers. Those B-17s were hell-bent-for-election, and we believe it was Parks who lost 14 ft of wing to one of the B-17s. Parks recovered and dropped his bombs with the group that day; the B-17 was not so fortunate. We hope the crew was able to bail out. This was one of the great mysteries of the war; how could those B-17s never seem to be able to see lower flying Liberators?

'Regrouping accomplished when Whitehead's crew experienced the second exciting event of the day. The stage was set for the unfolding plans for the day. Fifty-two 100-lb clusters of incendiaries comprised the bomb load carried by the *Mrs.* I, as all radio operators, rode the bomb bays on all bomb runs. The bomb bay doors of the Lib' were given to creeping shut and on occasion; bombs were known to hang up after release. I had repositioned myself in the bay after the second bomb run began.

'The first of several flak bursts hit the *Mrs* at about this time. Shortly after this hit, there was a flicker of light in the right rear bomb bay section. We were accustomed to watching static electrical charges play around in the interior of our bombers. The addition of a little light playing around was no cause for alarm, but caution required you to keep an eye on the area. Lt. Christburg, bombardier, chose this time to ask if the bomb bay doors were

open. I answered in the affirmative and concluded by saying, "Chris, you may have to drop these bombs."

'Chris asked: "What did you say?"

'I said: "Drop the damn things."

'The flicker had developed into a small magne-sium fire. No further questions were asked and Chris salvoed the entire 52 clusters.

'The bombs had hardly cleared the bays when a rather large hole appeared in the right side of the rear section of the bays. This hit cut our hydraulic and fuel lines on the right side of the rear bomb bay. (Later, we were to find a 12-inch section of main fuel line was missing.)

'Reason never understood, but my next move was to remove the flak helmet from my head and use it as a seat. No sooner than making this move than we received a burst of flak through the left side, near the nosewheel. This burst severed the hydraulic line and electrical line leading to the nose before cutting the nosewheel strut and penetrating the number two bulkhead. There was enough of the flak piece to rebound down the walkway and knock the helmet out from under me. Now, I know why the helmet had been removed. Contem-plating this, I stepped out on the catwalk, only to have the next burst cut in two some six inches away.

'A habit begun in Casper, Wyoming, the placing of a roll of friction tape in a rear pocket also took on meaning. The electrical wires cut in the nose were shorting out and a small electrical fire had started. This coupled with the hydraulic fluid, were reason enough to put the tape to good use. Taking the tape from my pocket, the job of taping loose wire ends began. It was necessary to take a position on the nosewheel doors to reach the loose wire ends. The small fire extinguished and the taping task completed, return to the flight deck was in order.

'Reaching the bomb bays, there was quite a sight to behold. Standing on the left front bomb bay door were Ed Hermann, co-pilot, and Russ Harriman, engineer. They were busily engaged in a fruitless task of stemming the flow of fuel from ruptured lines suffered the same time of the nose hit. Martin Boone, 2nd engineer and right waist gunner, was tearing up first aid kits in an attempt to find something which would help in the fuel loss task. Martin even tried chewing gum – the effect was short-lived.

'Continuing my journey to the flight deck, I flopped into the co-pilot's seat and reported the situation to the Boss. Finishing the assessment of

Reaching the bomb bays, there was quite a sight to behold. Standing on the left front bomb bay door were Ed Hermann ... and Russ Harriman ... They were busily engaged in a fruitless task of stemming the flow of fuel from ruptured lines suffered the same time as the nose hit. Martin Boone ... was tearing up first aid kits in an attempt to find something which would help in the fuel loss task. Martin even tried chewing gum – the effect was short-lived. (Frank Thomas. [L-R:Martin Boone, Kaylor C. Whitehead, Frank Thomas, Charles Christburg, Taylor])

our condition, I asked him if he knew where Ed and Russ were at this time. His answer was "No, where are they?" I may have said, "Those damn fools are standing on the bomb bay doors." One hundred and twenty lbs of pressure was enough to pop those doors out. The only thing holding them is the air pressure pushing up. Whitehead then asked me where I had been. Sitting on the nose-wheel doors taping up electrical wire ends. Thirty-five lbs of pressure is supposed to open them, I was informed. Who was the biggest fool?

'There were several amazing things connected with the experience, from the comparatively short time lapse from the first hit until everything that could be done had been done – and everyone had returned to his post. The second thing that amazed us was the realization that all four engines

were still running. Thirdly, no-one in the crew had been wounded and we were getting fuel to all engines, thanks to Russ. Transfer from main tanks was routed through the wing tanks to the engines as all our main lines were out and direct fuel feeding was impossible. Our remaining concerns centered around avoiding contact with fighters and having fuel to make it back to England.

'The realization that the latter was impossible was not long in coming. Exact location is the next major concern. Can we make it into friendly territory? We called for "little friends" to no avail (learned later that our ability to transmit was out along with our ability to receive radio messages). Nearing the Belgian border, we spotted an English Typhoon, so Whitehead decided to keep close and follow the RAF 'plane into its field. The Typhoon was flying in a northerly heading. We followed that baby in to a fighter base located at Vitry, France.

'We did not realize how close we were were to the front at this Me 109 base, until later. This information came from the wing commander when Whitehead told him we would taxi to the other side of the field to get out of the Typhoon's way. With true English calm, he replied: "I wouldn't do that as there are enemy snipers in the hangers in that area!"

'We were asked to join the wing commander for some food, which we were happy to do. We had just eaten breakfast at 2:00 a.m. that morning. We were now some 14 hours later and now that we were safe, food seemed like the very best of ideas.

'After we had eaten, the mapping out of our plans began. The method in which we hoped to get the *Mrs* ready for the flight back to Old Buck' was of top priority. Whitehead would take five of the crew members and co-ordinate a search for parts from crashed airplanes in the area. Ed, Russ, George Roby and I would stay with the 'plane and begin repairs, and make ready for other repairs. Added to our problems, was the fact that some ATC personnel had decided they would salvage the *Mrs* on the spot. Their belief was that it was impossible to get a B-24 airborne from 3,800 ft of dirt. We made it perfectly clear that there would be no salvage operation conducted on the *Mrs*.

'The search for parts that afternoon was short-lived due to the time of day and the uncertain military condition of the area. Boone found an SS helmet and a Mauser rifle. What fun it would be to frighten the rest of the crew. With this thought in mind, he donned the chrome plated helmet, shouldered the Mauser and began his advance on the rest of us. Luckily, he was grabbed before being spotted by one of the British infantrymen. His fun was spoiled but his life may have been saved.

'The time of day dictated that the Boss head for Douia or Arras and find lodging for the six searchers. Ed, Russ, Roby and I would stay with the 'plane and continue what repairs we could do. We were interrupted at approximately 8:30 p.m. by a French gentleman and his 12-year-old son. He asked if his son could peek into an American bomber. He was taken on a royal tour of the plane. He was duly impressed and probably had a great deal to tell his friends the next day. The four of us probably enjoyed the treat of having the visit equally as much. While the tour was being conducted, the wing commander returned to inform us that the field had been secured and there would be no further worry about snipers.

'A long day was drawing to a close and it was decided we should head for Arras and shelter. Catching a ride on an English lorry was easy and we thought we had it made. One catch: we disembarked too early and left ourselves quite a walk into Arras. After a two-mile walk (estimated), we saw a man returning home in his automobile. Luckily, he spoke very good English, and when he heard our story, invited us in. He was a manufacturer of bicycles in the Pas de Calais area. He and his wife informed us they had room for one of us. We decided Ed should stay there and we would

seek further. He called his neighbour, M. Charles Pottier, Transport Industrials, 32 Rue l'Arras, Saint Laurent, Blangy, who had room for the three of us. Russ, Roby and I had a room on the third floor and never did a bed feel more wonderful. We had coffee with M. Pottier and some of his friends before returning to the airfield the next morning.

'The wing commander assigned two welders to aid us in repairs of fuel and hydraulic lines. These were two of the most competent welders we had ever seen. The 12 inches of missing fuel line required 13 welds. This is a good indication of their proficiency and the trouble our scroungers were having. Late afternoon of this second day, most of the repairs we could accomplish were completed. Ed, Russ, Roby and I hitched a ride on the last lorry in a PoW convoy. We had agreed to meet the balance of the crew at a little caf they had located in Arras.

'We had learned our lesson from the night and stayed with our transportation until we arrived at the agreed location. Our green flight suits and leaving a PoW convoy, caused a little concern among the French populace, until one realized we were American flyers. We exchanged greetings with many people before entering the caf. We spent the night at a hotel in Arras – what a night's rest after our ordeal. Anyone who slept on bunk beds with those biscuits for mattress substitutes, can appreciate what a king-sized bed with silk sheets did for us. The scroungers had found a fighter pilot who had been evading the Germans for some six weeks. He had made arrangements with Whitehead to return to England with us, so we now numbered eleven.

'Returning to the field early the next morning, we assessed the remaining work needed before preparing take-off. Our friend, the wing commander, agreed to give us 900 gallons of fuel, the maximum he could part with. This of course, was sufficient for our trip to Old Buck'.

'We were very anxious to get on our way, but we would miss this RAF group. This base was a very busy place during that time with the Typhoons flown by English, Canadian, New Zealand and Australian pilots. We had begun to feel almost like a part of the operation.

'Many of the French residents had gathered for our 2:00 p.m. take-off. I guess word had spread that there was no way to get that bomber out with only 3,800 ft of dirt. We believed then, and still prefer to think, they were well-wishers and not curiosity seekers!

'The time had come to give her a try. Taxiing to

Clint was to see the day when he was just as happy when Crow's Nest returned after almost one month of absence from the base. (Frank Thomas)

the south end of the field, the Boss lined her up with the take-off route. Brakes were locked, throttles were shoved, the limit and booster pumps were opened. Whitehead and Herrmann held her until she began to slide, brakes released and the *Mrs* jumped forward. The entire north end of the field was lined by viewers; closer and closer, we bore down on them. Flying speed still to be reached, suddenly, those well-wishers began to have doubts and scattering was in style. Running, pedalling and all means were employed to get out of our way and give us the additional space. Really not airborne nor at flying speed, the Boss and Ed hauled her over the fence, marking the end of the field. Luck was with us, there was enough space on the other side of the fence to allow the *Mrs* to gain flying speed.

'The climb was a relief for a short time only. Suddenly, there were four runaway prop governors and no response to the attempts to bring them under control. Our friends on the ground were looking upward and waving. With props under control, the Boss asked if we should give them a drag job. The unanimous decision was, of course. According to Chris, who was in the bomb bays, and Rubbo, the tail gunner, the Boss cut four

swathes of grass as we made the pass across the field. Boone was heard to mutter: "I am sure glad they wouldn't let Chris and I load that German motorcycle on board." He now understood what the extra weight could have done.

'Middleton was ready with a heading by this time and England-bound we were. We had hopefully repaired the transmitter, but had made no attempt to repair the damage to our receiver. Approaching the coast, I sent a message to base explaining our situation and why we were using a three-day-old code identification group. The IFF was working, or at least we hoped so. Something happened as we crossed the coast without any problems. Our fighter pilot friend had already informed everyone he could reach, of the fact that he would never fly with a bomber crew again. "You guys are nuts," was all he would give as a reason.

'Apparently, the failure to be airborne before reaching the end of the field had convinced him that fighters was the only way to go.

'About the time we were passing Norwich, our ground crew were eating their evening meal. John N. Wilson jumped up from the table and shouted, "Here comes the *Mrs*". Carr, crew chief of *Lucky Penny* said: "It's a B-24 all right, but you're nuts to think it's your baby."

"John, she has been junk for at least two days," Clint Colvin added. Clint was to see the day when he was just as happy when *Crow's Nest* returned after almost one month of absence from the base.

'Ignoring all comments and opinions as to his sanity, Wilson headed for his hardstand, and was standing there with tears in his eyes when the *Mrs* was wheeled into place. He even acted as if he were glad to see us, grabbed each of us in turn and said: "You brought her home."

'We were not so welcome at the Mess Hall. Here, we heard from the Mess Officer, "No one told me you would be coming in this late." Made you feel really loved. He did offer to feed us for Boone's Mauser and the 2,000 rounds of ammunition. I believe Chris promised him the business end if he didn't snap to. Suddenly, his attitude changed and we then realized that Rubbo and Taylor had already started to eat while we were arguing. Seldom does one gain much from arguing the point.

'The next ego builder came when we returned to our nissen hut barracks to see the large banner proclaiming WELCOME HOME WHITEHEAD'S TOURISTS. Chum Schaumberg, *Crow's* radio operator had managed to secure the material for this most welcome sight. The name was to remain our trademark. Tomorrow was to bring new surprises.

'Some of the men in the hut were carried away with their ideas of what we should have done while in France. They were kidding us also about the possibility of us thinking we were heroes because just because we landed and repaired a B-24. They reminded us that the toughness of the B-24 itself was probably responsible for our being able to do it; no argument from us on that statement. Leroy Barnett was disappointed that we were not gone long enough so he could have shot our bomb, suspended above our door, full of holes. He said that Chum guarded the thing all the time that we were away.

'The next day arrived and our surprise developed. Whitehead reported in and returned approximately one hour later with some bad news. Each bomber crew member carried an escape kit in his gear. The escape kit included, among other things, maps of the area of your target and routes to work your way back to areas where the underground had a chance to pick you up. There was French currency in the amount of $120 to be used when necessary in your escape. We had used most of this money for food and lodging while in France. Whitehead had been told that all of the money had to be returned. Some of the men said it looked as if the 453rd did not place much value on the return of a B-24. Truth of the matter is, we

would have stayed and repaired the *Mrs* if it was to have cost us double the $120 each. Our biggest disappointment was due to the loss of our little dog. He waited until mid-afternoon of the third day for our return and then disappeared. He sat in front of the hut looking toward the flight line during this time.

'The balance of the repairs needed took an additional three days. Seems that a lot of what we had done in France was temporary and permanent repairs were made. The fuel and hydraulic lines that had been welded were taken out and replaced with new. The most aggravating problem seemed to be with the hydraulic system. The fluid used by the USAAF was of petroleum base, while that used by the RAF was vegetable base. The two were not compatible. The results were some really gummed-up valves and cylinders. Every time Wilson saw Russ, it was "What in the hell did you do to my 'plane?" Boy, was I glad that my classification was radio and not engineering. Wilson held the flight engineer responsible for all damage done. Another surprise we had was the knowledge that orders had been given while we were away that all bikes had to be gotten rid of in 10 days or they would be picked up. We gave 10 bikes to one of our little English friends from Old Buckenham.

'Late afternoon of the third day, the *Mrs* was ready to be slow timed. The entire crew wanted to be present when she was put through her paces. We all piled in and off we went. The problem showed itself immediately after take-off. When the wheels came up, the bomb bay doors opened, when the bomb bay doors were closed, flaps dropped. Back to the drawing board. Boy, did old Russ catch it this time. Wilson wanted to know why in the hell he put that vegetable oil in the hydraulic system. That night, with help, the entire hydraulic systems reserve tank, valves and pumps were exchanged for new parts and the *Mrs* was as good as new. Within a week or 10 days, Wilson had even forgiven Russ for fouling up his love.

'We were back in the swing of things in short order and flying most every day. If not on a mission checking out new crews, slow timing overhauled planes, etc. We flew the first day the *Mrs* was ready and the mission was Wissenhorn, Germany. I guess the target was secondary to the purpose of that trip. We were removed from the low low left and told to fly 1,000 to 2,000 ft above the group and by ourselves. My, what a feeling as we thought we were being ostracized for having spent some time in France. We learned the reason shortly when the target and secondary purpose of the mission was given. It seems the 2nd Wing had been selected to attempt to locate some AA batteries that had been moved. Our job, above all others, was to map the locations of AA batteries that opened up on us when and if they did. We felt right then that the "if" could have been removed. A total of nine hours was spent in our search but we did find some. The first one located had our altitude correctly, so we were very busy in evasive action, and found it difficult to pinpoint the source of our aggravation. They dropped their level and the next burst was a direct hit on the lead 'plane of the high high right element. We saw one man leave the rear escape hatch and spill his 'chute inside the 'plane.

'We made a couple of gasoline hauls to Clastres, France, during September. Wilson accompanied us on these hauls as Russ was absent for some reason. Flying is something that Wilson baulked at. Needless to say, we were surprised when he agreed to make the gasoline hauls with us. He wouldn't admit it directly, nor would he deny it was to repay us for the faith we had in him and his crew's ability to keep the *Mrs* mechanically sound. He felt he should repay this trust. We were very happy to take him for his first and maybe his last flight over Europe.

'We were there in September when the 445th was nearly wiped out. The 2nd Wing, 389th, 445th and 453rd, had drawn another one of those search and find missions. This time, it wasn't AA batteries but Goering's yellow-nosed fighters they wanted to locate. We found them and the 445th suffered the brunt of that find. Twenty-seven down there and another six failed to make it home.

'We went on to get credit for 26 combat missions and about seven more we at least thought we should have credit for. *Never Mrs* was to achieve $69\frac{1}{2}$ abortion-free missions accomplished on the four original engines. She crashed after a direct hit somewhere in the Ruhr Valley on 11 November. Five, including Lt. John H. Friedhaber, pilot, were still on board when she crashed. When we went to Sweden on 21 November 1944, flying *Dolly's Sister*, we had served since 8 August 1944 in the number one spot on the alert sheet. There had been no rotation for Whitehead's Tourists.'

Frank E. Thomas, radio operator, 'Never Mrs', 453rd BG

DITCHING

*'Only death in a cold, cold grave
for that brave crew their lives they gave
Instead of dying in that infernal machine
they should have lived to glory in a B-17'*

'We left Thorpe Abbotts before daylight on 19 May 1944. Our flight was to Berlin. We were hit with light to mild flak over the target. So we thought we had a good flight. On our way back over Denmark we were flying low squadron and "tail-end charlie" position when we were attacked by Me 109s and FW 190s. They made about six passes at our position before my left waist position gun was completely blown out and I was wounded in the head. They removed me to the radio room for aid. They began to throw out equipment to lighten the ship. Already, two engines were gone. Finally, the pilot, Julian P. Rogers, told our crew to prepare to ditch in the sea. We made a rough landing. They threw me out of the top window in the radio room and I came out on the wing and

Standing, L-R: Julian P Rogers, pilot; Robert B. Lawler, co-pilot; Frederick Mead, navigator; Beartrial Liabermann, bombardier. Kneeling, L-R: Richard Kendall, top turret; Thomas Gurlaski, radio; Russell Gately, ball; Carroll W. Brooks, right waist; Clarence F. Cherry, left waist; Alfonso Fiore, tail. (Clarence F. Cherry)

Finally, the pilot, Julian P. Rogers, told our crew to prepare to ditch in the sea. We made a rough landing. They threw me out of the top window in the radio room and I came out on the wing and started to float away from our sinking Fortress. They pulled me into the life raft. It was shot with cannon holes. (Author's Collection)

it was a great many. I saw some explode, others trailing smoke, others with wings on fire and many, many parachutes open as the crews bailed out. But one sight stands out above all others on the way home. As we crossed the North Sea, I began to see 'planes ditching in the water. It was like watching a motion picture. I was so detached from the action! Some of the 'planes would glide to the most gentle stop and the men would climb onto the wings, but others would hit a swell in the water and seem to dive nose first in a crumpled heap. It was obvious that almost no-one could survive the shock. British PT boats were on hand to pick up survivors.'
Lt. John W. McClane Jr., navigator, 44th BG

started to float away from our sinking Fortress. They pulled me into the life raft. It was shot with cannon holes. We were close to two islands off Denmark. We could hear the small engines on the boats in the harbour. Julian said to us: "Row out to sea." We were not going to be PoWs. I don't know how far we rowed.

'Later on a Fortress came low and made a fix on our position. Some 40 hours later an RAF Lock-heed ASR 'plane came over us and dropped a smoke flare on the water for wind drift. They dropped a wooden boat from their 'plane which had three parachutes attached to it. It dropped very close to us in the sea. We climbed aboard and started towards England. We ran into two Danish fishing boats and they interned us on their boat. They were going to take us back to Denmark as PoWs, but the British flying above us told them to stay put or be sunk. An ASR launch was on its way for us. We were taken to Great Yarmouth Hospital. All of my crew were saved. I stayed at Great Yarmouth hospital for a few days and then went back to flying and completed my tour.'
Clarence F. Cherry, gunner, 100th BG

'Many 'planes were damaged and just would have made it home under the best of conditions, but with the delay caused by this strong head wind, some could not make it. I don't know how many 'planes I saw go down that day on the way to the target, over the city and on the way home! I know

HIGHWAYS OF THE SKIES

There have been some great traditions
Through a thousand years of kings,
Long centuries of battles fought,
Crusades, campaigns and things
That gave to many regiments
Traditions tried and true,
Honors aged and multiplied,
As they fought decades through

The echo of the trumpeter
Whose repertoire at large,
Embraced but one great battle call:
'Forward! Bayonets! Charge!'
There's the spirit of the Alamo,
of courage unsurpassed;
Concord Bridge and San Juan Hill,
Verdun's 'They shall not pass!'

Such fighting makes tradition.
But today, unlike the past,
A fledgling code, without prelude
Becomes tradition fast.
The Air Force carved its heritage
On the highways of the skies,
Blazing there the fighting code
Of every man who flies.

Yet few know this tradition
The armadas built upstairs,
Where the bombers blazing fifties

Defy the flak, and dare
The fighter packs, the rocket bombs
And shell blasts – to attack!
It's a mighty proud tradition
To have 'never been turned back!'

Men of the 'Fortress,' Cpl. Ellsworth B. Laurence

'The clouds had continued their build-up and as we climbed on course, we suddenly found ourselves surrounded by fog so thick that we could barely see our own wing tips. Everyone was really scared, but all the pilots could do was maintain a set rate of climb at a set airspeed, with absolutely no deviation in course. We finally pulled up through the tops of the clouds at about 25,000 ft altitude. Luckily, our group came out in perfect formation, but the group ahead was not so lucky. We were eye-witnesses as two of them came together just as they emerged. There was an explosion and both ships disappeared back into the clouds.'
George M. Collar, 445th BG

'In my opinion, the worst problem experienced on missions was being extremely cold flying at high altitudes. Our heaters were inadequate and the electrically-heated suits were not always effective. We suffered more from the elements than the attacks from the Germans. There were times when I almost wished I could bail out and get down to where it would be relatively "warm", compared to the $-25°$ to $-35°$ temperatures we had to contend with.'
Ralph L. Nasch, co-pilot, 92nd BG

'I spotted the Dortmund-Ems canal coming up and was synchronizing on a nice railroad bridge, when all of a sudden, Frederick Jacobi, a young intelligence officer flying on his first mission, in the nose turret, came on intercom in an excited voice, shouting, "There's an airfield down there." He broke my concentration and I knew I couldn't hit the bridge, so I immediately raked the ship over in a steep bank using the course knob and autopilot, trying for the airfield. Needless to say, I didn't have time to kill the rate, and the bombs overshot and fell into an adjacent wood.'
George M. Collar, 445th BG

'Dick Houlihan had completed a tour in the Mediterranean but he kept going with us and flew 73 missions in all. Bill Willis held the right bomb bay door open with his feet to permit the bombs to fall clear. Nason braved the thirty-degree-below weather to crank open the bomb bay doors. Men had to give first aid in this cold at altitude. One had to throw overboard the dead body of his crewmate to lighten the ship to get back.'
Allan Healy, 467th BG

'It was terribly cold in the air and just miserably cold on the ground. Two or three oxygen masks would freeze up on each flight. People would wear their flying gear on the ground to keep warm and it would absorb moisture, which would then freeze when they were airborne ... adding to the frostbite problem, of course. It was just plain miserable.'
Col. William Cameron, pilot, 44th BG

'The mission I remember clearly is the last one, on 12 July 1944, to Munich. We were hit on the outskirts and barely made it to the target. We dropped our bombs and tried to keep up with the squadron, but on three engines this proved futile. We had lost a lot of gas' and found we had only enough to get us to the beach head in France. About this time a P-51 Mustang came alongside. Across the nose was *Hurry Home Honey* from the 357th FG. He (the pilot) suggested we try for Italy but was informed by our navigator, Lt. Ginn, that we would not make it over the mountains. Capt. Wilson, our pilot, asked the navigator to lay course for Switzerland. The pilot of the P-51 wished us luck ... (I found out later he was Maj. Richard A. Peterson of the 357th FG based at Leiston).

'We met a few Me 109s and Focke Wulfs but they were either out of ammo or nearly out, so they made a few half-hearted passes and left ...

'As we neared the Swiss border, the Germans had laid out a large red cross and were firing red flares for us to land. We were losing altitude. The fighters had damaged another engine but our pilot decided to fly inland as far as possible. We finally landed at Altenrheim/SG near Lake Constance. We were told it was the shortest landing a B-24 ever made. We landed in a swamp and the wheels were half hidden by mud ... '
Rocky Starek, gunner, Fat Stuff II, *712th BS, 448th BG*

'I can still remember a mid-air collision in dense fog. It happened in front of us and the resultant explosion burned a clear hole in the fog that must have been at least a quarter of a mile in diameter.'
Lt. Col. Tom S. Belovich, 446th BG

'His right "Tokyo tanks" were on fire. The Fortress dropped back in a medium spiral just before it trailed from view, belly to the sky, its wing a solid sheet of yellow flame.'
Beirne Lay, 'I Saw Regensburg Destroyed', 17 August 1943

'Capt. McLoughlin spoke into his oxygen mask to his tired crew and Col. Peaslee, sitting beside him.
   "We've flown this far for Uncle Sam, from here we fly for 'U.S.' – us."
Col. Budd J. Peaslee, CO, 384th BG, Schweinfurt, 17 August 1943, 'Heritage of Valor'

'I remember looking down somewhere after Eupen and counting the fitful yellow-orange flares I saw on the ground. At first I did not understand them. Here were no cities burning. No haystack could make a fire visible in broad daylight 23,000 ft up. Then it came to me as it came to others – for I remember my headset crackling with the news – that these were B-17s blazing on the ground.'
Lt. Elmer Bendiner, navigator, Tondelayo 379th BG, Schweinfurt, 14 October 1943

'We came off the target and re-grouped. I looked around at the group and there wasn't much of us left. In my squadron we started with six ships; two three-ship elements, and being in the lead ship I saw all five of them go down. Out of 18 aircraft we had six left.
   'Lt Jeffries said: "That's the government's half, now for ours."'
Henry C. Cordery, co-pilot, 306th BG, Schweinfurt, 14 October 1943

'We had survived. That is all that mattered. It was no use crying over spilt milk.'
B-17 pilot upon returning from Schweinfurt

'Suddenly, it was on a wing and flipped over. It broke in half in the middle of the radio room, fell down and back. When my crew realized that this was a crew we had trained closely with we immediately had a weak feeling in our stomachs. I had never lost a close friend before.'
Larry Goldstein, radio operator, 388th BG

'Up in the nose of the 'plane, Mac had his helmet and oxygen mask knocked off by flak and the nose compartment caught fire. Elliot Kolker, the navigator, put the fire out with a carbon tetrachloride fire extinguisher. Little did anyone know at this time but experts later determined that carbon tet' on hot metal creates poisonous phosgene gas. Mac got quite a dose of this while he was without his mask. He is probably the only air crewman to receive a chemical warfare wound.'
Wayne E. Cose, top turret gunner-engineer, 486th BG

'One rocket site in the Pas de Calais was "more extensive than any concrete construction in the U.S. with the possible exception of the Boulder Dam."'
Christopher Elliott

'On 8 August 1944 we were supposed to bomb a buzz bomb site at haute De Foret Dieu in the Pas de Calais, but after making about four passes we could not find the target, so we were forced to jettison our bombs in the North Sea. The bombs we were carrying were RDX and we were not allowed to land with them.'
George M. Collar, 445th BG

PERSONALITIES

'Here's a toast, to the host, of those who love the vastness of the sky.
To a friend, we'll send a message of his brother men who fly.
We drink to those, who give their all of old,
Then down we roar to score the rainbow's pot of gold.
Here's a toast, to the host of men we boast,
The US Air Corps.'

The US Air Corps Song

'By bombing the devils around the clock, we can prevent the German defences from getting any rest.'
Point Three of Maj. Gen. Ira C. Eaker's eight-point memorandum to British Prime Minister, Winston Churchill

'The logical distribution of the strategic 'round-the-clock offensive, the two directions of attack from the west and from the south, and the extensive area to be defended, together with the sheer numerical increase in attacking strength, brought German air defence face to face with the three most difficult problems.'
Generalmajor Adolf Galland, 1953 Air University Review

'Captains Steinbacher and Johnson were waiting to be assigned to fighter 'planes and while waiting, volunteered to fly five extra bombing missions. I got to know Capt. Steinbacher quite well since he had the bunk next to mine in our quonset hut. He was from Williamsport, Pennsylvannia, and he had played football for Penn. State. After he got into P-51s, he came over Tibenham one evening and gave us a royal buzz job. Later on, he came to a dance at our Officers' Club and celebrated his first victory (an FW 190 shot down over Munich). Steinbacher was killed as a result of a high-speed stall while buzzing Tibenham later on.'
George M. Collar, 445th BG

'Looker walked with a slouch and shambled along. He was standing in the barracks as I checked in and fingering a .50 calibre shell in one hand and telling stories of Ploesti to scare the hell out of the new men. But it was the stories he told of Marreckech and Casablanca, on leave with Arab women and prostitutes that shook up the recruits. He said whole crews had to be grounded because they got VD and others got so drunk they ended up in native jails infested with lice.'
Forrest S. Clark, gunner, 44th BG

'I'd flown with many bombardiers, most of whom usually said: "Let's get the hell out of here," after "bombs away", but one fellow I'll never forget said very quietly instead: "Die you bastards!" Like love, hate is a very personal emotion.'
Abe Dolim, navigator, 94th BG

'Charley McMahon had completed his tour and was a "happy warrior" but on Christmas Eve, when we put every 'plane we had up, he took the assembly ship to the target armed only with carbines in the waist.'
Allan Healy, 467th BG

'Our Capt. Dick Grace, famous Hollywood plane stuntman, who flew in World War One, did a tour with the 1st Division in B-17s and then a tour with the 448th.'
Maj. Newton L. Mclaughlin, Special Services Officer, 448th BG

'Right after we landed Gen. "Hap" Arnold and a party of high brass arrived at the 'field and the general gave the boys a pep talk. I was real surprised to see Clark Gable, the movie actor, in a captain's uniform and later found out that he had gone on five raids and earned his Air Medal. He was well thought of by everybody and was going back to the States . . . '
Capt. Franklin 'Pappy' Colby, pilot, 94th BG

'We flew on Capt. Calhoun's wing and Clark Gable flew with him and handled the radio hatch gun. Claude Campbell, my pilot, could quite easily see the Hollywood film star grinning at him over enemy territory.'
Howard E. Hernan, gunner, 303rd BG

'Everyone had nothing but praise for Stewart, for here was a man with nothing to gain and everything to lose taking such risks over the best defended targets in Germany.'
Harry H. Darrah, 389th BG, talking about James Stewart, movie star

'They used to come up to London for leave and stay at the Reindeer Club for officers in Cork Street, of which I was manageress. One day while in the dining room with the American Red Cross director, I saw an officer sitting at a table whose face was very familiar. I asked my director and she said, "Oh that's Jimmy Stewart, the film star."'
Mary Thompson

'On a mission to France he flew *Wham Bam*, our assembly ship, over the normal "race-track"

My pilot . . . could quite easily see the Hollywood film star grinning at him over enemy territory. (Author's Collection)

course around the Group's homing beacon, "Buncher Six". Then he pulled out to the left about a quarter of a mile and flew on ahead to allow the lead ship to take over. However, contrary to procedure, he stayed in this position: all the way into France! Finally, the major turned *Wham Bam* around and came home, much to the relief of his crew.

'He said: "If anyone breathes a word, I'll kill ya."

'Col. Ramsey D. Potts, the Group Commander, probably wanted to know where he had been for the past six hours!'
1/Lt. (later Lt. Col.) Bernard H. Fowle, lead navigator, 734th BS, interview about Maj. James Stewart, film star and 453rd BG Operations Officer

'Our assembly ship was an old, war-weary B-24D, an original aircraft that came to England with the 44th even though she was late getting off and a survivor of the Ploesti raid. She was known as *Lemon Drop*. It had been stripped of all armament and repainted with alternate bands of black and bright yellow. When it was not my time to lead, I was a number of times assigned to be the assembly navigator in the *Lemon Drop*. We often referred to this assembly ship as the "Striped Ass Zebra". The assembly ship was necessary to prevent pilots from assembling in the wrong formation. We would take off before the combat planes and reach the designated assembly area. The crew chief would fire off many flares to attract our group. When all the 'planes had gathered, I would lead them in the right direction and place at an exact time. The group proceeded on the mission, we returned to base.

'On one occasion, I became so angry at the pilot on one of these assembly missions that I told the CQ that I would never again fly with this particular pilot, even if I were court-martialled. What brought me to this state of mind was an event that happened after the assembly had been accomplished. The pilot asked me where the field was, I told him it was directly below us. At this, the reckless pilot put the *Lemon Drop* into a steep spiral, just short of a spin. I looked at the air speed indicator, it was beyond the red line. Where the bomb sight had been removed, an aluminium plate had been installed; it was buckling. I had survived a number of missions but I thought my end would come in this foolish manner. I screamed at the

Finally, the major turned **Wham Bam** *around and came home, much to the relief of his crew. He said, 'If anyone breathes a word, I'll kill ya.' (John W. McClane Jr. via Steve Adams)*

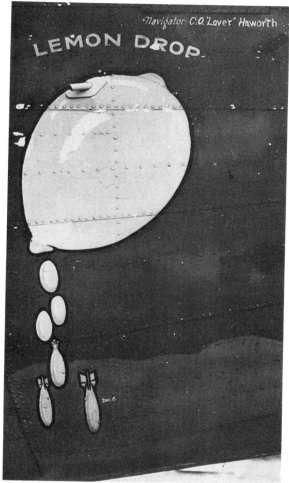

Navigator C.O. 'Lover' Haworth

LEMON DROP

The reckless pilot put the **Lemon Drop** into a steep spiral, just short of a spin. I looked at the air speed indicator, it was beyond the red line. (USAF Official)

pilot to pull the 'plane out of this dangerous dive. I was so mad, I was foaming at the mouth and only God knows what names I called the idiot.'
1/Lt. John W. McClane, navigator, 44th BG

'The tall, slender, boyish-looking pilot walks in a somewhat effeminate manner and you really have to look closely to see that he does indeed shave. He wears the only fur-collared summer flying jacket in the squadron and is one of the few who keeps his grommet in his dress hat. But he has been in the outfit long enough to have brought back shot-up bombers a couple of times and has recently been wounded – not seriously, however. Those of his friends who know him well know he

has a doting mother and five older sisters – that's all.'
The Graceful Pilot. November 1944, Abe Dolim, navigator, 94th BG

> 'Although it looks July 4th
> The pilot never shirks
> His eyes are on the leading ship
> Not on the fire works
> Navigator and bombardier
> Are wont to view the fight
> As do the eager crewmen Sir
> Through a machine gun sight'

'The most popular man in the squadron is the generous navigator from Oklahoma whose mother sends him Southern fried chicken packed in lard in a three-pound Crisco can about every 10 days. The other lucky stiff is the kid from the Bronx who quite often gets a whole salami from his girlfriend back home. One time the salami arrived badly mildewed and everybody moaned as he chucked it into the trash bucket. One of the guys plucked it out of the bucket, got his trench knife and pared the salami. Then he sliced it into quarter-inch thick pieces, stuck a couple of them on a fork and began to toast them over the pot-bellied stove. No sooner had the aroma wafted around when a mad scramble began for the remaining pieces of sausage.'
Ol' Buddy Winter 1944–45, Abe Dolim, navigator, 332nd BS, 94th BG

'One could walk into a room full of airmen and in a short time pick out with considerable accuracy who held what position just by observing the mannerisms of those present. Navigators were easy to sort out. Just look for a hypersensitive guy, someone who can't hold still one minute, an eager beaver asking questions unrelated to the interest of anyone else. It helped to be a little odd, but I loved the job.'
1/Lt. John W. McClane Jr., navigator, 44th BG

'I was very fortunate to be one of three young officers that was selected to receive first-hand training and counselling from a real "pro" of formation bombing. Gen. LeMay, our wing and Division commander, met with us in his office several times to give us his views as to the role of a formation command pilot. The information in these sessions was very valuable when I flew as a command pilot on missions to Berlin, Hamm, Munich, Hamburg, etc.'
Richard E. Perry, pilot, 390th BG

'Out of the darkness walked a strange chap in USAF uniform with both RAF and USAF wings. His chest was splattered with combat decorations and he sported a long handle-bar moustache. In a crisp British accent he introduced himself as Flt. Off. Vance Chipman, mentioning that he had just been transferred to the 25th BG. He would be assisting in Mosquito pilot training. I noticed that his mouth was watering while staring at our drinks so I poured him a stiff one. After several drinks together in the Officers' Club, we began to call each other by our nicknames. His was "Chip" and I was "Tip".

'Several weeks later I was going to London on leave. The little train left Watton about 2 p.m. for its 15-mile trip to Thetford, where connections were made with the 4 p.m. express train to London. The general procedure was to wait in the pub directly across the street from the Thetford railway station. The pub owner always made sure we Yanks never missed the train. Chipman was in the pub and on his way to London also, so we teamed up for the journey. By the time the London train arrived we were in "great shape", boarding the train with more than an adequate

supply of Scotch and ale. I guess we made a big splash upon arrival at Liverpool Street station. Getting a hotel room in London was almost impossible. I had made friends with the desk clerk at Russell Square hotel and he was able to arrange rooms for "Chip" and me.

'We wound up in some pub that night and having a great time. Suddenly, I thought my ears were playing tricks upon me as "Chip" had dropped his British accent and was speaking in a strong Russian voice. He had everyone in the pub believing he was a Russian pilot sent over to help their American and British allies. All night I wondered just what game Chipman was playing. The next morning I went to his room to awaken him. To my amazement, he began to speak with a typical American mid-western accent. I asked him point-blank, "Just where in hell did you come from?" Laughing, he replied that he was a former race track driver from Chicago. He had joined the Royal Canadian Air Force when war started in Europe.

'At breakfast that morning we agreed to meet in

In he strolled with a monkey on his shoulder. (Ralph Tipton)

the hotel pub at opening time. At 11 a.m. I was there, but not "Chip". About 30 minutes later, in he strolled with a monkey on his shoulder. "Chip" explained that as he was walking past a pet shop, this monkey saluted him (or so he thought). The monkey seemed to be searching for a long lost friend. Chip bought the monkey for £20. For the remaining two days that monkey accompanied us on a tour of pubs, causing quite a commotion I must admit.

'Upon return to Watton, the next evening at dinner some chap seated next to me asked if I knew anything about some monkey romping through Officers' BOQ. The Group CO, Col. Leon Gray, was on the warpath. It seems that the monkey had gotten into Col. Gray's quarters and opened tooth paste, shaving cream, talcum powder, etc. and decorated his room in a most non-military manner! He added something about Col. Gray was looking for "Chip" or "Tip" and that was enough for me!

'I left my food, quickly eased out of the Mess, mounted my trusty bike and dashed off to the safety of the Flying Fish pub. By closing time I had regained my courage and rode back. As I passed the Manager's Office there was a familiar voice – Smitty's who asked me to come into his darkened office and to watch the show in the bar. Chipman was sitting at one end of the bar drinking Scotch, with the monkey perched on his shoulder. "Chip's" personal pewter mug was filled with ale. The monkey would jump down, take a large gulp of ale, and leap back onto "Chip's" shoulder – much to the amusement of the bar patrons.

'The next thing I knew, "Chip" was having a duel with fire extinguishers with some high-ranking officer. Men were dashing out of both doors so I got the hell out of there, too. The following day, while visiting the Flying Fish, I heard rumours about what happened. One was that the monkey had set off a flare somehow and "Chip" used a fire extinguisher to clean up the mess. Many 25th BG pilots were soaked in an acid/soda bath in the process, plus some damage was done to the club furniture. Col. Gray banished "Chip" to a 30-day residence in a pup tent erected on the lawn in front of the Officers' Club!'

'Vance Chipman was later shot down flying a secret "Mickey" mission and was a German prisoner. After his liberation and return to Watton, "Chip" told me he once tried to escape by stealing an Me 109. He was recaptured before he could start the engine.'
Ralph Tipton, 25th BG

'I'll never forget the day I met Joe Kennedy Jr., USN, (oldest brother of President Kennedy). He landed his B-24 at Watton. Lt. Kennedy had volunteered for the "Mother" and "Drone" missions over V1 and V2 rocket sites and German submarine pens. These missions were code-named 'Aphrodite' and 'Anvil'. I never saw Lt. Kennedy again as he was killed on one of these dangerous missions on 12 August 1944. His 'plane was filled with highly explosive Nitro starch in boxes with detonators connected to each container. The 'plane – the baby – was to be headed toward a German secret weapon site at Mimoyecques. Joe Kennedy was to parachute out of the bomber into the sea and be picked up by an RAF high-speed boat. Hopefully, the huge "flying bomb" would strike the submarine pen. Lt. Kennedy's plane blew up before he exited, however. One of our "Bluestocking" weather patrol Mosquitoes was flying directly behind the ill-fated bomber and was nearly downed by the debris. It's mission was to photograph the flight and its results.'
Joe Capicotta, 8th Combat Camera Unit

'Down a lonely road on a cold black night
a miserable beggar trudges into sight
and the people whisper over their beers
There goes the last of the bombardiers

What is a bombardier? – no reply
But men grow silent and women sigh
as a death like silence fills the place
With a gaunt grey ghost of a long lost race.'

'The Last of the Bombardiers'

PIN-UP

'The American gal
Is a peach of a pal
To the boys who are guarding our nation,
She girds for the fight
By the dawn's early light
And her war job is done with elation!
She always responds
When she's asked to buy war bonds –
No critic can label HER flighty,
And because it's in style
To conserve with a smile
She's conserving by day and by nighty!'

'Patriotic Gal' by Phil Stack

Below: *I drew a girl on the plane and my buddy Michael Otis Harris Murphy from Montgomery, Alabama, did the painting. There was not a brush stroke showing ... painted the name on using the style from a Carnation Cream can and Doris was the girlfriend of the pilot. (Harold Darrah via Jake Krause)*

Above: *GI's DREAM OF AMERICAN BEAUTY!* (Rackheath Memories)

'Patriotic Gal'; Heavenly Body, 'They'll Always Be a Christmas'; Warning Signal; Military Secrets; Matrimony Preferred; Torches at Midnight; Shoo Shoo Baby.
B-17 and B-24s named after Varga pin-ups of 1943, 'Esquire' magazine

'Uncertain of the future, but fearing the worst, we read a prospectus about the 1941 calendar that 'Esquire' is urging on its readers – a dozen pages of nepenthe, each illustrated by Varga, an artist who could make a girl look nude if she were rolled up in a rug. "Order it, look at it, feel it quiver; set it to the music of a slow drum ... "'
"Talk of the Town" 'The New Yorker', 11 January 1941

'When George Petty, Alberto Vargas, Gil Elvgren, and other talented artists created their stunning girls, no doubt these men had no idea how far their talent would reach ...'
'The History of Aircraft Nose Art', Jeffrey L. Ethel, Clarence Simonsen

Right: *A Varga girl so beautiful, so perfect, so typical of the American girl, that I can put that picture in any part of the world, without any signature ... and they will say: that is the Varga Girl. (Harold Darrah via Jake Krause)*

Centre: *Each crewman had his favourite pin-ups on the wall behind his bunk. These were highly prized and usually came from Yank magazine. (Pete Henry: 'The Sack Shack', Shipdham, 31 August 1944. [Henry in top bunk, Lee in bottom bunk])*

'I drew a girl on the 'plane and my buddy, Michael Otis Harris Murphy from Montgomery, Alabama, did the painting. There was not a brush stroke showing. Murphy ran the colours together and then dabbed with the end of the brush to blend the colours. It was an amazing work of art. He even had the reflection on her nails and lips. The picture was on a Vargas calender that I talked the top sergeant out of its position in headquarters. I painted the name on using the style from a Carnation Cream can and Doris was the girlfriend of the pilot [Bill Graff]. I painted a large Good Housekeeping Seal of Approval just below the rock she is seated on. The very next morning after the girl was painted on, along came Jimmy Stewart who flew the bird on a tough mission.'
Harry H. Darrah, 389th BG, co-artist Delectable Doris, *July 1944*

'A Varga girl so beautiful, so perfect, so typical of the American girl, that I can put that picture in any part of the world, without any signature ... and they will say: "that is the Varga Girl."'
Alberto Vargas, 'Esquire' *artist*

'Each crewman had his favourite pin-ups on the wall behind his bunk. These were highly prized and usually came from 'Yank' magazine. The favourites were Betty Grable, Chili Williams in the two-piece polka dot bathing suit, and Rita Hayworth in a silk negligee, the picture that was in 'LIFE' Magazine. Sometimes the movie stars sent autographed photos in response to requests. I had one of Ginger Rogers which she had signed. A friend gave it to me. I still have it. I never saw a

Right: *The favourites were Betty Grable, Chili Williams in the two-piece polka dot bathing suit and Rita Hayworth in a silk negligee. (Author's Collection)*

Eve Whitney

Elaine Shepard

Helen O'Hara

Roth

Kay Boc

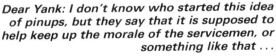

Dear Yank: I don't know who started this idea of pinups, but they say that it is supposed to help keep up the morale of the servicemen, or something like that . . .

How many of you GIs would like to go home and find the room of your wife or girlfriend covered with pictures of a guy stepping out of a bathtub, draped only in a skimpy little towel, or see the walls covered with the pictures of a shorts advertisement or such pictures? ('Yank' magazine)

lewd picture as this was before pornography killed off the pin-up.'
S/Sgt. Ben Smith Jr., radio operator, 303rd BG

Dear Yank:
'I don't know who started this idea of pin-ups, but they say that it is supposed to help keep up the morale of the servicemen, or something like that. Here is my idea of the help it is. In the first place, I would say that 24 out of 25 of the men in the service are either married or have a girl at home whom they respect and intend to marry as soon as this war is over . . . How many of you GIs would like to go home and find the room of your wife or girlfriend covered with pictures of a guy stepping out of a bathtub, draped only in a skimpy little towel, or see the walls covered with the pictures of a shorts advertisement or such pictures? None of you would. Then why keep a lot of junk hanging around and kid yourself about keeping up morale . . . ?

'I would much rather wake up in the morning and see a picture of a P-51 or '39 hanging above my bed or over the picture of my wife, whom I

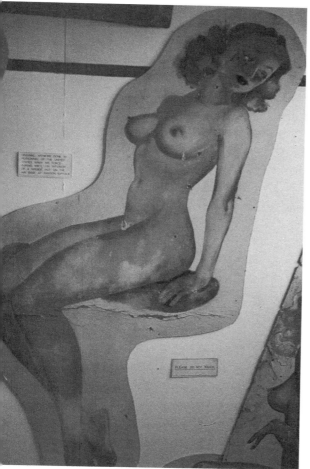

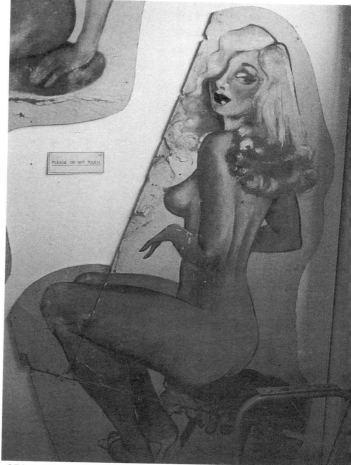

350th FG wall nudes, on display at IWM, Duxford (Author's Collection)

think is the best-looking girl in the world, than of some dame who has been kidded into, or highly paid for, posing for these pictures.'
Pfc. Joseph H. Saling, Myrtle Beach AAF, South Carolina, 'Yank' magazine, 1943

MOST ADMIRED AMERICAN FEMALE (the Whole Package):
Rosie the Riveter. (1943)
The girls who'd dance with you at the USO and make you believe they meant it. (1944)
The one you were married to – or would be as soon as this damned thing was over (1945)
'Yank' magazine

MOST ADMIRED AMERICAN FEMALE (Limbs only):
Rita Hayworth. (1943)
Rita Hayworth. (1944)
Rita Hayworth, for Christ's sake! ... (1945)
'Yank' magazine

'Now that we soldiers overseas are allowed to select the contents of our packages from home, here are four types of gift boxes that we would like to receive:
A – One Lana Turner and one case of Scotch.
B – One Diana Shore and one case of Scotch.
C – One Rita Hayworth and one case of Scotch.
D – One Scotch and one case of Jane Russells.'
Cpl. James O'Neill 'Yank' magazine, 2 July 1943

Dear Yank:
'We boys do not approve of your very indecent portrayal of the spicy-looking female in a recent edition of our much-loved and eagerly read *Yank*. It seems the intelligent-looking Irene Manning

'MOST ADMIRED AMERICAN FEMALE (the Whole Package): Rosie the Riveter. (1943)' (Harry Gann, McDonnell Douglas)

would never pose for such a suggestive-looking picture ... Is this the much publicized "Pinup Girl" that the Yankee soldiers so crave? We have our doubts! Miss Manning is well dressed, but the pose – phew! (Hays office, please take note.)'
Sgt. E W O'Hara, Britain: 'Yank' magazine, 1943

'The All American Girl was the Statue of Liberty rather than a pin-up. The number of missions completed stretched from the nose way back to the tail and I would judge it was in the sixties when she was lost.'
Bill Carleton, 351st BS Engineering Officer, 100th BG

Dear Yank:
'I do not like your magazine! It is a trade paper for professional soldiers. I am not a professional soldier. There are comparatively few professional soldiers. I like civilian life. I like civilian life pictures. So I can see what I'm missing and fight a bit harder to get back to it. *Sad-Sack* is OK. I am

Sad-Sack is OK. I am OK. We're all OK. ('Yank' magazine)

THE SAD SACK — "THE PROPOSITION"

SGT. GEORGE BAKER
Copyright 1943 by George Baker

It seems the intelligent-looking Irene Manning would never pose for such a suggestive-looking picture. Is this the much publicized 'Pinup Girl' that the Yankee soldiers so crave? ... Miss Manning is well dressed, but the pose – phew!' (Connie Richards)

OK. We're all OK. But *Yank* isn't.'
Cpl. W.H. Dundas, Britain. Mail Call, 'Yank' magazine 1945

TWO GREAT NATIONS, DIVIDED BY A COMMON LANGUAGE

George Bernard Shaw

> *'We see them try to jitterbug,*
> *They twist and turn and pull and hug.*
> *It's enough to make Red Indians jealous,*
> *Yet Yanks are civilized, so they tell us.'*

The GIs, *by a WAAF at Shipdham*

'Landing at an RAF base after a mission, they always fed us fresh farm eggs and French fried potatoes ["chips"] after we had had a dram or two of spirits. I always wondered, where did they get the eggs; we did not have them on our base.

'This base being a Photo reconnaissance base had a great number of women. Photo interpreters with whom we were billeted. Interesting to say the least; learned that it was vulgar to use the term "fanny" in mixed company, but alright to use "ass".'
Col. Robert H. Tays, pilot, 392nd BG

'When we had gone overseas we had painted a nude on our B-17 and called her the *Sad Shack*. I said I was going to kiss her fanny every time I got back from a mission. When I wrote to my parents that I had seen "fanny" that day they knew I had completed another mission.'
Bernal 'Rusty' Lewis, co-pilot, 379th BG

'We were caught in a rain storm while bicycling home from the river camp. Like the others, I got pretty wet. After arriving at the house, the family members were able to change into dry clothes, but I had no extra clothing. Therefore, I made the suggestion that perhaps Fred would loan me a pair of his pants until mine dried. I could always tell when I said something wrong. Suddenly, everyone would stop talking and an awkward silence would set in until their composure returned. In this case, as he always did, Mr Colman took me aside to inform me that in England only women wore pants, men wore trousers.

'On another return trip, we rode into a swarm of flying insects. As I slapped at the little beasties, I said something to the effect that I wished these bugs would go away. Again, I knew at once that I had put my foot in my mouth. Mr 'C' informed me later that "bug" was a contraction for "bugger", which was a vulgar word in polite society. There were other words or expressions, such as handbag versus pocketbook, that amused the family and vice versa, but all in all, we communicated well.'
1/Lt. John W. McClane Jr., navigator, 44th BG

'On one of our trips to London, I needed a tube for my radio. I was told I could find it in London so I went into a radio repair shop to buy the type desired. The clerk asked if he could be of assistance. I said, "Yes, I need a tube for my radio." At this request I got a most puzzled look from the clerk. He asked me to describe what I wanted, said that he did not comprehend my need. Now I was puzzled, how could he not know what I needed?

'I pulled a piece of paper out of my pocket with

the tube number on it. The clerk took one look and said he knew what my need was, I wanted a "valve". The shop had in stock the desired item. We parted after a good laugh at our difference in Anglo-American terms.

Another difference was that the English do not refer to blocks as we Americans do, but rather will tell you to walk so many "minutes", with parting words, "You can't miss it."'
John W. McClane, navigator, 44th BG

'We have gone far fast. That might be said of everybody who lives in these times; civilians and military alike. Everybody is a survivor.

'I see survivors on trains here I have ridden. The trains are like toys compared to America's big cars and big locomotives. The train passengers are survivors of bombings, air raids, death, I tell myself. Riding a British train is different; the seating arrangement is different. The entry into the cars here is through many doors from the side, not one door at the ends of a car.'
S/Sgt Robert T. Marshall, B-17 radio operator, 384th BG

NO BALLS AT ALL

'Hitler has only got one ball.
Goering has two, but they're too small
Himmler is something similar,
But poor old Goebbels has no balls at all.'

'No-ball': Code word for V1 target.

No Balls At All; Cannon Ball; Fireball; Eight Ball; Lucille Ball; Linda Ball (Major Ball's baby daughter); *Spitball; Snowball; Screwball; Speedball; Highball; Foulball; Spareball.*
B-17F Flying Fortresses, 511th 'Ball Boys' BS (commanded by Maj. Clinton Ball), 351st BG

'We proceeded to Sioux City air base, Iowa, where we received new B-17F models and flying and

'Screw Ball' (the late Allan Healy)

maintenance crews were assigned to them. Our combined crews named our airplane *Big Red* after 'Man of War,' the famous racehorse.'
M/Sgt. Frank W. Grover, Crew Chief, 388th BG

'Our call sign at Flixton was 'Beach Bell' and my aircraft was 'C for Charlie' and our group call sign was 'Balance'. The squadron call sign was 'Accept.' These I remember well.'
Lt. Col. Tom S. Belovich, 446th BG

'The young lady wants to see her boyfriend's bomber. She is curious about the name *Frenesi*. She asks the young sergeant what the name means.

'He replies: "Oh, you know, it's from the title of the song, 'Frenesi'."

'She hesitates and says: "Oh, you Yanks can't fool me. 'Frenesi' means free and easy – and that's the way you like your girls." '
Abe Dolim, radio operator, 94th BG, summer 1944, Bury St Edmunds. (Frenesi – Spanish/ Portugese definition – Frenzy, Fury, Rapture)

'The pilot has just returned to his squadron from two months' leave in the ZOI and has been down to the line to watch the bombers return from an early mission. As he pedals back from the ramp toward the Mess, he notices the hulk of a bomber lying in the muck as though it might be used for ditching practice. The camouflage paint marks her as an old timer and then his eyes spot the numbers on the vertical stabilizer – 9775 – it rings a bell. He pedals around to the front quarter of the wreck and notes the sitting nude with crossed leg. She stares at him with knowing eyes. His mind wanders to a day when "bogies" were abundant and how the old girl undulated off his left wing. So old *Frenesi* has finally bought the farm – the hard way.'
Abe Dolim, End of a Queen, Autumn 1944, 94th BG 'Swamp' Bury St. Edmunds

'V-mail is quicker,
Air Mail is thicker.'
Pvt. Raymond Carlson, Mail Call, 'Yank' magazine

'I read "Stars And Stripes", the GI's newspaper. It waves the flag and I like that. London papers sold on the base drive me to the "Stars And Stripes". The nationalism of their tone is English, of course. I should expect that. The guys really go for a London paper that has a comic strip that features a nude woman. I check out that strip, too. Day after day she is without clothes. Can this be a newspaper?'
T/Sgt. Robert T. Marshall, radio operator, 385th BG

Lena The Hyena; Dogpatch Express; Sweet Moonbeam McSwine; Mammy Yokum; Daisy Mae Scragg; Marryin' Sam; Hairless Joe.
Al Capp Dogpatch characters from Lil' Abner.

'We were known by one and all as 'The Flying Eightballs', a title bestowed on the group in its pre-combat period when things just could not go right.
1/Lt. John W. McClane Jr., navigator, 44th BG

'We had been assigned a new all natural aluminium B-24H #295260, code named P-260, for which Peritti selected the name of *Lili Marlene*. How he came by this name I have no idea. He also arranged to have the picture of Lili painted on the right side of the nose of the plane. She was sitting on a bomb and, as one might expect, mostly nude. *Lili Marlene* was a beautiful 'plane. Bright, unpainted silver with our squadron code letters of 'WQ' painted in large letters on either side of the fuselage just aft on the side gunner windows. The two vertical stabilizers were left silver except for a broad vertical black stripe and the letter 'P'. The left side of the nose had our 'Flying Eightball' logo as did all 44th BG 'planes. We completed our tour of combat duty in October 1944.
  '*Lili Marlene* crashed killing Lt. Bledsoe and his entire crew on 28 December 1944. We loved *Lili*

V-mail is quicker/Air Mail is thicker. (Author's Collection)

Marlene. I was sure she would fly until old age sent her to the 'Great Haven In The Sky,' where old bombers go. I know she is there now even if she did meet with a premature death.'
1/Lt. John W. McClane Jr., navigator, 68th BS, 44th BG

Tondelayo: From a character played by Hedy Lamar in the movie, White Cargo.

Memphis Belle: From the wayward southern gal played by Joan Blondell in the film Lady for a Night described in the dialogue as a 'Memphis Belle'.

Red Ass (Referred to as *The Bungay Buckaroo*): B-24 Liberator in the 446th BG.

S.O.L (Shit Outa Luck) and *4Q2*; 458th BG Liberators.

Nine-O-Nine; Inspired by the B-17's last three serial numbers.

No Nothin': Inspired by the B-17's last three serial numbers.

DO-JIN-DON: Donald Duck-inspired B-24J, 706th Bomb Squadron, 446th BG.

Pickle-Barrel; Bombardiers claimed they could place a bomb in a pickle barrel from 22,000 ft.

'No doubt many have often wondered why the names on some of the 'planes. I know a lot of reasons that can't be printed in a book, but regardless of what they were they were good morale builders for the crews that flew them. The Old Squaw was a complimentary term in the state of Mississippi at one time. When the Choctaw Indians occupied Mississippi, the term was one of respect bestowed on the oldest female in the tribe. She was considered "good medicine" and was the only woman permitted to attend tribal meetings. Of course, Andrew Jackson drove the Choctaws out of Mississippi in 1830, so they went down like our 'plane. So maybe it wasn't such a good name after all. It seemed appropriate at the time.'
Howard E. Hernan, gunner, 303rd BG

'I was co-pilot of WQ-V of the 44th BG which took part in "Market Garden" on 18 September 1944. The pilot was Lt. Elvin L. Barnhart. The original name of the aircraft was *Puritanical Bitch*,

Lili Marlene was a beautiful 'plane. Bright, unpainted silver with our squadron code letters of WQ painted in large letters on either side of the fuselage ... two vertical stabilizers ... left silver except for a broad vertical black stripe and the letter 'P'. (USAF Official)

complete with original painting, but when a WAAF was assigned to the base Col. Snavely ordered the 'B' changed to a 'W'. During the Eindhoven delivery mission we were leading the right element, so Barney had to keep eyes left in order to maintain position. This left me with the unenviable task of watching ahead for church steeples, power lines or anything else which appeared to be higher than we were and calling his attention to it, preferably in time. I was never so scared in my life, especially since my attention was divided – we had a super-charger fire in #3 engine (we also had #3 throttle cable cut and, as we discovered upon touchdown, the left tyre punctured). It was not "our" airplane; contrary to common belief, we did not (at least during my tour) have our own 'planes – we flew what we were assigned each day.'

Lt. (later Col.) Harry C. Stubbs, 44th BG (10 first with the 458th BG and 25 more with the 44th)

'"Paddlefoot" was a caricature used by the Minnesota Gophers football team and the idea of crew member Glenn R. Matson. Although I didn't do the original, I duplicated it in miniature on the flight jackets of all its crew members. This was a fairly common practice . . . *Little Lambsy Divey* was named after the popular song of the same name and was flown by one of the lead crews . . . *Ten Gun Dottie* was our squadron commander's plane (Maj. Jamieson) and named after his wife. It depicted the five twin gun emplacements of the Liberators . . . *Wolfgang* was also painted for a lead crew but subsequently removed as it was thought to be too "offensive" to the Germans and if its crew were captured – who knows.'

Harold J. Johnston, base artist, 458th BG

'Shortly after completing 20 missions, I had my A-2 flight jacket painted. The leather jacket and the 50 mission crush hat were the distinct mark of a combat flyer; therefore, the painting required special consideration. I found an enlisted man, who as a civilian, had worked for Marshall Field Department store in Chicago. Saw some of the work he had done and was impressed. He did it for £10, about $40. It is a true work of art and I treasure it to this day.

Col. Robert H. Tays, pilot, 337 Oombriago, 392nd BG

Piccadilly Lilly was flown by Lt. Murphy, who I believe was an airline pilot. He was an excellent pilot and completed 15 missions, had shot down eight Nazi warplanes and had been on two diver-

Shortly after completing 20 missions, I had my A-2 flight jacket painted. The leather jacket and the 50 mission crush hat were the distinct mark of a combat flyer. (Alfred R. Lea, 452nd BG)

sion missions. These were shown on the 'plane as a "sitting duck" or "decoy". Each bomb indicated one combat mission, which would have completed their tour.

'Lt Barker, our Operations Officer, and a close friend, was flying with Lt. Murphy the day they failed to return. Of our original 'planes and crew, we had only one crew out of 12 finish and that was Lt. Dye who flew *Going Jessie* which was parked in front of the engineering shack. While there were other individuals from the original cadre that finished, his was the only crew.'

Bill Carleton, 351st BS Engineering Officer, 100th BG

'Back from central France, the crew finally gets a good look at the B-17F they have flown that day. It was pretty dark when they clambered aboard at 06:30 that morning. The nose of the old crate is decorated with the head of a medieval court jester surrounded with swastikas and yellow bombs representing enemy fighters shot down and missions flown. There are 14 swastikas and at least 50 bombs.

'Off to his right are the words *Idiot's Delight*. The red-eyed snaggled toothed joker leers at the crew and he seems to be saying, "Scared hell out of you bastards, didn't I?" The crew chief is happy with what he sees. In the Plexiglas above the single nose gun there is a hole big enough for him to stick his head through.'
Jokers Wild, Abe Dolim, 94th BG, 30 April 1944, 332nd BS hardstand, Bury St. Edmunds:

'Sky Scorpions came from Lt. Caldwell's aircraft of that name in the 565th Squadron. He had a black scorpion on it. The formation ship was the *Green Dragon*.
Earl Zimmerman, 389th BG

'Lt Marion Brown had a B-24 called *The Big Brown Jug*. His brother flew the *Little Brown Jug*, a P-47. Mission after mission, they would look for each other and eventually they teamed up after a raid. But the P-47 came in close and was immediately shot at by one of the gunners who mistook it for a FW 190. When they got on the ground Brown chewed him out. His brother had come in at 1,500 yds off the wing and when fired on had lifted the wing and whipped over the fuselage to show everyone his big white stars.'
Earl Zimmerman, radio operator, 389th BG

'Our belly gunner, C.J. Alexander we all called "Swoose" after the popular song of the day "Alexander the Swoose".'
1/Lt. John W. McClane Jr., navigator, 44th BG

'The filming mission of a B-17 carrying two time-fused, 2,000-lb, steel-nosed, radio-controlled glide bombs, 18 ft long, was code-named "Disney". A running film of the operation was needed to find faults in new methods, to improve accuracy in operation and assess results. On occasion a steel-nosed, time-fused glidebomb would penetrate the concrete and steel U-boat pens and explode within the concrete complex. The damage would be difficult to assess since the film would show only a pin hole in the thick, reinforced protective shield.

The pin hole, perhaps 30 to 36 in. diameter and the churning, undulating waters outside the pens, would evidence a strike, but only when the evidence was on film.'
Dean H. Sanner, Mosquito pilot, 25th BG

'The "Disney Bombs" really taxed the 'plane for flying manoeuvrability and formation flying. It sure took all the skill I had and knowledge to get this awkward flying machine into formation. We therefore had a pretty loose formation. With these two big bombs underneath our wings you can be sure we were very careful. But the nice thing was when we approached the Dutch coast. There was no opposition, only a little bit of flak. It was something to see when these bombs were released and the rockets cut in. I felt proud to fly this mission.'
Bill Rose, pilot, 326th BS, 92nd BG on the first 'Disney Bomb' mission

---

'Our ground crew chief, John N. Wilson, was unofficially in a race with Clint Colvin, crew chief of *Crow's Nest*, another B-24H with an appropriate name and nose art. Completing the hard stand area assigned to these two 'planes was *Balls-O'Fire*, featuring Snuffy Smith in the nose art. *Balls O'Fire* still carried the olive drab paint and had developed a reputation of never having had a crewmember killed while flying in this odd ball. She also had a unique reputation of needing serious repairs each time she went out on a mission. We can never recall her returning at the same time as the group – she was always 30 minutes to one hour behind on the return. *Balls O'Fire* was left on her hard stand when the 453rd was recalled to the States. It seems she had a tree limb run through one wing, picked up on the Rhine crossing support mission.'
Frank Thomas, radio operator, Never Mrs, 453rd BG

SWEATING IT OUT

'Oh pity the poor co-pilot
His forehead dripping wet
Nine men are working for their lives
While he, for 10, must sweat.'

BEACON
PHONE
ODM/DIST
Q SITE
I/C
FLAREPATH
C
I/C
WEATHER
BA OBB OFF OFE REMARKS

'That familiar phrase, "sweating it out" was no idle collection of words. When I was flying combat in the summer of '44 I literally had grainy salt deposits on the OUTside of my thick leather GI shoes!

'I'm not ashamed to admit that I was sweating every minute we were over enemy territory!'
Bob Maag, pilot, Skinny, *94th BG*

'Icicles kept forming in my oxygen mask even though it wasn't too cold. Later, when I took off my helmet, ice chunks fell out from around my ears. These had evidently formed from the vapour while breathing oxygen for hours. The frozen skin peeled for months thereafter.'
Joe Wroblewski, pilot, 351st BG

'When we were in a battle and the guns were firing, I could smell the cordite. It was long after the war before the smell of gun smoke would not bring fear back to me. Also the excitement would make me sweat. I would have a cake of ice on my forehead where my perspiration was coming out

Above: *That familiar phrase, 'sweating it out' was no idle collection of words. (USAF Official)*

from under my helmet. I pulled it off in little chunks.

'When the action got hot and heavy, even though it was 40 below zero or more, I would always perspire so heavily that sweat would come out from under my flight helmet and freeze along my forehead. I would pick the ice off with my fingers when the action was over . . . '
John McClane Jr., 44th BG navigator

'It was always bitter cold and noisy at our altitude. I wore an electric heating suit. Sometimes all the parts of the suit didn't work. Once one of my electric slippers didn't function. My foot hurt so badly that I was afraid to remove the boot after landing to look at it. I constantly had to squeeze my oxygen mask to break the icicles from the chin part of my mask to keep it in operation. Many times my face got frost bitten, and for many years

Above: *It was always bitter cold and noisy at our altitude. (Geoff Ward)*

Below: *We returned with a few holes in the ship. (Author's Collection)*

The ground crews always sweated out the returning bombers. (Col. William B. Cameron [left])

my face would have red patches on the cheeks during the winter months.'
Lloyd W. Hughes, gunner, 453rd BG, Berlin, June 1944

'We returned with a few holes in the ship. The trip was rather long and it was cold at altitude. Returned safely to the field but can truthfully say that I "sweated" a bit today.'
Larry Goldstein, radio operator, 388th BG

'The ground crews always sweated out the returning bombers.'
Jim Brock, 882nd Chemical Warfare Co., Attlebridge

'I was awakened about 3.00 a.m. and had a good feeling as to where we were going. My next to last mission. I began to sweat this one out. Berlin was our target. If any one of us had our own way we would have all gone back to bed.'
1/Lt. Joe Wroblewski, pilot, Shady Lady II, 351st BG, 7 May 1944

> *Come gather round me boys*
> *And I'll give you all the poop.*
> *I'll tell you 'bout the fighters*
> *I'll tell you 'bout the flak*
> *The last one to take off*
> *But the first one to get back.'*

Air Corps song to the tune of 'McNamara's Band'

'On April 1 1944, Col. Thompson was reported KIA and on April 3 1944, Col. Jerry Mason took command. He hastened to correct conditions but moved a little too fast. When he ordered class "A" uniforms at retreat the men rebelled, stayed in their barracks and used emergency rations for their evening meal. This resulted in Col. Mason asking to be relieved of command.'
Maj. Newton L. Mclaughlin, Special Services Officer, 448th BG

DISCIPLINE

> *'Oh me name is Col—*
> *I'm the leader of the group*

'When the truck came to deliver coal, it was always driven by a crew of GIs who were in the guard house for committing various offences, mostly for staying out when their passes were over. They would maybe be free for a day or two and would come into the Red Cross Club in their best uniforms, go off to Norwich for the evening and

OFFICE OF THE STATION SURGEON
ARMY AIR FORCE STATION #155
A.P.O. 634

M-A-3

314.7   February 21, 1944

SUBJECT: History of Health of Command for January 1944.

TO: Public Relations Officer, AAF Station 155, A.P.O. 634.

    1. In general the health history for January 1944 was very
good, i.e., no serious outbreaks of disease threatened the Command,
no airplanes failed to take off on Combat Missions because of
lack of physically fit aircrewmen to man them, and an excellent
comparative Combat record was maintained.

    2. Statistically the following were recorded:

        Flying Personnel   All Personnel

    Frost Bite   8   Resp. Infection   52
    Aero-otitis   30   Venereal Disease   9
    Venereal Disease   4   Injuries   31
    Resp. Infection   91   All Other Diseases   96
    Battle Casualties   21   Total Number of Cases 188
    Flying Fatigue   0   Total Days Lost   1126
    All Other Diseases or 39   Mean Strength   2879
            Injuries
    Total Number of Cases 196
    Total Days Lost(Flying)2065
    Mean Strength   765

    3. As long as the premises stated in ppl can be accomplished,
this office will continue its present policies.

                              Williston P. Bunting,
                              Major, Medical Corps,
                              Station Surgeon.

Above: *History of Health of Command for January 1944. (USAF Official)*

promptly be back in the guard house next day. The MPs (Military Police) always patrolled the city in two's and had the nickname of "Snowdrops".
Phyllis Smales, Rackheath teenager, American Red Cross Club, 467th BG, 1944

'I had the unpleasant honour to be the defence counsel for the pilot and navigator of a lead squadron crew who put a beautiful bomb pattern on the railroad yards in Basle, Switzerland. They thought they had bombed Freiburg, Germany, and were tried in a general court for culpable negligence in the performance of duty. We achieved an acquittal after a week-long court, longest in the history of the 8th Air Force.

'Because the questions were those of navigation, I was named to the defence board by Gen. Peck. The court was held at our group base at Horsham St Faith. I was named defence counsel because I ranked the two lawyers on the defence board. These were Lt. Max Sokarl and Capt. Irving

Below: *President of the court was Col James Stewart ... the motion picture actor. (USAF Official)*

Goldman. President of the court was Col. James Stewart ... the motion picture actor. Trial Judge Advocate was a Lt. Kranawitter, an attorney in civilian life. Law member of the court was an officer who was, in civilian life, a municipal judge in

Cartoon (Rackheath Memories)

He ran a tight base and, despite cries of 'Chicken' from new, and some old, men, it paid off. (the late Allan Healy)

100 OPERATIONAL BOMBING MISSIONS IN 140 DAYS!

THAT'S THE RECORD THIS GROUP HAS SET FOR 2ND BOMB DIVISION OF THE FAMED 8TH AIR FORCE IN ENGLAND.....

FLYING 2372 SORTIES, THESE B-24 LIBERATOR BOMBERS HAVE RAINED 5440 TONS OF BOMBS UPON GERMANY AND THE OCCUPIED COUNTRIES .... IF YOU CAN PICTURE 108,800 SACKS OF FLOUR, WEIGHING 100 POUNDS EACH, THEY WOULD EQUAL THE WEIGHT OF DESTRUCTION THESE BOMBERS HAVE DROPPED ON ENEMY TARGETS ....

Col. Albert J. SHOWER
WEST POINT GRAD, COMMANDING OFFICER OF THIS B-24 HEAVY BOMBER GROUP.....

LISTEN TO THE PURR OF THOSE ENGINES!

PRIDE AND JOY — OF M/SGT. JOE RAMIREZ, OF LOS ANGELES, CAL., IS A B-24 BOMBER NAMED "Witchcraft" WHICH HAS COMPLETED 70 MISSIONS WITHOUT A MECHANICAL FAILURE! M/SGT RAMIREZ IS THE GROUND CREW CHIEF.

His character moulded the group. He brought men home alive. (the late Allan Healy)

Los Angeles. Lt. Gen. James Doolittle was asked to explain what had gone wrong by Gen. Spaatz who went to Switzerland at the request of Gen. Eisenhower to apologise.'
Jackson W. Granholm, 458th BG Navigator, on the American bombing by 2nd Air Division Liberators of Basle and Zurich on 4 March 1945

<hr>

'Col. Albert J. Shower, West Point, 1935, – "Black Al" – was the CO. There are probably as many different views as to what he was like as there were men in the squadrons. There can be only one view of the character he put upon the group by his leadership. He made it a well-trained group – he insisted on arduous practice missions, tight formations, perfect peel-offs, exact take-offs, all of which paid off in giving the group its low loss rate. He liked blouses and ties worn, strict "military courtesy", a more than well-kept base. He ran a tight base and, despite cries of "Chicken" from new, and some old, men, it paid off ... His character moulded the group. He brought men home alive.'
Allan Healy, 467th BG

<hr>

'Col. Westover, a young West Point officer and son of the former commanding general of the Air Corps, advised me the day he took command, to

M/Sgt. Joe Ramirez (the late Allan Healy)

throw the rule book out of the window and he would back me to the hilt. He kept his word to the extent of overriding higher authority in taking the Post Exchange away from the quartermaster and turning it over to me, an Air Corps Officer.'
Maj. Newton L. Mclaughlin, Special Services Officer, 448th BG

<hr>

'Some of us found the *Brickmaker's Arms* one black night as we were riding about on our newly acquired bikes. When it got dark we found ourselves lost. It was at the "Brick" that I got instructions back to our base. I soon returned there and it became "my" pub for the duration. I asked Ma Brister who I could go hunting with and she introduced me to Ernest Knights. He and I hunted rabbits and I hunted pheasants when the opportunity presented itself.'
Charles H. Mills, one-time military policeman, 2nd AD HQ, Ketteringham Hall

<hr>

'To: Superintendent O. Carter, Sir,
I respectfully beg to report First Sgt. Charles H.

Mills of 315 Signals Co Wing, A.P.O.. 634, United States Army, Horsham St Faiths, for (a) killing game, one cock pheasant during unlawful season, (b) killing game without a game licence and (c) trespassing in pursuit of game during daytime on land owned by Mr J.R. Mealing Mills of 456 Unthank Road, Norwich, at a grass meadow adjoining Curzon Hall Farm, East Carleton, on Friday 17th Sept, 1943 about 11-45am ... I later spoke to the owner of the land, Mr J. R. Mealing Mills, and he wished for no action to be taken in the matter stating that he would have prosecuted for trespassing in pursuit of game, had the offender been other than an American. He also said he had had previous trouble with Americans trespassing on the land with guns and had warned them off.

'The pheasant, subject of the above, I have placed in cold store at Mr W. Dann's Butcher, of Great Melton Road, Hethersett, for evidence if required ... Your obedient servant, James Hurrell P.C.36.'
Statement by James Hurrell, P.C.36, 20th September 1944

'Our landlord, Sir Eric Teichman, would send an invitation for three officers to dinner. I was invited and asked if I could go pheasant hunting. He said an invitation would be sent to the CO for two officers next Wednesday. I got my name on the list. Instead of pheasants they shot Norfolk partridge. Beaters drove the birds over the guns. I did not do

'Tighten formation! Tighten formation!' (via Ian McLachlan)

well as all shots were overhead.

'I was invited to return the next week for pheasants. This time I wore Class A uniform and took a sergeant as a loader with two 12-gauge automatic shot guns. Again, all guns lined up and the beaters drove the birds over us. I requested Sir Eric to let me go with the beaters as we do in the US. I walked through the bracken with three beaters on each side. I had the kind of shots I knew. For the day I totalled 26 pheasants and two woodcocks. Sir Eric invited me to return. Unlike the US, the game belongs to the landlord. Pheasants brought 10 shillings in the mark .t. Each gun was given a brace.'
Lt. Col. George H. Parker, Station Engineer, 466th BG, Attlebridge, Norfolk.

'I'm going outside to stop that damned poaching.'
Sir Eric Teichman, at Honingham Hall estate, near Attlebridge, Norfolk, on the afternoon of 3 December 1944

'The old man said: "Wait a minute. What are your names?" Smith said: "Get back Pop" ... I shot him.' *Pte. Leonard S. Wojtacha's statement of how Pte. George E. Smith, a 27-year-old cookhouse worker at Attlebridge Air Base, murdered Sir Eric Teichman in cold blood at Smith's Court Martial on 8 January 1945. (Smith was found guilty and hanged.)*

'Smith is a schizophrenic and incapable of knowing right from wrong. He has the mental age approximately of a nine-year-old child ... '
Smith's defence lawyer, 1/Lt. Max Sokarl

'We didn't want any Hairbreadth Harry types. We wanted beady-eyed guys just absolutely holding the course, sweating and working hard to keep the subtle settings right in.'
Harry Crosby, 100th BG

'Tighten formation! Tighten formation!'
Gen. Robert Williams, 1st Bomb Division commander

'If a unit wished to score well in bombing accuracy it was necessary to make a straight, unswerving bomb run with no evasive action to avoid flak; but this resulted in greater losses.'
Gen. Maurice 'Mo' Preston

'The truck drove to the helmeted MPs at the main

gate that opened in the link fence that protected the area. It was fairly flat countryside and we drove down the one main road of the base, past clustered areas on the left and right of wood and tar paper barracks. Every so often there would be a painted sign that could be read from the road. One was, "This Group flies the tightest formation in the ETO."

'Another read, "This Group takes no evasive action on the bomb run."'
William C. Stewart, gunner, 92nd BG; arrival at Podington, January 1945

'The pilot who flew all the way to Rackheath, only to nose up his aircraft with a broken nosewheel strut after landing down wind on the shortest runway on the field, was demoted to co-pilot, in which ignominious state he flew several missions. After taking the bump in graceful manner I was happy to give him a crew, and he was a very good aircraft commander. At one time there was a bombardier who was a disciplinary problem in his unit. Someone asked me to take him, so I agreed, having a good fatherly talk before sending him to a squadron which had a rather strict commander. By working with him and keeping him busy, he became one of the sharpest bombardiers. He liked a bit of fun and had a very likeable personality.'
Col. Albert J. Shower, CO, 467th BG

'This being our last mission, we shot a green flare upon landing. It sort of upset our base commander, Col. Romig, because this was against orders. He threatened us but all we had to do was go on a practice mission two days later.'
Joe Wroblewski, pilot, 351st BG, completing his tour on 19 May 1944

'I wasn't sorry the mission had been "scrubbed". It meant another day to live.'
8th Air Force combat crewman

'The scavenger, the guy who goofs off at sick call. He is still here. I avoid him and I feel sorry for him. Before we went to the 94th, I didn't like what he was doing; whether it was necessary or not, I don't know. I just want nothing to do with him. I used to think he was a malingerer. He had something going; he would go to sick call on mornings we drew the tough targets and guys caught on. Ear trouble, he said. I give him the benefit of the doubt; you don't accuse somebody of trying to get out of flying a tough mission. One guy did and they almost fought ...

If a unit wished to score well in bombing accuracy it was necessary to make a straight unswerving bomb run with no evasive action to avoid flak; but this resulted in greater losses. (Author's Collection)

'The malingerer/scavenger picks and chooses his missions, it seems. He makes his move after he checks the flight line. Things like ground crews filling "Tokyo tanks" cause him to have ear problems. Bomb loads affect him.

'Altitude does things to guys with bad ears; same with guys who have colds in the head. I think if he is sick, he ought to be grounded permanently so he can avoid the bad feeling that builds against him. If he is a malingerer, he is pitiful and deserving his agony. I wish he weren't around.'
T/Sgt. Robert T. Marshall, radio operator, 385th BG

'Our losses weren't there because of the discipline the guys had. Other units were strung out all over the skies, making them easy targets for the fighters. Our guys got in close and stayed so. A good formation gave you a lot of supporting firepower, which made you the last ones the enemy fighter planes wanted to take on .... 'We never sent the word to leave us alone tomorrow. We always said that we can make it, get a box together, even if they all landed out of commission ... 'It was a disgrace to turn back.'
Gen. Lewis Lyle, 379th BG

'In order to reduce losses units would demand that

pilots return to base with any aircraft found to be in a questionable condition at the start of a mission. This, of course, led to a high abort rate.'
Gen. Maurice 'Mo' Preston, 379th BG

'On a mission over the Ruhr, on the way back we had a fighter get on our tail. I took evasive action which, in formation, consisted of skidding the B-17 sideways first one way and then the other. We were limited to how far we could skid out of the formation and then when you skidded back in you could get over or underneath the other man's side. The B-17 was a very stable aircraft and very hard to skid. I put all the pressure I could on the rudder. A fighter just sat out there. I was on intercom with the tail gunner and I pleaded, "Shoot him down!"

'When I skidded into the formation and then reversed my skid, he let his 20 mm's go. The

Death and courage and devotion to duty were a part of our history. (USAF Official)

incendiary bullets came into the cockpit through the oxygen tank, ploughed into the armour plating behind the co-pilot's head and richocheted off and went through the top turret gunner's leg. They ended up in our chest-type parachutes and ignited them. The rubber bands which held them closed burned and the parachutes came open. We immediately went on emergency oxygen. A part of the tank hit me in the shoulder but I could still use my hand and fingers.

'I looked at Doug Maxwell and he was trying to get his oxygen system on. He was not paying attention to flying the ship so I said: "Hey, come on, let's check with the Engineer." I could see him sitting with his finger in his leg. He was bleeding and behind him was a fire. Eventually, one of the crew stamped the fire out. This was the last time Maxwell flew with us. When we had needed help most he was too concerned with his own well being. He went on another crew and was later shot down.'
Bill Rose, pilot, 326th BS, 92nd BG

DEATH

'The bells of hell go ting-a-ling-a-ling
For you but not for me;
And the little devils how they sing-a-ling-a-ling
For you but not for me.
Oh Death, where is thy sting-a-ling-a-ling
O Grave, thy victor-ee?
The bells of hell go ting-a-ling-a-ling
For you but not for me.'

'Maj. Saltsman returned with two bullet holes. One went through the tailwheel so he landed with a flat tyre. Also, the navigator was hit and lost quite a bit of blood. The sight of this turned the stomachs of the other crew members, but as I was raised on a farm where we did our own butchering, this never bothered me. Consequently, for the rest of the war it was always my job to clean out the ship whenever we had wounded on board.'
94th BG ground crewman

'Death and courage and devotion to duty were a part of our history.'
Allan Healy, 467th BG

'One of our B-17s was hit by a Ju 88. It was firing rockets at the time and set the Fortress on fire. It

A returning Liberator crashed near the field as it tried to land on three engines and all were killed but for one man who walked away unhurt.' (93rd BG)

lost power and started to fall behind our formation. The squadron leader requested permission to stay with the Fortress. We could not break formation and so we had to watch as it fell behind and finally plunged into the North Sea. There were no survivors.'

Leonard W. Herman, 95th BG

'A German fighter pilot dangling from a cream-coloured parachute passed within range, just under our formation at one o'clock. It would have been easy to kill him as he floated past our right wing. Over at 11 o'clock I saw a B-17, straggling and losing altitude, fire sweeping its entire belly while the crew bailed out. An airman left the right waist hatch, his open parachute on fire. I believe I am more afraid of fire than anything else. God what a miserable way to die.'

Abe Dolim, navigator, 94th BG

'Remnants of left service shoe size 8C
Remnants parachute harness
Remnants of fleece-lined flying boot
Silver air crew wings marked M.D.
Fingerprints: fingers missing.'

Dimitrie Jimmy Siladie

'A radio operator who forgot his code-book and went back to get it, only to walk directly into a live prop. It was goodbye. Happened in the 44th.'

Forrest S. Clark, gunner, 44th BG

'Death would come in many ways. We lost two men falling into the North Sea. A runaway turret shot down one of our own 'planes on a practice mission when the formation was over the sea and only Capt. Taylor and five enlisted men were saved by Air Sea Rescue after riding their parachutes down. On one occasion a returning Liberator crashed near the field as it tried to land on three engines, and all were killed but one man who walked away unhurt. We lost crews in forced landings and in take-off accidents. A take-off on 29 December 1944 was made in ground fog that shrouded the sides of the runways with 15 killed and four wounded. Two other 'planes were damaged on this take-off and one crash-landed at Attlebridge and one was headed for enemy territory, and its crew bailed out.'

Allan Healy, 467th BG

'My engineer got out after I did and when a shot down airman returned to England he had to be verified, so I went down to London on 1 May 1944 to identify Sgt. Thompson. He was in the last batch to get out of Turkey. After we had all got back from Africa, they tried to reunite the crew. I flew as a spare radio man for a time but Lt. James, the pilot, was made gunnery officer of the 565th Squadron, later transferring to a Mosquito outfit. We lost our co-pilot in Africa – he quit flying. The bombardier and navigator were killed and severely injured respectively. Most of the gunners returned. I was grounded later for a few missions with ear trouble, during which time the gunners flew a mission and did not come back. That left me and Harold Thompson, the engineer. We were treated as mascots because we were two of the original

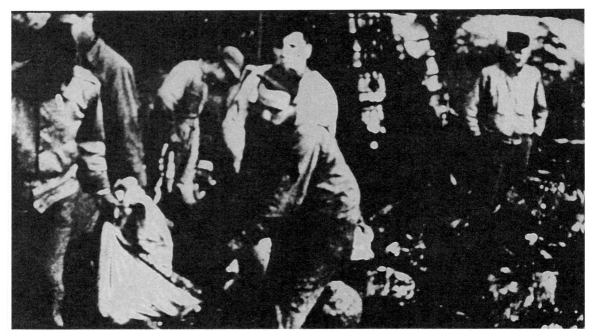

surviving and we were put with the ground crews, flying as spares now and again. On the morning of 21 November 1944, Harold left for a mission. I could hear bombers forming up over "Buncher Six" and a loud explosion followed. Later, I discovered that two of our B-24s had collided over Hethel. Harold and 16 other men were killed. All were buried in the same casket at Cambridge.'
Earl Zimmerman, 389th BG Ploesti veteran

'A .30 calibre armour-piercing shell entered the waist gun area and went right through the steel helmet of Sgt. Leonard A. Baumgartner and struck him in the head. I went to the back of the airplane to administer to him. Baumgartner took his last breath in my arms.'
Richard E Perry, pilot, 390th BG

'I slipped the burning Fortress out of formation and released the bombs over the marshalling yards of Cologne before advising the crew to bail out. Eight took my advice before I dived to just 4,000 ft. The flames were extinguished in the dive and I was able to land in Belgium. The controls had been badly damaged, the instruments shot up and more than 200 holes had punctured the skin. As I crawled out I noticed the tail gunner still at his post. "Some trip wasn't it?" The tail gunner did not answer. He was dead.'
Douglas L. Johnson, pilot, 390th BG, Cologne raid, October 1944

We lost crews in forced landings and in take-off accidents. (Thorpe Abbotts Memorial Museum)

'It appeared to me that every section of this huge city was on fire. An ugly pall of smoke was blowing to the southwest. It looked the way that one might imagine Hell to be.'
1/Lt. John W. McClane Jr., navigator, 44th BG, describing Hamburg on the morning of 21 June 1944 after the RAF had fire-bombed the city, while en route to Berlin

---

'I was told by one of my B-17 friends that during the night, Jerry also dropped a vicious anti-personnel bomb called a "Bouncing Betty" that would hop up about waist-high if it were stepped on and then explode. In order to rid the grass field of these devices so our B-17s could take off, they rounded up the local Russian peasants and lined them shoulder to shoulder and walked them across the field to explode the "Bettys". The 'planes were more valued than the lives of the people.'
1/Lt. John W. McClane Jr., navigator, 68th BS, 44th BG, Shuttle bombing mission to Russia

---

She was full of rattles, groans and squeaks
and an awful hissing from oxygen leaks
They banked to the right and turned around
and that shivering Lib' was England bound

*Number one cut with an awful noise
and it really worked the 'suicide boys'
Number three quit with a hell of a roar
then they feathered number four*

*The crew were worried and tried to leave
just as the Lib' gave a final heave
Then like a rock she dove for the ground
and never a body or piece was found.*

'Wreckage was scattered over a large area. The bottom cone of the hole was filled with aluminium that had melted from the intense heat of the burning wreckage. Not too far away was a crew of three men. They had placed a rope around the trunk of the body of one of the pilots. Both of the unfortunate pilots were still sitting in their heavy metal bucket seats; their arms had been burned to stumps as were their legs. All of their bodies, including their heads, were burned charcoal black. The clean-up crew gave a tug on the rope, expecting to extract the body but instead, the torso simply pulled apart like an overdone roast. On the way to my observation point, I saw an unburned electric flying glove. We always needed an extra glove so I was not above usurping this one for my emergency bag. When I picked it up, it took me no time to let it go again, as I noticed it still had a hand in it.'

1/Lt. John W. McClane Jr., navigator, 44th BG

Above: *The torso simply pulled apart like an overdone roast. (Author's Collection)*

Below: *... a returning Liberator crashed near the field as it tried to land on three engines and all were killed ...*

'On the return from the mission to a rail station at Leipzig, Lt. Walter A. Wesley landed his Fortress on the Podington runway and taxied away to dispersal. While removing guns, the top turret turned and caught the engineer between the turret and the side of the aircraft, crushing his head and

I walked into the Officers' Mess and I heard this horrendous noise. I thought it was some sort of welcome for me. Then a huge lump of shrapnel landed about 20 ft away ... It seemed the explosion was caused by some engineers who were unloading bombs from a truck to the bomb dump. (Dan Winston)

neck and causing death by asphyxiation.'
92nd BG history, 27 February 1945

'I walked into the Officers' Mess and I heard this horrendous noise. I thought it was some sort of welcome for me. Then a huge lump of shrapnel landed about 20 ft away and that was my introduction to the base.'
Lt. Calvin Shahbaz, 491st BG, Metfield

'It seemed the explosion was caused by some engineers who were unloading bombs from a truck to the bomb dump. The bombs were not primed and the men were kicking them off the truck and on to the ground. While they were being unloaded in this fashion, one went off. The grass from the bomb dump to the hangar was scorched and the bottom of the hangar ripped out. Sometime later the truck's differential axle was discovered in a village about a mile from the scene of the explosion, thrown there by the blast!'
Mr Pye, Chief Foreman of Trades

'In a few minutes we were over Metfield. What a mess. For hundreds of yards out from the centre of the blast, a large blackened area of destruction lay before our eyes. Buildings and 'planes were destroyed everywhere. It seems that ordnance personnel were unloading "high explosive" bombs when one accidently detonated. This in turn set off 1,200 tons of other HE bombs and incendiaries. The blast killed six men and was heard for 40 miles. Property was damaged as much as five miles away. Five B-24s were wrecked and six others badly damaged.'
1/Lt. John W. McClane Jr., lead navigator, 44th BG, describing a flight over Metfield after the bomb dump explosion on 15 July 1944 at 19:30 hrs

*From my brother's sleep, I fell into the state,
And I hunched in its belly till my wet fur froze.
Six miles from earth, loosed from its dream of life,
I woke to black flak and the nightmare fighters.
When I died they washed me out of the turret
with a hose.*

Randall Jarrell, 'The Death of the Ball Turret Gunner'

'A shell burst just 20 ft from our right vertical stabilizer, sending a piece of shrapnel through the tail turret, killing our tail gunner, S/Sgt. W. E. Jackson.'
S/Sgt. Gene H. Gaskins, gunner, 448th BG, 9th May 1944

'When a large quantity of chaff being thrown out by a forward 'plane hit his compartment, it startled him. His bombs fell on one of our own landing strips, killing four men and wounding 14 others. In addition, he destroyed two P-47 Thunderbolts. Another bombardier, who was leading his squadron, was trying to free a faulty mechanism which in turn salvoed his bombs accidentally. When they left the bomb bay, it was a signal for 12 following 'planes to drop their bombs, which they did. This incident killed 16 of our ground troops and wounded 60 more.'

1/Lt. John W. McClane, lead navigator, 68th BS, 44th BG, bombardiers' accidental tripping of the bomb release switch during abortive carpet bombing tactical attack in support of US 1st Army, St Lo, 24 July 1944

'We reached our base and landed after five hours and 30 minutes in the air. Capt. Peritti was instructed to pull up in front of Group HQ rather than go to our usual hardstand. When I lowered myself out of the 'plane and looked up, the first thing I saw was Col. John Gibson, CO of the 44th BG. My heart sank. I could see a very serious look on his face. He stepped out of his jeep and looked straight at us. With a wide rapid motion of his right hand starting at knee level swinging up over the top of his head, he demanded in a loud voice, "YOU FOLLOW ME." He also ordered that the camera be taken out of our 'plane and the pictures be developed at once.

'Needless to say, we did follow Col. Gibson into the de-briefing room. He spread a map in front of him and pointing to me said, "WHERE WERE YOU?" In a stammering voice filled with trepidation, I began by explaining what had happened over the Channel and why we had changed course away from the lead squadron. Suddenly, I was greatly relieved because Col. Gibson said to forget about what happened on the way over the Channel. He wanted to know where we had dropped our bombs. All this time I thought we were in big trouble for having left the formation and now he did not give a hoot about that.

'I knew exactly where Warga had dropped our squadron bombs and pointed out the spot on the map, as did Warga. How it was accomplished so quickly I do not know, but Intelligence came up with the pictures taken from our 'plane. They even had pencilled lines over our designated strike area and almost every bomb was inside the lines. At this point Col. Gibson's whole personality changed back to the usual good-natured and likeable person

he was. A smile broke over his face from ear to ear. The 44th was not at fault for a grievous error; word had filtered back that bombs had fallen short of the drop zone, crossing the road coming out of St Lo, and into American lines, killing many of our men. Later I was told it was 260 men including Gen. McNair. Ours were the first bombs to drop so the target area was very visible. But the groups following us could see nothing through the dense dust and dropped their bombs into the cloud until corrected by P-51s flying to indicate the correct drop area ... I have talked to several men who were on the ground that day. Chester Rotter was a Captain with the infantry. He said that whereas his company was not able to advance one hedgerow the day before, that after this tremendous carpet bombing he led his men 5,000 metres before they found a German who could stand up and fight. All the others were either dead or near dead with blood coming out of their nose, mouth and ears. Dr Rotter said the one thing he most remembers is that all the cattle were laying on their backs with all four legs up in the air.'

1/Lt. John W. McClane, lead navigator, 68th BS, 44th BG, describing the carpet bombing tactical attack mission in support of the US 1st Army at St Lo, 25 July 1944

'The 506th Squadron was perhaps a half mile ahead of us or less. As they approached the river, very heavy and accurate flak burst in their formation. I was looking directly at it when one of their 'planes started to burn. The 'plane fell out of formation and the crew bailed out just in time. As I looked directly at it, the 'plane exploded in front of us. There was a monstrous explosion, the 'plane literally disintegrated before my eyes. This was a bright cloudless day with unlimited visibility, the sun was shining bright. The 'plane blew to bits. The motors were torn from the wings and went tumbling through the sky with their props windmilling as they fell in a large non-linear arc. The wings and the fuselage and the tail were torn to shreds. As the pieces of aluminium drifted and twisted while they fell, with each turn the sun would be reflected off their surface back into my eyes as if they were mirrors. It was like watching a thousand suns turn on and off in a rapid random fashion. But the most spectacular sight was the gas' tanks which had been torn from the wings. They did not explode their gasoline but rather it burned in huge orange flames streaming out behind the tanks as they fell in a wavy fashion towards the earth below.

'I was fascinated with the sight that I was witnessing until, all of a sudden, I realized that our squadron would be over the exact same spot in a minute or two. I know it sounds cowardly but I became obsessed with an uncontrollable fear. I got it in my mind that we would be the next 'plane to be literally blown out of the sky. As the flak began to reach us, I was paralysed until we passed beyond their range. I had never experienced such an intense emotion before or since.'

1/Lt. John W. McClane, lead navigator, 68th BS, 44th BG, describing the end of Lt. John Millikin's B-24 Passion Pit *42-95150 on the mission to Rouen, France, 13 August 1944. The crew, who were on their 30th and final mission, were captured and made PoWs; except Millikin, who escaped.*

'It was a nice clear, crisp morning on St. Patrick's Day 17 March 1945. There were no flak or fighters which was great. On the way home we flew in our own contrails to hide from any possible fighters. As we were about five minutes inside Germany, the 'plane below me came up underneath me and collided in mid-air. That 'plane broke in half and went down. We had damage to our aircraft. The Plexiglas nose was gone, two engines on the right side were out and two holes from two props were opened up on either side of the front fuselage. A man from the other 'plane was sucked up into my plane. He had no arms, no legs and no head. Just the torso. John Gann, my bombardier, was pushed to the ceiling by the chin turret and hurt his back. Some of my crew took him in the back of the radio room and laid him

Someone sang over the interphone that the flak was thick enough to land on. (Geoff Ward)

there. They covered him up with a jacket. At that altitude it was −60°F.

'The radio operator on my 'plane had tried to put his 'chute on and it opened up in his radio room. I told everyone by radio that I had control. DO NOT BAIL OUT. We had lost some altitude. We followed the same direction that the group was going and started to let down. There were two layers of clouds and after we got through the second layer, a P-47 saw my predicament and came up close and waggled his wings as he wanted me to follow him to his base near Brussels. In order not to break radio silence I instructed my engineer to shoot flares and I then landed at that field. The torso was identified as the radio operator from the other plane after examining his name tag on the back of his vest.

'That night, my crew and I got drunk and we were thankful to be alive. A couple of days later we were returned to our base at Eye and flew seven more missions and then the war was over.'

Lt. Robert H. Tenneberg, pilot of Rat Poison, *490th BG, which collided with another 490th BG B-17 after a squadron in the 385th BG cut through the clouds, causing the 490th B-17 to veer upwards.*

FLAK

'The last time I saw Paris
From 20,000 feet
The flak was poppin' round my head
And underneath my feet!'

'When the flak bursts were thickest and closest I'd sing "Home on the Range" over the interphone (probably off key!) to relieve the tension.'
Bob Maag, pilot, Skinny, *94th BG*

'Someone sang over the interphone that the flak was thick enough to land on.'
Karl W. Wendel, navigator 447th BG

'Our crew only had two missions under our belts and didn't realize what was ahead of us. The first one to Bremen, on 26 September, only involved a relatively few puffs of flak which didn't seem to be close enough to register. Little did I realize the punch behind those puffs at the time. On the second mission, however, to Mainz on 27 September, I took back my thought, "Is this all there is to it?" when a B-17 disappeared in front of us with a single direct hit burst of flak. Wow, nine men and a 'plane gone in one puff – those Germans are out to get us!

'On the Merseberg mission we soon found out that the Germans were really guarding their oil with walls of flak. The bursts were getting closer and closer. The thin aluminium skin was really taking a beating. In fact it was beginning to look like a sieve. There were huge holes in the wings where the flak pierced the self-sealing gas' tanks. Some of the engines were taking hits and beginning to falter.'
Wayne E. Cose, top turret gunner/engineer, 486th BG

'All was going quite well until just before the IP. A piece of flak shot through over my left shoulder and hit the ratchet motor of the 522 VHF equipment which changed the channels of the cockpit for the captain. The flak was about the size of the top rim of a coffee cup. Needless to say, our transmitter was now jammed.'
Herman L. Hager, pilot, 398th BG

'We neared the IP that was to last 12 to 15 minutes before "bombs away". There was no more evasive action while on this run. I remember quite well how intense the flak was because the Germans were really trying to save the oil plant.'
Herman L. Hager, pilot, 398th BG

'A flak burst hit squarely in the nose and blew practically the entire nose section to shreds, obscuring my vision and that of the co-pilot, Philip H. Stahlman. What little there was left in front of me looked like a scrap heap.'
1/Lt. Lawrence deLancey, pilot, 398th BG, describing a mission to Cologne on 15 October 1944

'We received a direct hit in our left wing. The great amount of smoke seemed to fill up the entire aircraft. We didn't seem to be able to maintain the speed nor the altitude needed to stay with the formation, so Fred Wismer left his position and tried to hang on at "Purple Heart Corner".'
Herman L. Hager, pilot, 398th BG

'Clouds had covered the target and we did not have a "Mickey" ship. We made a 360 over Hamm; still could not see the target and went for a target of opportunity which turned out to be Osnabruck. Our squadron lead navigator took us right into the Ruhr Valley on the way home and we really took a pounding. We lost two 'planes from

We received a direct hit in our left wing. (Author's Collection)

another group who had tagged onto us over the North Sea on the way in and the rest of us took plenty of holes. Gerry E. Meyer, our radio operator, was hit and received the Purple Heart. I still have a piece of flak that missed me by one foot. Everyone else on the crew had a near miss.'
Herbert Shanker, 359th BS, 303rd BG

'I broke out in a sweat and was glad to get into the flak before they could make another pass. Flak was the lesser of the two evils. It was heavy but inaccurate and we only picked up a few holes and one piece tore away the tail gunner's shoe. He received no injury.'
Joe Wroblewski, pilot, 351st BG

'Munster had the heaviest concentration of flak I had ever seen. It blotted out the sky.'
Perry Rudd, 457th BG

'There was flak before the target and plenty after. The sky was really black. I couldn't see how it was possible to get through the stuff. The oil refinery was built in a once destroyed area; the Germans must have thought we wouldn't hit the area again.'
Howard E Hernan, gunner, 303rd BG

'The flak over Sottevast was unbelievably accurate! Every 'plane received hits and damage. Bernard Palmquist, the ballgunner on Ralph W. Wright's crew, was hit and the flak went through his shoulder. He told me later that he had never seen such flak. This was the only time he could actually "smell it".'
John A. Miller, waist gunner, 100th BG

'We took off at 04:45 on 20 June for Hamburg again. We went over the target at 24,000 ft; a suicide run. The flak was the heaviest I'd ever seen. The navigator and co-pilot were hit with flying glass in the eye and leg respectively. Our plane had 40 to 50 holes in it. We lost some 'planes as we went over the target. We each dropped our 18 250-lb GP bombs and flames leapt three to four thousand feet. We could still see the smoke even after we were over the North Sea.'
Howard Herman, 92nd BG

'Over Berlin, we flew through 20 miles of flak batteries, as many as 520 guns. This was a horrible experience and something to be dreaded. The guns fired in batteries of four, a burst would go off in front of us, we instantly flew through black smoke. A second burst would be a little closer, a

Munster had the heaviest concentration of flak I had ever seen. It blotted out the sky. (Cliff Hatcher [94th BG, Munster, 11 November 1943])

third would be almost on our nose. I was sure the next would blow us to Kingdom Come but by the grace of God would go off at our tail. I was almost frozen with fear by the time the third exploded.'
John McClane Jr., navigator, 44th BG

'When we neared the IP, I turned the turret facing forward and could see the black bursts of flak directly in front of us at our level. We flew to that place in the sky where the black was heaviest and I heard the bombardier shout, "Bombs away!" The 'plane rose in the air and settled back.'
William C. Stewart, ball turret gunner, 92nd BG

'Nearing the target, I saw this "boiling mass" of flak. We started to make a 360 turn and I thought, "Thank God we don't have to fly through it." However, I was soon to discover that another group had cut us off and we were only waiting our turn. God it was awful. I could see 'planes falling from all over the sky. When the first flak burst was at our altitude I knew we had just "bought the farm".

I heard the bombardier shout, 'Bombs away!' The 'plane rose in the air and settled back. (Ian McLachlan)

'It was a hell of a ride through that stuff. Our group just simply dissolved.'
S/Sgt. Adolph J. Smetana, tail gunner, 351st BG

'De-briefing was held at the same time we were eating our evening meal. We were given one shot of whiskey before eating and I felt a little light-headed afterwards. The debriefing officer asked his questions and it was then that I learned, when the other crewmembers answered, that the flak was "meagre". I thought it was worse than that but this was only my first mission. I was to learn later on what "intense" flak really was.'
William C. Stewart, ball turret gunner, 92nd BG

'In spite of the flight helmet with earphones and the flak helmet and the roar of the motors, I could hear the flak hitting the 'plane. It sounded like gravel on a tin roof when hitting my navigation compartment, which was covered by the metal skin of the fuselage . . .

'One of my duties was to inform the crew when it was time to put the flak vest and helmet on and

when it was safe to remove it. The helmet was a modified GI steel helmet and the vest was a series of over-lapping metal plates sewed into a cloth jacket which covered our torso front and back. The helmet covered down over our ears and the back of our neck. There is no doubt as to the added protection all this gave our bodies, but equally as important was the psychological value of doing what you could to "hide" from danger.'
Lt. John H. McClane Jr, navigator, 44th BG

'The flight over Denmark was beautiful and uneventful. Such a peaceful looking land to be occupied by the hated Nazis. We broke the coast and when I felt safe, I told everyone that they could remove their flak vests and helmets. We were out over the water and I had no reason to believe that any more danger existed from anti-aircraft fire. I was wrong. About the time we pulled the straps that let these heavy protecting vests fall to the floor, wham bang, four very accurate flak bursts went off close to us. It frightened the holy heck out of us. I looked down to the water to see where the AA was coming from and low and behold, the scoundrels had stationed a barge off the coast fitted with an AA battery. By the time we got our vests back on, it was too late. This taught me a lesson I never forgot,

from then on I looked to be sure all was safe before announcing time to drop our vests.'
Lt. John H. McClane Jr., navigator, 44th BG

'The Germans had their own psychological tricks also. On one mission over northern France, the flak exploded with red smoke instead of the normal black. It did not make the flak more deadly but sure as heck scared the fire out of us not knowing what it was.'
Lt. John H. McClane Jr., navigator, 44th BG

'There was one piece of the anatomy much beloved by the flight crews. This was shown by the extreme lengths they went to protect it − the groin. All who had sitting jobs in the aircraft sat on a piece of armour, as most shrapnel travelled upward. All sorts of ingenious methods were devised to protect the "family jewels". The fact that this fragile piece of equipment would avail them little if their head was blown off seemed not to matter; they surrounded it with armour plate. The married men were particularly solicitous in this

behalf, although I am afraid we all overdid this piece of business. I think that all these elaborate safeguards were more symbolic than protective. It was just one of the many things we did to foster the myth of our continuity.'
Ben Smith, radio operator, 303rd BG

'We went through the southern part of the Ruhr Valley and it was an awful experience. The "Happy Valley Boys" can really throw up a heavy barrage of flak. It was very heavy today and Jack Kings had a close call. Flak entered just below his gun position but armour plate deflected it. After "bombs away" the pilots used evasive action and really threw the plane around the sky. It was the heaviest flak I have yet to see. Thank God there was no fighter opposition. We sweated this one out. Many 'planes went down and we settled for quite a few flak holes. Returned to base with a few flak holes, one of which necessitated a wing tip change.'
Larry Goldstein, radio operator, 388th BG

In spite of the flight helmet with ear phones and the flak helmet and the roar of the motors, I could hear the flak hitting the plane. (Lt. Col. Laurence Gilbert, 392nd BG Operations Officer, 4 November 1943)

'I remember the first combat mission I flew, which was on 29 June 1944. Capt. Steinbacher came down to breakfast with us to get some fresh eggs. During the meal, some of us rookies expressed some concern about flak. He said: "Don't let it scare you, because if you can see those black powder puffs you will know that they have missed. If they have yellow centres, they are getting pretty close but don't worry, you'll never see the ones that hit you."'
George M. Collar, 445th BG

'As we made landfall over Schoewen Island on the Dutch coast, up came the flak, and they all had yellow centres.'
George M. Collar, 445th BG

'A replacement for Lt. Murphy was a Lt. Flak and

Piccadilly Lilly No. 2. Since he had red hair he was known as "Pinky" Flak. He was a lousy pilot who burned up his engines and one time returned with only one engine operating. On another occasion he failed to pick the 'plane off the ground and ran *Piccadilly Lilly* right off the end of the runway and across the ditch into the mud, bombs and all. That was the end of *Piccadilly Lilly No. 2* but "Pinky" Flak did live to complete his tour and be sent back to the States, much to the relief of the engineering department.'
Bill Carleton, 100th BG

'The first five missions were average but our sixth, on 30 November 1944, was the roughest one we flew. It was to Meresburg, where we were to hit an oil refinery. They had about 1,000 flak guns there. We saw six B-17s blown up and go down in flames. The 8th Air Force lost 54 ships from flak alone. The navigator on the crew whose wing we were flying off was killed. How we were lucky enough to get through is hard to see. We had about 50 holes in our ship when we landed, but none were serious. When we were lucky enough to get by that time we thought we would be lucky enough to finish our required 35 missions.'
William B. Sterrett, bombardier, 100th BG

'At some point in time, I again came back to reality as I remember our approach to the City of Berlin. The flak was intense. The Nazi defenders had 520 anti-aircraft guns trained in a 20-mile arc on us. The sky was one huge black cloud of exploding metal. The guns fired in batteries of four, or so it seemed to me. When it was bursting at some altitude other than our own, we had little to fear, but as soon as they zeroed in, trouble was at hand. I never did get over the fright of seeing a flak burst right in front of us, then a second a little closer and a third even closer yet. With each burst, the plane would almost instantly fly through the black cloud. One could easily sense the cordite smell. At this point, you knew the next burst would be inside your plane . . .'
Lt. John W. McClane Jr., navigator, 44th BG

'The time was late 1944. I was co-pilot on a lead crew under Capt. Clark McClain. At this time we had flown about half our missions and were beginning to "wise-up" about the statistics of casualties and what caused them. Flak was our major problem – much more so than fighters – so we learned all we could from our armaments officers about the specific techniques the Germans used in firing their anti-aircraft. There were three distinct patterns. One (used often on clear days) was the four-gun battery fired one at a time, tracking a particular 'plane, usually the leader, and correcting between shots. Another was the "blanket" method of filling an air space with bursts predicted to be where the 'planes would be. But the third was a precisely calculated and deadly method where all the AA guns would fire simultaneously at a small target, such as a squadron, taking their aim from the central gun battery. This was the kind of barrage we learned early to identify and to fear. We also learned that the time required between bursts of this kind was 20 seconds.

'One night a bunch of pilots were sitting at the Officers' Club at the 93rd station at Hardwick, milling over the odds of bombers on a straight and level bomb run versus those fantastic German gunners. That night four things came to me in a flash. One was that we were bombing the Ruhr Valley, which on the Flak-Map was one big blob of red – no way to avoid the guns. Another was that we, at that time, began to break up into squadrons, rather than groups, to drop our bombs. Still another was that we were carefully instructed to reach our IP and allow a full 30 seconds between squadrons in order to avoid prop wash and also to

maintain a reasonably uniform bombing altitude (for what that was worth). But most important was the simple fact that the Germans could fire every 20 seconds, thus taking careful aim on every single squadron that passed.

'We reasoned, with simple logic, that if we closed up our formations (in line, one squadron after another) to something less than 20 second intervals, and compensated for potential prop wash by flying a few feet higher or lower than the preceeding squadron, we could statistically cut in half the potential casualties, for the simple reason that each anti-aircraft battery would have only one shot for each two squadrons.

'There were no senior officers present that night at our "bull session" but I decided we would initiate this procedure. On the next day's mission we led the 2nd Division on a trip down the Ruhr Valley, and as lead crew pilot, I instructed all the squadron commanders of our "new procedure" while in the air: "Close up to 15 second intervals."

'Happily, though we encountered fantastic flak,

Winnie *did some skating. I thought she would never stop but finally she hit a ditch and stopped. Then it was very quiet. I thought for a moment I was dead. (Dick Dugger [left])*

and had heavy damage, our losses were only about half what they had been on previous missions in that part of Germany.'
Lloyd T. Smith, lead pilot, 93rd BG

'We were returning from a mission to Hannover. The sky was clear, the clouds were solid below us. There were bursts of spent flak in the area and then I saw eight bursts at our altitude and some distance behind us. I called ''Flak'' over the intercom and the crew started to throw out chaff. The next eight bursts were half the distance from the last bursts. I'm sure all of us were saying a prayer for help as I sat there in the tail turret feeling completely helpless. I knew the next eight burst would be among us and that some of us were not going to make it. But at the same time the bursts were due they did not come. As we flew along I looked down and could see the sun sparkling of the chaff as it fell to earth. It was more than 1,000 ft below and there, right in the middle of it were eight black puffs and then eight more. The hand of the almighty had made the gunners on the ground change the settings on their fuses, and not a

MISSION COMPLETED! 'FLAK' HEAVY!
(Rackheath Memories)

moment too soon.'
Henry A. DeKeyser, 576th BS, 392nd BG

'The flak was the heaviest I ever saw. I kept thinking, we will never make it. We constantly saw the instant red flash of the flak explosion and heard the shrapnel hitting the airplane. We were hit by flak many times and several times lost an engine. This happened to everyone flying and was taken as part of the mission.'
Lloyd W. Hughes, gunner, 453rd BG, Berlin, June 1944

'Flak destroyed 3,501 American planes in 1944. This was 600 more than met their doom by fighter plane opposition.'
1/Lt. John W. McClane Jr., navigator, 44th BG

'Suddenly, all hell broke loose as the flak guns opened up. Just before the bombardier pushed the button our ship was hit and it plummeted from 23,000 ft to almost ground level! . . . I was in my turret, spinning around above the radio operator and the force was keeping me pinned in. We plunged downward.

'It was a mess but the pilot finally got the ship under control, although we were at tree-top level

and flying round the target area with other squadrons dropping their bombs all about us. . . . *Windy Winnie* flew low over a German airfield – so low that we nearly hit a flak tower. German pilots were getting in their fighters to come up after us.

'We flew on over towns, where we were hit many times, and also over countryside. *Winnie* had so many large holes in her, it was like flying outdoors. The back end was a mess; oil and gasoline was everywhere but she was still flying. The pilot was giving it red line power on all four engines when number four engine was hit and we continued on three engines. A Liberator does not fly well with three engines at tree-top level, but we kept in the air by throwing out everything we could – radio equipment, supplies, and even the guns.

'We did not know if we were in Germany or whatever, but we knew we were on a westerly heading. The ground was still white and we could not see anything apart from some large power lines in front. The pilot pulled back on the stick and barely missed them and the bomber began to fall slowly to the ground. She hit it and started to bounce. Small trees were cut down and with her wheels up *Winnie* did some skating. I thought she would never stop but finally she hit a ditch and stopped. Then it was very quiet. I thought for a moment I was dead.'

S/Sgt. Richmond 'Dick' H. Dugger, top turret gunner, 448th BG, mission to Dortmund, Sunday 28 January 1945

'Finally, we got back into the flak which was really close. We could hear the shells as they burst, which is too close for comfort. On our mission to Frankfurt I told the boys that I could hear the pieces of shrapnel beating on the side of the ship and they had all said I was getting "flak happy". I knew they would agree with me this time.'

William B. Sterret, bombardier, 100th BG

FLAK-HAPPY

'Down in Ruhr Valley
Flying so low
Some chairborne bahstaad
Said I must go
Flak loves big bombers
Fighters do too!
P-51 Boys how I love you'

'Down in Ruhr Valley' to the tune of 'Birmingham Jail'

'Numerous men were known to be "flak happy". There was definite evidence of fatigue (irritability, sleeplessness, battle dreams) to some degree in 60 to 65 per cent of combat crews after 35 missions.' *Extract from 9th BC report*

'Everyone who flew these missions had fear. It made sleep hard to come by, when your name was up. For some it could effect a change in personality. Nervousness, drinking, overindulgences of all sorts showed it. At first many were insecure and were put on the defensive – you became overly self-assured, or diffident, very loud or mouse quiet. You either spoke too often of combat, or avoided the subject. You perhaps drank a bit more. You thought you wouldn't ever be afraid. During the first five missions you changed. Perhaps the first few were an unreality like a movie that you saw and weren't in. You didn't know enough to be scared. Somewhere by the fifth or tenth mission you had experienced real fear and knew you could deal with it. You knew that skill and training counted . . . Some in these early missions, or later, had more than the usual harrowing experiences and their problems were greater. Yet almost all, by their tenth mission, became effective fighters, quiet and cool on the ground and in the air, took responsibility and acquired esprit de corps. Despite the anxiety of sweating out the tour they could tolerate the tension and stress with tranquillity. All attention was given to the job, drinking was more a thing for passes when it could act as a catharsis to the dirty real job one had. But somewhere, from the 12th to the 16th mission, operational fatigue came to the soundest individual as a result of the exhausting effects of the tension, the frequent briefings, flying at altitude, loss of sleep, and the practice and real missions. The doctors said this

was 50 per cent fatigue and 50 per cent the emotional strain. There was no shame for this result of fear and stress. You were just "flak-happy" and this phrase explained how you felt and much of what you did.'
Allan Healy, 467th BG

'I saw many men who absolutely refused to fly another mission after seeing their buddies go down on a raid or be victims of mid-air collisions.'
Larry Goldstein, radio operator, 388th BG

'When new B-26 groups arrived, 9th Bomber Command discovered that they were short of 150 navigators which meant that they had to fly more missions without relief. Replacements at that time were being based on a total of 57 crews per group but the groups themselves were operating on a basis of 87 crews per group. Official policy was to release a man from the air war after 50 missions. In an attempt to ease crew shortages the 50 mission limit was cancelled and the consequent event was a drop in morale . . . '
Extract from 9th BC report

'Maximum leaves for light and medium bomber crews "under normal conditions" were set at one week between the 25th and 30th mission and two weeks between the 40th and 50th mission. The new policy did not apply to aircrewmen sent to rest homes due to operational fatigue . . . '
Extract from 9th BC report

'As it turned out, St Nazaire was Spook Bender's last mission. He'd lost a lot of weight and was usually shaking like a leaf. Who could blame him? All he could talk about was "all them Focke Wulfs" and "all that flak". It was about this time that Bill Lindley and Spook went to see a movie in the nearest big town, Ipswich. They sat in the first row of the balcony but the projectionist made a big mistake when he showed the latest newsreel before the movie, with nothing but German fighters attacking B-17s of the Eighth Air Force. Spook went slightly berserk. He crouched down behind the rail of the balcony and kept screaming for his gunners to "Shoot! Shoot! Shoot!"

'Bill managed to calm him, got him outside, and then they took a taxi back to Horham . . . Bob stayed in hospital for a rest and they finally sent him home to the United States. He suffered a massive heart attack a few years later and died. He was only 25 years old.'
Don Merton, co-pilot, 336th BS, 95th BG

Spook went slightly berserk. He crouched down behind the rail of the balcony and kept screaming for his gunners to 'Shoot! Shoot! Shoot!' (Ian Hawkins)

'The crew that we resided with were on their 28th or 29th mission and they were all crazy. One in particular would wake up in the middle of the night and shoot his .45 off at mice. A .45 reverberates and makes quite a bit of noise and disturbs your sleep!'
John A. Holden, navigator, 731st BS, 452nd BG

'We had a gunner who started in a B-17 as engineer and who would call off enemy fighters when they turned out to be spots before his eyes. He finally was grounded and went to the ground

crew. Bill Kuban, who was on our crew had a habit of knocking his head against a post in the barracks the night before missions. He claimed it cleared his head and relieved the tension. He was wounded on the Oslo mission. The last time I saw him he was stretched out bleeding by the ball turret and I thought, here was a gonner.'
Forrest S. Clark, gunner, 44th BG

'The squadron flight surgeon drank with us and palled around with us but kept a very watchful eye on us. He knew what shape we were in, how many combat missions we had flown and what the crew situation was. He was the one who dispensed the pills. In February – March 1944, I was on pills to put me to sleep and on the morning of a mission I was on pills to wake me up and get me going. Sleeping at night became so bad that we started taking pills from our escape kits.'
Bill Rose, pilot, 92nd BG

'We had four officer crews in one nissen hut. The night before a mission I would go over to the barracks and write letters and get some early sleep because you never knew when you would be alerted to fly a mission the next day. One night one of the officer crews packed all their belongings. It made me wonder what insight they must have had when they knew they would not survive the next mission. Sure enough, the next day they went down.'
Bill Rose, pilot, 92nd BG

'We had another crew who went on a bombing mission to southern Germany. After bombing the target we turned around and came home, but this crew took off for Switzerland. When we got back I checked their clothes in the hut. Everything was there except for their Class A uniforms which they had worn on the raid to prove their identity. They had just given up fighting.'
Bill Rose, pilot, 92nd BG

'After losing 12 hours yesterday in our longest raid thus far, and one which not only was long, but also pretty rough, we were all pretty tired and worn out at 03:00 this morning when we were called for another mission. This last day of the week which was to go down in history as the biggest week of aerial combat of the war, found us rather dulled at the prospects of another long mission … We had arrived at that mental state where one more extra long, extra tough raid, meant almost nothing to us. It was just another raid. As for myself, at least, I'd grown calloused. The tougher the raid now, the better I liked it.'
Lowell Watts, pilot, 388th BG, Big Week, February 1944

'One of the boys from the Bronx came back and caused quite a disturbance. He got drunk every chance he could, he knew he would get killed the next time out; but this particular night he did not come straight in. He went out to the ship in a stolen jeep, rounded up the Very pistols, burned up several wheatfields during his riot and finally ended up in our barracks. He opened one door and started firing Very pistol shots into the barracks, setting fire to clothing and bedding. The door on the other end of the barracks had a traffic jam. Because of the firing they got down on their hands and knees and crawled into the ice and snow. I went next door and called the MP. He was interested in the information but said there was no way he could make his appearance until things quieted down.

'They still did not send the boy home. They just confined him to barracks and counselling.'
Emmett D. Seale, 446th BG

'Some of the boys were developing the equivalent of "shell shock", in spite of all our doctor's efforts. The nervous strain of continuous raids had been more than some of them could take. It raised the very rough command problem as to how long these lads would still be fit to fly a combat mission, especially the pilots whose nine-man crews were trusting him with their lives. I finally had to go to Col. Castle about one pilot who was rapidly coming "unstuck" as the British say, and they sent him to the "Rest Home" in southern England. He didn't like it and I felt real sorry for him, but Col. Castle agreed that it was no longer safe to send him on combat raids.'
Capt. Franklin 'Pappy' Colby, Squadron Commander, 94th BG

'I was sent for a "flak furlough" at Coombe House shortly after the Brunswick mission of 11 January 1944, when we lost eight B-17s. We were in such bad shape our flight surgeon, "Doc" Miller, went along with us! He too was getting "flak happy" riding along with his boys.'
Cliff Hatcher, 94th BG pilot

FLAK LEAVE

His hair was long, his hands were thin
His back was bent like an old pin
His eyes were two empty rims of black
And he faintly mumbled, 'Shack, Shack, Shack!'

'The Last of the Bombardiers'

'A "flak shack", that delightful, full-fed, pleasant English country estate, helped to cure both operational and flying fatigue.'
Allan Healy 467th BG

'We reached 17 without anybody suggesting a rest home to us.'
Larry Goldstein, radio operator, 388th BG

We got to go to a rest home run by the Red Cross, which was much needed.

'After the Schweinfurt raid we got to go to a rest home run by the Red Cross which was much needed. The officers went to Stanbridge Earls while we went to Moulsford Manor. We were treated royally and got to wear civilian clothes. There were butlers, waiters and maids to take care of us.'
Howard E. Hernan, gunner, 303rd BG

'The rest home on the Thames River, outside of London, was a wonderful invention. When the bosses decided that a crew was sufficiently combat weary ("flak happy"), they allowed the crew a few days' rest and recreation at one of the rest homes. We didn't think we were really that bad off, but finally agreed to take off a few days from combat to join the other "flak happy" troops. We were really pleased to find that our rest home was a renovated mansion on a large estate. There were two to four men assigned to comfortable bedrooms. There was a nice dining room and lots of recreation facilities. The American Red Cross and their British counterparts managed and staffed the rest home. We were not allowed to wear uniforms. In

fact, we were issued an old pair of blue jeans, a shirt, and a pair of tennis shoes, and that is all we had to wear while we were there. Recreation facilities included tennis, golf, horseback riding, punting on the Thames, British croquet, and many kinds of club games (chequers, dominoes, cards, etc). We were particularly delighted with one special treat – breakfast in bed most any time we wanted it from about 6:00 a.m. to 9:00 a.m. This

We were issued an old pair of blue jeans, a shirt, and a pair of tennis shoes, and that is all we had to wear while we were there. Recreation facilities included tennis, golf, horseback riding, punting-on-the-Thames, British croquet, and many kinds of club games. (Bill Cameron Collection)

was served by one of the waitresses, who would knock on the door at the time we requested the night before. In establishing this time, however, it did take us a while to get accustomed to the British use of the English language when the young lady at the desk would ask:

"What time would you like to be knocked up in the morning?"'
Capt. Alvin D. Skaggs, pilot, 448th BG, May 1944

'From 23 to 30 June I spent a quiet week at Aylesfield House, Alton (the "Flak House" to the trade), where we slept late and let ourselves be pampered by butlers and the Red Cross ladies.'
Abe Dolim, 94th BG

'On the staff were the most beautiful American and English Red Cross girls I had ever seen. Perhaps they looked more beautiful because we had just come off combat flying duty. We had flown quite a number of missions. Constance was the typical English beauty, complete with the alluring accent of the British and the complexion to fit. She was the objective for a date with all the men stationed at this English manor house on a large country estate surrounded by acres of green lawns, gardens and woodlands. There were many walks about the estate that lent themselves to romantic interludes with the girls. As was common among war-weary airmen of the time, there was always one or two who boasted how they could make out with any of the girls. I became frustrated by their claims and decided it was time to do something about them.

'Constance, or Connie, was a popular companion on these walks and it was not uncommon among the men to bid for the privilege of accompanying her. Since she could accompany all the men, lots were drawn to see who would get to walk with her the following day. I drew one of the lots but as luck would have it, that day turned out to be a typical English soaker with rain and mist most of the day at intervals. Nevertheless, we did take the walk and using umbrellas we managed to walk a considerable distance in the woodland, out of sight of the estate. Half way around I got the courage to try to kiss Connie, but this was against the rules and she let me know it. Not to be outdone, we decided that I would teach the other airmen a lesson and so it was agreed that we would stay out longer than the usual time and make it appear we had done some prolonged and heavy romancing in the shelter of the woods. It was a cruel illusion but one that delighted me at the time. How cold and damp we got sitting in a

On the staff were the most beautiful American and English Red Cross girls I had ever seen. Perhaps they looked more beautiful because we had just come off combat flying duty. We had flown quite a number of missions ...

greenhouse and under a shelter to make the time pass. There was nothing whatever between us, not even an embrace. We were examples of puritan discretion. However, to make the others more jealous, Connie agreed to smear some of her lipstick (a rare enough item in wartime Britain) on my cheek to make it appear we had experienced some hot and heavy romancing). I shall never forget the looks on the others' faces when we emerged from the woodland what seemed hours later. The jealousy was so thick it was palatable.'
Forrest S. Clark, gunner, 44th BG

'I remember the flak house on the Broads. I went there for a rest and went pubbing by boat and learned to play hearts with shillings.'
Mary Carroll Leeds, American Red Cross girl, Attlebridge, June 1944 to May 1945

'The day after Christmas 1944, my crew was sent to Knight Hays Court near Tiverton in the Lands End area. The manor house had 99 rooms, well kept by its owner, vaulted ceilings, fire places, dining room, library, game room, and special rooms like one might expect a knight to have. Several thousand acres belonged to Knight Hays which were worked by its tenants and supervised by gardeners, game wardens and others. Wearing civilian clothes given to us by the Red Cross, who operated the place, we romped in non-military fashion for 10 days. A herd of cattle grazed near by so the crew challenged me to ride rodeo style. They were very docile and soon all were riding. The Texas image faded. Playing much bridge, eating well, drinking well, playing golf in civvies, the war was forgotten for a few days.'
Col. Robert H. Tays, pilot, 392nd BG

'The combat crew had just returned from the "Flakhouse" and the pilot has decided they must do what is in fashion and "buzz" the house with their B-17. The navigator declines, saying, "No thanks, combat is enough risk for me." The pilot is angry at this rebuff and replies, "That is an order."

'The navigator says, "OK, get the ops officer to tell me I've got to go."

'The pilot is really sore now and says, "I'll kick your ass off the crew."

'Then the navigator flares up and says, "Listen, if you think I fly with you because I'm in love with you, you're crazier than hell – I fly with you because I think you're a damned good pilot – if you want another navigator, that's alright with me."

'They fly only one more mission together – their last one for the combat tour.'
A Case of Nerves, July 1944, 332nd area: Abe Dolim, navigator, 94th BG

R & R

We see them in the train and bus,
There isn't any room for us,
We walk and let them have our seats,
Then get run over by their jeeps.

The GIs, by a WAAF at Shipdham

'Soon after dark, while some of us were sightseeing or pub-crawling, Al became acquainted with an Irish lass and the only place in which to be alone with her was one of those small, shallow openings between the brick row houses. It did not disturb Al that his feet protruded a few inches onto the sidewalk. An innocent bicyclist, flying blind in the blackout, ran over Al's legs, inflicting painful, but superficial wounds. Al's demands for a Purple Heart were, in the interest of propriety, declined.'
Hazards of R & R (Rest & Recreation) in Belfast

'Much of America was imported for our comfort, though we could not have an American drug store or see women dressed as American women are. We had a PX, of sorts, a place where you went for your weekly rations: five packs of cigarettes (once down to four), four candy bars, some gum or peppermints, an occasional bonus of fruit juice, cookies, soap, razor blades, and other oddments that meant so much in personal living. It was little and meagre compared to American Army posts.'
Allan Healy, 467th BG

'The weather was severe and the enlisted men had

They roamed the local villages, looking for rural pubs, which they enjoyed very much ...

no recreational centre. The quartermaster had turned the gym into a warehouse. The engineers had filled the squash court with salt for de-icing the runways. The Post Exchange merchandise was extremely limited and of poor quality and the quartermaster said he could not stock regulation quantities due to the rat problem.'
Maj. Newton L. Mclaughlin, Special Services Officer, 448th BG

'Cambridge was not too far away and for some there was great attraction in its University atmo-

Bicycling was a major pastime. English cycles were issued to many of the ground men. The air crews felt free to borrow ...

sphere, the Cam and the "Backs", King's College Chapel, the Bull Hotel taken over for GIs, bookstores and antique shops. Oxford was farther away but it, too, was visited. A few even took the special week's course there that gave them some insight into English history and places, took them to Stratford, gave them teas with interesting English people.'
Allan Healy, 467th BG

'We passed through Reading and I thought of Oscar Wilde and Reading Gaol. As we neared Oxford, I could see the spires of the colleges and the ornate facades of the town buildings and green squares. When we got off the train at Oxford, a group of English girls, seeing our American uniforms, came running over. They asked if we wanted to go to a dance that night. Sgt. Abe Sofferman, whose place I was to take on the crew after his death, said he didn't want to go because he was in Oxford to learn something about history. He was a bookish fellow in that way. We dwelled for a day or two amid the gothic splendours of Oxford, visiting the rooms and dorms, the pubs and the riverbank. For a brief period we were in that citadel of learning away from the dreariness and danger of our bases. Oxford and Cambridge were relatively untouched by war in the physical

sense. They were touched in another way as many of the students were in the allied forces.
'Passing the plains and fenlands I saw Cambridge and Ely cathedrals above the flatness. I could see them from the train window en route to Norwich and back to base. Frequently, I would see these spires partly obscured by mist and a curtain of rain and fog, but always when it cleared, they stood out firm and inspiring.'
Forrest S. Clark, gunner, 44th BG

'How they roamed the local villages, looking for the rural pubs, which they very much enjoyed. They bought anything that looked like a bicycle and learnt to ride. I remember them coming from the pub riding single file, wobbling all over the road, and shouting at each other, so it was quite easy to know they were coming.'
J. Gogle, Shipdham

'Bicycling was a major pastime. English 'cycles were issued to many of the ground men. The air crews felt free to borrow. "Borrowing" became so bad that on one occasion all 'cycles were called in by the MPs and their numbers checked. Many were then returned to their original owners.'
Allan Healy, 467th BG

'The British Government, under the Reverse Lease Lend programme, sent three goods-wagons of bicycles to 3rd SAD for assignment to officers and airmen for their personal use. Since a bicycle was

English 'cycles were issued to many of the ground men. The air crews felt free to borrow. 'Borrowing' became so bad that on one occasion all 'cycles were called in by the MPs and their numbers checked. (the late Allan Healy)

considered to be a vehicle and vehicles were Ordnance property, Base Ordnance inherited the job of caring for the bikes. We assigned them to personnel at 3rd SAD, kept spare parts, and performed the maintenance on every bike. Most of the bikes were Raleigh and another make, but there were a few Royal Enfield models. The Royal Enfields were far superior in quality than the others and it was a status symbol to "drive" a Royal Enfield. Since I was ranking non-commissioned officer in Base Ordnance, naturally I had the best Enfield on the base!

'The first three 3rd SAD men lost were killed while riding bicycles. One crashed head-on into a GI truck; one lost control of a bike and was killed when his head struck the concrete runway; the third was hit by a truck at night by Griston church. And for every death, there were 5,000 injuries! What few bicycles left in serviceable condition when we left Griston were loaded up and given to an orphanage in Norwich, maybe some to Ipswich.'
Wiley S. Noble, 3rd SAD, Watton-Griston

'Many had bicycles, those fine, low-geared, light English bikes whose handlebar brakes caused many a spill, arse over teakettle.'
Allan Healy, 467th BG

'The CO and the other three colonels had cars provided. My boy friend was Col. Shower's driver, Cpl. Raymond West from Roswell, New Mexico, and after he had driven the CO to various local places in the evenings, his time would be free until he had to return for him. Little did the colonel know I rode in his car almost as much as he did. Any officers below the rank of colonel had to use bicycles. Dozens of officers could be seen in the evenings making their way to Horning Ferry Inn and some even cycled as far as Surlingham Ferry.'
Phyllis Smales, Rackheath teenager, American Red Cross Club, 467th BG, 1944

'At the first opportunity we ventured into Thrapston to buy some bicycles. I purchased a little sports model with 24 in. wheels for £5 and used it for cycling around the base, into Thrapston and for trips to buy fresh eggs. T/Sgt. John A. Dougherty, the engineer in Pense's crew who shared our hut, purchased a 26 in. wheel bike. His had more speed but mine had more power so we hooked them together. It was the most contrary thing to ride but we made many trips on it. When he was shot down I dismantled the tandem. I vowed there and then that whatever crew replaced

Pense's I was not going to make friends. I would be sociable and as pleasant as I could, but it was too hard when you lost them. Even to this day I cannot remember who moved into the hut or even what they looked like.'

Howard E. Hernan, gunner, 303rd BG

Above: *Any officers below the rank of colonel had to use bicycles. (the late Allan Healy)*

Below: *Thanksgiving Day, November 24 1944, we prepared the traditional food for the celebration – turkey with all the trimmings, and pumpkin pie. (Jake Krause)*

'Each evening when the bar closed, I would walk through the Mess kitchen. I was looking for leftovers to take to the hut. I usually found bread, cheese, cake, etc. Thanksgiving had been a snowy day with lots of good food and drink. Leaving the bar and wandering through the kitchen, the Mess Sergeant had a whole turkey left over. He insisted I take it to the boys at the hut. He wrapped it up in a pan, I got on my drunken bicycle and headed for the hut. Bicycles operate poorly on packed snow. The first turn I came to my bicycle went one way, my turkey another, and I was totally disorientated. I crawled to the hut and nobody believed my story. We found it next day beside the road in the snow.

'Those of us who drank excessively slept the night before a mission; the others did so intermittently. Ten minutes on pure oxygen the next morning, you were clear as a bell and ready to meet the day's challenges.'
Col. Robert H. Tays, pilot, 392nd BG

'On this bike trip we wandered into a village where we went to a tea shop and had tea and biscuits. We were given some rather stern looks by the patrons – older ladies – and it took us a while to figure out why. And then it dawned on us that as Yanks we were getting better food than English civilians and they must have resented our consuming their biscuits.'
Robert L. Miller, pilot, Son Of A Blitz, 863rd BS, 493rd BG

'On Thanksgiving Day, November 24 1944, we prepared the traditional food for the celebration – turkey with all the trimmings, and pumpkin pie. Most of the British staff had never tasted the latter, but it was delicious; the flesh was scooped out from the pumpkins, sweetened and cooked to a pulp, cinnamon and raisins added and baked in a crusty pie. All the cake mixing was done by hand and as I was a only 4ft 11 in tall, I had to stand on duck boards to reach down into the galvanized baths in which we mixed the cakes.'
Phyllis Smales, American Red Cross Club, Rackheath

'Our first introduction to the Yank was his arrival at the pub in the evenings. Plenty of money to burn and looking for a good time. In summer they used to spend their rest periods in properties along the riverbanks. We young lads and lassies were welcome to visit them and make use of the dinghies paddling up and down the river. Also, there were special treats, such as sweets, cigarettes and tinned fruit.'
Neville Firman

'A popular British pastime in Norfolk was to go sailing in small sailboats along the canals and small streams. This pastime prompted us to develop another sport of trying to blow over or capsize these boats while on training flights. On one

'A favourite stunt was to drop .45 calibre ammo' in the little pot-bellied stove.'

HOME, SWEET HOME! IN THE E.T.O.

occasion we made a couple of passes but couldn't capsize one, so we made another pass very low and directly at it. This must have been too much for the sailors because they dove in the water as we pulled up to go over the top of the mast.'
Lt. Alvin D. Skaggs, pilot, 448th BG

'One evening, during the summer of 1944, my father, brother and I, took two horse-drawn carts of hay to the Red Cross Club where I worked, and about two dozen Yanks and their girlfriends loaded themselves onto the carts and we went for a hay ride. We took them to Salhouse Broad where they all disappeared, along with bottles of Coca-Cola. We just sat around and waited to round them up at about 10 p.m. We managed to get them back to base at about 11p.m.'
Phyllis Smales, Rackheath teenager, American Red Cross Club, 467th BG, 1944

'In Belfast, we had our first experience at a British dance hall. The dance floor was very large with several hundreds of couples dancing. Whereas Americans dance in a small area of the floor, maybe getting around the whole floor once to a dance number, the British move fast, almost run, with the whole floor of couples moving like a wheel. Also, they did not like to talk much or carry out a conversation like American couples do. However, they will all burst out in song if a catchy tune gets their attention. This was our first experience of a mixed group singing a song that to us seemed a little off colour for mixed company. The title was, "Roll Me Over in The Clover".'
1/Lt. John W. McClane Jr., navigator, 44th BG

'We fixed up a small open bay at the end of our barracks, which was building 200, so we called it the '200 Club'. It was a place for parties and sitting around "shooting the bull" when we didn't have anything else to do. A favourite stunt was to drop .45 calibre ammo' in the little potbellied stove, secretly of course. That used to stir things up. I once let go a smoke bomb ... almost ruined our clothes and bedding with the stench. On one occasion I was definitely the "square" of the group although part of it. It was decided to strip me of my clothes. The girls thought it was very funny but I got as mad as hell (this about 3 a.m.) and almost had a fist fight with Bob Brown, one of my best friends. He would have killed me. I was the type who got into trouble trying to do the right thing ... like getting transportation for the girls at 4 a.m., when all my buddies went to bed and left them there.

'On one occasion I woke old George and "Gentleman" Jim at 5 a.m. for the practice mission ... not realizing they had a couple of girls in the sack with them ... and was met by a barrage of .45 gunshots over my head in the dark ... and I hit the floor of the hallway and crawled out! They were quite a bunch and when they were gone there was no-one who ever quite took their places.'
Lt.(later Col.) William Cameron, pilot, 44th BG

'In the early days of powdered eggs and brussel sprouts, we carried our Mess gear to the club. Beer was served from a barrel on a rickety table, using our Mess kit cups. At the end we had a fine club, linens, silver and all the rest, which we paid for, but it was never so welcome. We even built our own movie theatre, using materials bought from a bombed out movie house.'
Col. William Cameron, pilot, 44th BG

'About a week before the Group arrived, a neighbouring British battle school held their end of term party. We were invited to the party, at an old castle a few miles from our field. I upheld the honour of the air force with the Colonel in charge of Attlebridge. We were the only ones left standing at 03:00 hrs. Our staff car had disappeared so we walked back in a dense fog 'till 06:00 and finally found the field. Back to work at 08:00 – Tough life.'
Lt. Col. George H. Parker, Station Engineer, 466th BG

'That afternoon, who should show up unexpectedly but the Bob Hope Special Services Show with Frances Langford, Jerry Colonna and Jack Pepper, their guitarist. They put on a terrific show that did us all a world of good.'
Capt Franklin 'Pappy' Colby, 94th BG

'Our GI show, My Day, won the 8th Air Force cup. Our lightweight boxer, Vince Padilla, was the champ of the UK. We had good track, baseball, basketball and football teams. When Col. Westover made a sail boat out of a wing tank we had the only yacht in the 8th Air Force.'
Maj. Newton Mclaughlin, Special Services, 448th BG

'Carrow Road, the home ground of Norwich City Football Club, was the setting for a Wild West Show which was staged on 5 August 1944. It was jointly sponsored by the Special Services section in conjunction with the Norfolk War Charities Fund

We had good track, baseball, basketball and football teams. (USAF Official/FOTE News)

Great Yarmouth Hospital Week

First Time in Great Yarmouth!

REAL AMERICAN

BASEBALL

(Not Softball)

Wellesley Recreation Ground

At 6-45 p.m.   Gates open 6-15 p.m.

FRIDAY, AUGUST 11th

Two Specially Selected Allied Sides.

Play by Play Commentary and full explanation of the Game by Ace Commentator MURPHY, U.S.A.

Coach—**D. MAHER**, U.S.A. Professional.   A Unique Event you should not miss

Trophy to be presented to Winning Team by the Deputy-Mayor, Ald. F. H. Debbage

Admission to Ground 6d.   **Grand Stand 6d.**
                                              Extra

(Corporation Buses extended Half-an-Hour on all Services)

Selections by the Famous American 'Flying Deck' Band.

When you have read this, please pass it on to a friend—Thank You!

Yare Printing Co., Ltd., King Street, Great Yarmouth.

11 AUG 44   466 BG

and attracted a crowd of over 15,000, most of whom were unaware that only hours before many of the "cowboys" had been flying over Germany. One of the stars of the show was Lonnie Harvard, a Texan cowpuncher. He was a waist gunner with the 453rd and had flown his 19th mission that day with a visit to Brunswick. The ringmaster was Capt. Jack Maher, while Corp. Guy Rennie, a former Hollywood showman, was master of ceremonies to help make it an occasion to remember.'
Norwich newspaper report, 1944

'We gave parties in the Red Cross Club kitchen when a crew finished 30 missions – fried eggs ... For the group's 200th mission they sent me out to recruit GIRLS. The first place I went a stern WREN officer said "No". 'Didn't the girls have a good time at the 100th mission party?' I asked. I guess they did. She said it was several days before she got them back!'
Mary Carroll Leeds, American Red Cross girl, Attlebridge, June 1944 to May 1945

'According to one rumour, there would be 300 girls from Norwich and another 500 from London and Cambridge. One officer had said, "Confiden-

tially, they have to find their own quarters and absolutely be off the base in THREE days!"'
Richard Bing, radio operator, 561st BS, 388th BG

'Dances were held regularly in the canteen. WAAFs and ATS girls were usually invited and arrived in USAAF trucks. On special occasions, the canteen would be decorated gaily with garlands by the American girls who worked in the Club Director's office. When the air crews celebrated the 100th mission, exactly 100 cardboard Liberators about 18 inches long, were fixed to the ceiling dangling from string, as if flying in formation.'
Phyllis Smales, Rackheath teenager, American Red Cross Club, 467th BG, 1944

'Life at the base had its high moments of relief and relaxation. The two highest spots were probably the two parties given; one when we had flown 100 missions and the other after the 200th bombing.

**Dances were held regularly in the canteen.
(Rackheath Memories)**

These rivalled the Roman saturnalia. We were stood down by Division so that all could participate. The Aero Club and Officers' Club and the newer NCO Club were decorated in style. Girls came from far and wide. Liquor flowed freely. All the pyro-technics used on the base became fireworks for a tremendous display of rockets and flares. The parties lasted all night and many never got home at all. It was a bit of a shambles; nevertheless, a lot of pent up emotion was let off.

'The day after the 200th Mission Party, all gathered in the hangar to drink beer and witness an airshow of stunt flying in formation by P-51s and P-47s. The show was spectacular and done by experts. Unfortunately, a less experienced man came by in a '51 and tried to roll it at 100 ft but lost control and crashed by the gym – the graceful, purposeful power of the plane becoming a small pile of aluminium scrap amidst fire-blackened grass.'
Allan Healy, 467th BG

'The base was entertained by Mustangs of the

Life at the base had its high moments of relief and relaxation. (Col. William B. Cameron)

The two highest spots were probably the two parties given; one when we had flown 100 missions. (the late Lt. Col. John H. Woolnough)

The 'Divisionaires' band of the First Air Division provided the music and celebrations continued late into the evening. (the late Allan Healy)

364th FG. The "Divisionaires" band of the First Air Division provided the music and celebrations continued late into the evening. The party was a gala affair to which all the brass and all the civilians in the surrounding community were invited. An

English carnival was set up on the field and we had an American barbecue, including beef on a spit right on the airfield. Three bands were brought in and there were dances in the hangar, the Non-Coms' Club and the Officers' Club. Official contact was made with the other allied groups and special invitations were issued to the ATS, the WRENS and WAAFs. Gen. Doolittle and Gen. Spaatz were on hand as were many other dignitaries. Depending upon your viewpoint, the party was a smashing success or a disgrace to motherhood and the flag. The principal casualties were one chaplain who resigned and an investigation which gave us a clean (better strike "clean") bill of health.'

Bill Carleton, 351st BS Engineering Officer, 100th BG

'Once a month, we had a party at the Officers' Club. Eight or 10 trucks were sent to the neighbouring villages to pick up the young ladies that were eager to entertain or be entertained by those

At night we usually played cards or shot 'craps' in the hut. We didn't have much money and were paid only once a month so we tried to spread our funds over a long period and so usually bet small amounts in our games . . .

daring combatants. Americans seemed to fascinate these gals. Many of them would love to have married an American and come state side, or as they would put it, move to the colonies.

'A good meal was served followed by dancing and a floor show. One show was a take-off on Carmen Miranda. This person wore the loud, gaudy and revealing dress to a tee. Head decorations included the entire fruit world. Her dances were perfect imitations, exotic, provocative, and exuberant. After her performance, a major on the Wing General Staff made a hard play for her. We watched this with the knowledge that the lady was not a lady but a very young MP from another outfit. When the major had pressed luck as far as the MP could stand it, he was told the truth about the disguise – what a surprise with much embarassment. Parties needed hoaxes like this. It rounded out the lifestyle of combat fliers of airplanes, alcohol and sex.'

Col. Robert H. Tays, pilot, 392nd BG

'Test flights were discreetly scheduled on the days of major parties to insure that there was sufficient ice at the Officers' Club bar. Ice was made by taking a B-17 to 30,000 ft with containers of water sitting in the waist area. Ice formed quickly and the cool drinks preferred by the American flyers

became a reality, much to the amazement of the RAF liaison officers at Thurleigh.'
Russell A. Strong, 'First Over Germany'

'The "ice-cream" was made in the Mess and frozen in the air. Powdered eggs were put in egg shells to fool some of the troops.'
Harold Schultz, Aircrew Mess, Attlebridge

'Very near the end of the war, our bombardier and I went to Clacton-on-Sea. We saw a queue about a block long and asked what it was for. We were told that ice-cream was being sold, and we excitedly got in line. Then we observed that most of the people in the queue were children, and reasoned that most of the them had probably never even tasted ice-cream, so we quietly stepped aside.'
Robert L. Miller, pilot, Son Of A Blitz, 863rd BS, 493rd BG

'Combat aviators are known as notorious drinkers. We did drink. Combat flying is a very high tension-producing activity. Our flight surgeon recognized this fact and encouraged the use of alcohol. After

USO shows came to us in the hangar, about once a month. Bob Hope, Glenn Miller, and many more, a host of comely young gals with each entertainer. (Thorpe Abbotts Memorial Museum)

each mission, we were served a double shot of straight bourbon for medicinal purposes. Not having eaten since early in the morning and with empty stomachs, the effect was quite pronounced. At the 'O' Club, beer known as half and half or mild and bitters was sold by the pint. It took some time to get used to non-carbonated warm English beer. Scotch whisky with water and gin mixed with many things were common. No American beer or bourbon at the bar.'

Col. Robert H. Tays, pilot, 392nd BG

'On 4 August 1944, the 44th BG flew its 200th mission. One week later, on 11 August, the group celebrated this event with an all day of fun. All missions and training were suspended, all "rank" lost its privileges. Orders were out that no-one was to display his rank. Anyone caught with his uniform on was simply seized by any group of men nearby and taken to a large "duck pond" on base and thrown in, clothes and all. The base had a carnival-like atmosphere, all cares were set aside and the men had become boys again. We played baseball and pitched horseshoes, with a stage show that night.

'The highlight of the day came for me when almost everyone had gathered later in the afternoon in the area of the large "duck pond". I could not believe my eyes when I saw a group of men grab Col. John Gibson, who was dressed in his uniform, and heave him unceremoniously into the water. He came out looking like a drowned rat, but all smiles. He took his medicine like the man he was.

'About that time, up drives Brig. Gen. Leon Johnson in his jeep, CO of the 14th Combat Wing and holder of the Congressional Medal of Honor. Several men, with more respect than they had shown Col. Gibson, led him to the pond. He protested feebly but knew by looking at Col. Gibson and others who had gone before, that his protest was in vain. In he went with a big splash. You should have seen us all crowded around whooping and hollering like a bunch of Wild Indians. Both he and Col. Gibson endeared themselves to all personnel on the base and for days, it was the talk of the groups what "good sports" they were. What a glorious day of relaxation we had enjoyed. All of us needed this break from the strain and tension we were under.'

1/Lt. John W. McClane Jr., navigator, 68th BS, 44th BG

'USO shows came to us in the hangar, about once

a month. Bob Hope, Glenn Miller, and many more, a host of comely young gals with each entertainer. The shows were clean and much fun with GI participation. For an hour or two, we forgot that we were scheduled to fly tomorrow. A touch of home or something familiar always seemed to lighten the stress load. Glenn Miller played our base just a few days before he was lost.'

Col. Robert H. Tays, pilot, 392nd BG

'Glenn Miller's band, 'The Flying Yanks', lost their instruments en route to our 200th mission party from London when they stopped for lunch.'

Maj. Newton L. Mclaughlin, Special Services, 448th BG

'On a few occasions we visited Cambridge, and . . . found a music store, since I wanted to buy a clarinet for myself, having left mine at home in the States. I was studying music in college and clarinet was my instrument. I didn't want to bring my valuable instrument with me overseas and I bought this terrible metal clarinet for £100 − at the time a pound was $4.04 − which was extremely extravagant.

'Shortly after we began to fly missions, I was approached by a sergeant who asked if I would like to join the jazz band on the base. Having had a lot of experience in such groups in high school and college, I said, "You bet!"

'I was assigned a saxophone part and after a few rehearsals our group played for a dance at another field. Then the sergeant leader announced we were to play at a time I couldn't be there. He looked at me and said: "Are you flying COMBAT?"

I said: "Sure".

He said "I wish I had known that. You're replacing a guy who was shot down."

'They found someone who was less likely to need replacing.'

Robert L. Miller, pilot, Son Of A Blitz, 863rd BS, 493rd BG

'A Second Air Division show called, "It's All Yours Buddy" toured the bases in Norfolk and Suffolk. When I was the Special Services Officer at Attlebridge, I met the cast and the "Swingsters" band on the stage.'

Maj. Newton S. McLaughlin, Special Services Officer, 466th BG

'At night we usually played cards or shot "craps" in the hut. We didn't have much money and were paid only once a month so we tried to spread our

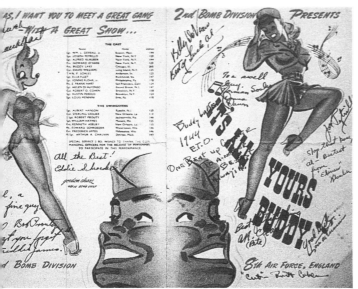

'IT'S ALL YOURS BUDDY' (Maj. Newton L. McLaughlin/Lt. Col. John H. Woolnough)

funds over a long period and so usually bet small amounts in our games. On our first combat mission our crew was not bothered by fighters, but a long distance off to our left we did see a group of 11 'planes being hit by enemy fighters and seven of the 11 went down, picked off one at a time.

'That night, when we got back to the hut, one guy threw his total wad on the floor and said: "Damn, if they're all going to be like this one, SHOOT IT ALL!"'
T/Sgt. Jack Kings, waist gunner 388th BG

'It seemed to me that our enlisted men could not hold onto money from one pay day to the next. I gathered from what I heard that within a few days of being paid, all their money was lost in crap games or gambling of some sort. I often would

SHILLING LIMIT!

loan them just enough money to get the necessities they needed from the PX; anything more would soon be gone.'

1/Lt. John W. McClane Jr., navigator, 44th BG

'If the weather was bad or our group was stood down, a lot of cards were played in the Officers' Club: bridge, poker and a game I never learned, called "Red Dog". The stakes must have been high, for both our bombardier, Jerry, and navigator, John, approached me for loans about the middle of each month because they had lost all their money playing "Red Dog". I saw crap games being played in a barracks when there were literally hundreds of pounds awaiting the outcome of the roll of the dice.'

Robert L. Miller, pilot, Son Of A Blitz, 863rd BS, 493rd BG

I saw crap games being played in a barracks when there were literally hundreds of pounds awaiting the outcome of the roll of the dice. (Rackheath Memories)

GLADIATORS OF THE AIR

Morituri te salutamos (We who are about to die salute you)

'I always carried a money belt but by the time we finished leave, the money was gone and all we had was the return train ticket back to London. We did every pub in Brighton, a resort town noted for its pubs. There was something like a front line men-

I always carried a money belt but by the time we finished leave, the money was gone and all we had was the return train ticket back to London. (Col. William B. Cameron)

tality about this seacoast city because it was only about 40 to 50 miles across the Channel to the Nazi-occupied France. During this time Brighton was the target of several hit-and-run type German bombing raids. But we thought there were more girls in Brighton.

'It was Tom Kinder, from Boontown, New Jersey, who got us lodgings in a small rooming house on Marine Parade, overlooking the sea. All the old Georgian style sea front hotels were filled with service men and women mostly on some kind of leave. The landlady was a Mrs Sutherland. She was very English and I had trouble understanding her. She referred to her establishment as a "billet". Even in the darkest days of winter she had flowers in the living room. She put us Yanks up for a couple of nights, but I am sure she wondered what we did all day. The beach was off limits and was filled with barbed wire barricades. I saw the Royal Pavilion and that was quite a spectacular sight for Americans.

'When the damp mists rolled in from the sea our wool uniforms became musty, and I can still recall the smell of that musty wool and the way it scratched your neck. We had to wear the winter uniforms by order. We tried to look jaunty but it was difficult with those bulky uniforms and the wet climate of southern England. After a few days of pubbing we presented a raunchy looking group and must have scared off many girls. Dave Edmonds, our bombardier, was a favourite drinking companion of the pub-jockeys I went on leave with. Dave was a handsome, tall fellow, the biggest man in our small group. He died tragically, as so many did in the air combat of World War Two. I liked him because he reminded me of a loner, a lost sheep and yet in his loneliness he managed to summon enough courage to fly combat missions, and that is the way he died. Perhaps in many respects he had more to overcome than we did. He would go through several transformations during the drinking hours. At one of these transformations, his eyes, which were dark, would turn the colour of mince in a pie. Therefore, we called him, simply, "Mince". We would all take turns looking intently at his eyes to see when they would turn this mince colour; a sort of mushy yellow-brown hue. It was at this precise time we knew he was getting drunk and so were we.

'Kinder, "Mince" and I, along with the Aussies, tangled with many Limey soldiers, but it was the Royal Marines who did us in. This was before D-Day and the Marines didn't think much of the so-called flyboys of the American air forces. We challenged them to all kinds of contests but it was chug-a-lugging that was the real test. Kinder would line up 10 beer mugs and start chug-a-lugging them. He got to five and collapsed. Then I would take over, followed by "Mince", until all 10 would be consumed. Not to be outdone, the Marines would line up 15 mugs and chug-a-lug them down, next 20, and so forth. Now, I knew our limit was about 15 mugs of beer. Kinder downed seven mugs, I did about five and "Mince" the last three mugs. The Marines, however, beat us by downing 20 mugs. We were flat out after about three such contests but the Marines were still going upright. The Aussies came to our rescue and downed the required 20. We couldn't take too much of the warm English brew and preferred Scotch. It was the Aussies who were the greatest beer drinkers.

'Our favourite pub was one owned by the British boxing champion of the time, Tommy Farr, a big bulk of a man who often tended bar. He liked Americans, having fought some bouts in the States. We would arrive a few minutes before the pubs would open, stake out our favourite pub for that day, and be there when the doors opened. We would start drinking Scotch or English liquor with mild and bitters for chasers. We started out from the first pub, making the rounds up every little alleyway and street and returning to the first shortly before closing time. The next day we would repeat the routine.

'These pub forays into drunkenness and oblivion were to obscure the grim realities. Many of those young gladiators of the air didn't make it through the war; the Royal Marines, who hit the Normandy beaches, among them. Nothing can detract from their heroism in the face of impending combat. Even their drinking had a noble quality to it, like youthful gods who died young, sampling the divine nectar, living and loving deeply and above all, loving each other.

'We had done much drinking from pub to pub and late that day we found ourselves in a roller skating rink, each of us with an English girl we had met somewhere along the way. We were just intoxicated enough to whirl our girlfriends around that rink at breakneck speed and clearing the floor of all others. We were having a great high time sending the girls flying in all directions, when

suddenly, the air raid siren sounded. Immediately, the place was cleared; the girls and the English disappeared, leaving only us Yanks and a few Aussies still skating around and around. An air raid warden came in and shouted, "Come on Yanks, you've got to get to the shelter. Make it quick!"

'We paid no attention and continued to skate, led now by the Aussies singing "Waltzing Matilda", directly down the street and toward the seafront! Now and then we could see the glow of bomb bursts but we never did go to the shelter. We must have skated into a plush beachfront hotel in the early morning hours. I awoke between satin-like

As I stepped out on the broad avenue ... a squadron of RAF fighters went over ... and headed towards France. I wished them luck. (T/Sgt Forrest S. Clark).

Lt. Rocky Griffith's crew. Back row, L/R: Lt. Weatherwax; Lt. Dave Edmonds; Lt. R. C. Griffith; Lt. W. Tinsman; Sgt. W. Kuban. Front row, L/R: T/Sgt. Forrest S. Clark; T/Sgt. J. Gibboney; T/Sgt. Abe Sofferman; T/Sgt. E. Parrish; T/Sgt. H. Hermon. (Clark)

SUPPLY AND DEMAND

sheets in the bridal suite. I don't know how I got there but I suspect it was the stalwart Aussies. The girls had difficulty explaining what they were doing in our hotel. One of them got our GI shoes which we had left at the skating rink. She was told, "Don't bring those crazy Yanks back here again."

'I felt very ashamed as I gathered my clothes together, dressed hastily and crept downstairs through the large ornate lobby and past the gaze of dozens of officer types. I thought it was a dream because the hotel was full of majors, colonels and high-ranking RAF officers. I may have saluted a few very weakly as I made my sheepish exit. As I stepped out on the broad avenue that was Marine Parade on a bright sunny morning, a squadron of RAF fighters went over the beach and headed out toward France. I wished them luck.'
S/Sgt. Forrest S. Clark, gunner, 44th BG

Who saw them first, the exiles returning, the fighters,
The Croix de Lorraine and the Tricolour flown
from the hull?
Who saw us moving more fitly to join the spectators,
The crazy, the crying, the silent whose hearts were
full?

St Aubin D' Aubign: Paul Dehn, August 1944

'After Paris was liberated on 25 August, we sent a crew with a case of Nescafé and they returned with a 'plane load of champagne.'
Maj. Newton L. Mclaughlin, Special Services, 448th BG

'The 466th had a mission to haul petrol to Patton for over a week. Our Intelligence Officer was an architect who studied in France and was a friend of the owners of Pomery & Greno at Rheims. He

arranged for good old Benney Weiner, our Club Officer, to purchase some of the finest champagne in France. The mission landed near Rheims. Benney brought back something over three tons of Pomery & Greno 1938!'
Lt. Col. George H. Parker, 466th BG

'On 29 August B-24s began "trucking" missions, transporting urgent fuel and supplies to the Allied ground forces in France. When the Allies launched Operation "Market Garden" using British and American airborne divisions against German-held Dutch towns on the Rhine in mid-September, the B-24s were once again called upon to supplement the troop carriers. We hauled boxed goods and five-gallon Jerry cans of gasoline initially, but soon we were hauling 80-octane gas' only, in our 'plane's outer wing "Tokyo" tanks, in tanks installed in the bomb bays and in fighter drop tanks carried in the waist area of the ship. These loads were about 2,700 gallons which were pumped off at the landing fields in France. In addition, we carried enough 100-octane in our wing tanks for the approximate five-hour round

Cognac, perfume, German war weapons and parts of wrecked aircraft were sought after. The Officers' Club was adorned with swastikas from Luftwaffe planes. (the late Allan Healy)

trip. At the height of the operation there were 150 airplanes at Rackheath. All armament was taken from the 'planes except the Martin upper turret guns and ammunition and we flew at altitudes of 1,000 ft or less, ready to go "on the deck" if attack by enemy fighters occurred.'
Philip G. Day, co-pilot, Lil' Peach, *467th BG, 11 September 1944*

'On 12 September the 458th BG at Horsham St Faith delivered just over 13,000 gallons of fuel to units in France. The first full divisional "trucking" mission on 18 September, including six specially modified Liberators from the 458th, delivered over 9,000 gallons of fuel to Gen. Patton's forces. During September, in 13 days of flying "trucking" missions, the 458th alone delivered 727,160 gallons of fuel to France.'
458th BG history

'From 19 September until 3 October, the 96th Wing flew no combat missions but established a forward base at the airfield at Clastres, near St Quentin, France, We ferried gasoline for Patton's tanks and motorized units.'
Col. Albert J. Shower, CO, 467th BG

'Planes were modified to carry tanks in their bomb-bays, many war-weary ships from other

Groups were brought to Rackheath to carry on the work. The many coloured fins and rudders denoting these Groups appearing on our field had the civilians about guessing as to their mission. Skeleton crews plus two sightseers went out in each 'plane. Often 'planes made two trips a day and overnight stops in France were frequent. There was much bad weather and sometimes planes turned back, unable to land in France.

'The interlude was welcome and provided much pleasure for those engaged in it. The chic of French women pleased. Cognac, perfume, German war weapons and parts of wrecked aircraft were sought after. The Officers' Club was adorned with swastikas from Luftwaffe 'planes. Until 3 October, when we again went back on operations, 646,000 gallons of gasoline were trucked by us to France. Then we went out to score our second 100.'
Allan Healy, 467th BG

'The 8th Air Force mission plan called for 28 squadrons of Liberators (252 aircraft) to drop supplies to the 82nd and 101st Airborne Divisions which had been airlifted behind the German lines the previous day. Briefing was at 09:30. With the Group's DB-7, *Lady Josephine V*, up as monitor aircraft, 40 B-24s were airborne by 13:27. At 14:33, B-17 117/J, which had aborted on the ground, took off to join the formation. Forty-one were now up and ready, and at 14:53 the lead aircraft departed the English coast at 1,500 ft for the 34-minute flight to Eindhoven, Holland. Coming off the targets the 491st 'planes were still all intact, although small arms fire had killed one crewmember and injured several others. Shortly after leaving the drop area the lead plane on the 'A' force (44-40210, Capt. James K. Hunter) caught a burst of flak in the right wing section. Hunter and eight others were killed as their aircraft demolished itself against trees and farm buildings. One of the casualties was Capt. Mitchell. Miraculously, one man did survive, S/Sgt. Frank DiPalma. S/Sgt. DiPalma was hidden in a Catholic church until the British Army liberated the town of Udenhout.'
'A history of the 491st BG' on the supply drop in Holland during the 'Market Garden' operation on 18 September 1944

'She took one bounce and struck some haystacks, exploding in a large orange flame. Our altitude was about 100 ft at the time. The tail gunner was the only survivor. He was hidden by some Dutch monks until liberated.'
Ted Parker, waist gunner, 491st BG, who watched

helplessly as the lead ship, flown by Capt. Jim Hunter and which carried Capt. Anthony Mitchell, the air commander, aboard, was shot down on 18 September 1944

'At the target I opened the hatch in the floor and had to work quickly because we would be passing the dropping zone fast and at low altitude. In my haste my leg became entangled in the parachute straps attached to the ammunition track and I was pulled out of the hole when the last bundle went out. I just managed to cling to the track, but my legs were dangling out of the hatch. The Quartermaster [who had "frozen" since take-off] ignored my calls for help. Finally, the tail gunner, David

'At the target I opened the hatch in the floor and had to work quickly because we would be passing the dropping zone fast and at low altitude.' (Ted Parker)

As we neared the target the small arms fire became intense. We were hit several times. One slug stopped in the back pack parachute of our tail gunner. (Dan Winston)

Slade, heard me and came to my assistance.'
Ted Parker, waist gunner, 491st BG, 18 September 1944 drop to the 101st American Airborne at Best, Holland

---

'The view along the route to the drop zone was incredible. Crashed C-47s, burned outlines of crashed gliders, gliders nosed up or on their back – a general mess. Our flight was over farming area. We could nearly see the flying feathers of the fluttering chickens; the cows were in full gallop – right through fences and bushes. The Dutch farmers were waving happily. It was certainly a different sight than we would see at our usual 22,000 ft altitude. As we neared the target the small arms fire became intense. We were hit several times. One slug stopped in the back pack parachute of our tail gunner.'
Dusty Worthen, bombardier, 93rd BG

During March 1945 the Second Air Division was again called upon to provide Liberators to drop supplies. (392nd BG)

'During March 1945, the Second Air Division was again called upon to provide Liberators to drop supplies, this time to Field-Marshal Montgomery's Second Army crossing the Rhine at Wesel. About 6,000 aircraft took part in the operation and murderous ground fire accounted for many of the 14 Liberators that failed to return. 104 B-24s returned to their bases with varying degrees of damage.'
458th BG history

HUMOUR

Where the heavy dew whips through the breeze
And you wade through mud up to your knees
Where the sun don't shine and the rain flows free
And the fog's so thick you could hardly see

Where we live on Brussel sprouts and spam

And the powdered eggs which aren't worth a damn
In town you can eat the fish and spuds
And down the taste with a mug of suds

You hold your nose when you gulp it down
It hits your stomach and then you frown
It burns your tongue, makes your throat feel queer
It's rightly named bitter, it sure ain't beer

Where you get watered scotch at four bits a snort
And those limey cabbies don't stand short
Where the prices are high and the queues are long
And the Yankie GI's are always wrong

And these pitch black nights when you stay out late
It's so bloody dark you can hardly navigate
There's no transportation so you have to hike
And you get your can knocked off by a GI bike

Where most of the gals are blonde and bold
And they think every Yank's pocket is lined with gold
Then there's the Piccadilly Commandos with painted allure
Steer clear of them or you'll get burnt for sure

The isle ain't worth saving I don't think
Cut the balloons and let the damned thing sink
I ain't complaining I'll have you know
But life's rough as a cob in the ETO.

RAF teletype operator, Shipdham

'I had just arrived in England and was unused to the black-out. The sun was shining when I left the base and walked into Norwich to visit the Lido ballroom. When I left it was pitch black and I did not know the way back to my base at Horsham St Faith. I asked someone the way and he said: "Just keep walking straight up the road outside. You cawn't miss it." I did as he said, one foot on the pavement and one in the gutter up the street in the dark. I hadn't gone more than a hundred yards when I walked into a lampost and knocked myself out.'
458th BG ground crewman at Horsham St Faith, near Norwich, 1944

We joined the effing Air Force 'cos we thought it effing right,
But don't care if we effing fly or if we effing fight.
But what we do object to are those effing Ops Room twats
Who sit there sewing stripes on at the rate of effing knots

'We stopped again to watch some RAF armourers load a 12,000-lb torpedo-shaped bomb on a Lancaster, its lower half protruding from a well in the bomb bay section. One of the RAF airmen said to a Yank gunner: "I suppose it will be a long time before you fellows carry one of these up in your Fortresses." The gunner replied: 'It will be a damned sight longer before you guys drop one of those babies on Berlin in broad daylight."
Abe Dolim, navigator, 94th BG

'In the early months of operations Boxted had several night visits from enemy intruder aircraft. On one very dark night bombs were dropped on the airfield and a large crowd at the Red Cross Aero Club scattered to a wood nearby for safety. One joker, in the quiet depths of the wood, imitated the shrill whine of a falling bomb and then threw himself in a watery foxhole. There was deep silence. A colonel broke the silence with, "I'll court martial that man when I find him!"'
History of 354th FG

'They took the Flying Fortress up to 40,000 feet,
'Cause they've only got a teeny weeny bomb . . . '

RAF Song

Colonel to his executive officers: 'Tomorrow evening at approximately 20.00 hrs Halley's Comet will be visible in this area. An event which occurs only once every 75 years. Have the men fall out in the squadron area in fatigues, and I will explain this rare phenomenon to them. In case of rain, we will not be able to see anything, so assemble the men in the theatre and I will show them films of it.'

Executive officer to squadron commander: 'By order of the colonel, tomorrow at 20:00 hrs, Halley's Comet will appear above the squadron area. If it rains, fall the men out in fatigues, then march to the theatre where this rare phenomenon will take place. Something which occurs only once in 75 years.'

Squadron commander to the lieutenant: 'By order of the colonel. In fatigues at 20:00 hrs

The isle ain't worth saving I don't think
Cut the balloons and let the damned thing
sink. I ain't complaining I'll have you know
But life's rough as a cob in the ETO.
(Rackheath Memories)

During the war the music hall joke was that 'Yanks' were 'Overpaid, Oversexed and Over here'. (Rackheath Memories)

tomorrow evening the phenomenal Halley's Comet will appear in the theatre. In case of rain, in the squadron area, the colonel will give another order, something which occurs once every 75 years.'

Lieutenant to sergeant: 'Tomorrow at 20:00 hrs, the colonel will appear in the theatre with

Ugly as a whistling shithouse and yet truly a magnificent lady. (Col. William B. Cameron)

Halley's Comet, something which happens every 75 years. If it rains, the colonel will order the comet into the squadron area.'

Sergeant to the squadron: 'When it rains tomorrow at 20:00 hrs, the phenomenal 75-year-old General Halley, accompanied by the colonel, will drive his comet through the squadron theatre in fatigues.'
BAD News, journal of the BAD 2 Association

'I was so very anxious to fly. When the RAF airman told me it would be 7/6d a day (seven shillings and sixpence, or about $37\frac{1}{2}$p) I told him I couldn't afford it. You see, I thought I had to pay them. I had always heard that to be a member of British Armed Forces you had to have a bit of money.

'The airman laughed at me and said: "No, we pay you 7/6d a day." I said: "You loveable fool. You could've had me for nothing."

'I really thought they were crazy to pay me to fly.'
Col. James E. Goodson, pilot, RAF 133rd Eagle Squadron/4th FG ace

---

'The story we heard later was that Col. Kane had been their guest of honour and during his carefully chosen remarks stated that before the war was over there were three cities he would like to bomb . . . "Berlin, Tokyo and London". He was asked not to come back.'
Col. Bill Cameron describing Col. "Killer" Kane's visit to a British Officers' Club in Benghazi

---

'In a further effort to conserve fuel I had the crew leavening off the four fuel tanks, switching fuel between tanks for as little as 10- to 12-second intervals. As the fuel supply inexorably diminished and we were switching between tanks, our bombardier, Lyle Haines, asked: "What do you want me to do skipper, make the next transfer with an eye dropper?"'
Bob Maag, pilot, 94th BG

'During the war the music hall joke was that "Yanks" were "Overpaid, Oversexed and Over here." I'm still here and I'm overpaid . . . Two out of three ain't bad.'
Anglophile Lt. Col. James "Goody" Goodson, Fighter pilot

'Ugly as a whistling shithouse and yet truly a magnificent lady.'
Col. Robert H. Tays, pilot, 392nd BG, describing the B-24.

'The banana boat'
B-17 crewmembers' description of the B-24

'A medium bomber'
B-24 crewmembers' description of the B-17

Of a B-24 they all make such fun
They say she was built in 1901
It is something I cannot deny
She looks like a box car in the sky
The tail is short, the wing is long
I hear it was put together wrong.
Maybe it was, but I'll bet
They'll find a use for the damned thing yet.

'Grenade carrier'
B-24 crewmembers' description of the B-17

'Needless to say, a pilot had a lot of pride in the aircraft he flew and the Fortress was no exception. When I began missions I would look down at squadrons of Liberators 4,000 ft below, struggling to get more altitude in an airplane that wasn't capable as the Fortress was. Then I would remember a common joke among us Fortress pilots where we mercilessly chided the pilots who flew the "flying box-cars" with "Oh, you fly the B-24 – isn't that the crate that ours came in." We Fortress pilots weren't too popular with Lib' pilots.'
2/Lt. Robert W. Browne, Fortress pilot, 487th BG

'Our engineering officer, Lt. Chernachowski, a really fine guy, had the misfortune of falling from his bike and dislocating his shoulder. Humour prevailed. Maj. Jamieson commissioned me to paint a "purple heart" award (the rear quarter of a horse). Then, in continuing good humour (by all participants), we had a mock ceremony and this recorded it for posterity. Humour was often expressed by our group "artists", particularly as they decorated their quarters. There was no limit to their imagination, including goblins, dragons and what-nots in a multitude of colours, poses and locations. Painted footprints were common, leaving a trail across a room, up the wall, traversing the ceiling, etc. A real tension breaker and indicative of the ever present GI sense of humour.'
Harold J. Johnston, base artist, 458th BG

'On the 16th mission when Keith Kent, the bombardier, was trying to see how his bombs were falling, flak hit the nose of the aircraft and he got some fragments of glass just over one eye. Turned out it wasn't very serious but it was enemy inflicted and drew blood so he'd get a "Purple Heart". One pretty good-sized piece hit next to me. I picked it up and tried to scratch a bloody place on one cheek just above my oxygen mask, but the weather was so damn cold and my face so cold and tight I couldn't make a scratch!'
T/Sgt. Jack Kings, waist gunner 388th BG

You can always tell a gunner
By his hands and vacant stare
You can always tell a bombardier
By his manner debonair
You can always tell a navigator
By his pencils maps and such
You can always tell a pilot
But you can't tell him much

'A buck private and a sergeant were court martialled for striking a colonel. Asked why he had done it, the sergeant explained that the colonel, while passing down the line of review, had stepped on his sore foot.

"Instinctively," said the sergeant, "I threw up my guard, like anyone would do, and let him have it before I realized what had actually happened. It was an accident, I can assure you."

'Then the buck private was asked for his explanation.

"Well, you see sir," he replied, "When I saw the sergeant strike the colonel, I thought the war was over." '
401st BG Newsletter

'She placed her machine gun in a corner, pulled down some purple bloomers and went about her business, pulled the bloomers on, shouldered her burp-gun and left. As a 20-year-old American, I was not prepared for such a show. I must have remained in partial shock for five more minutes.'
Paul E Montague, who bailed out over the Russian lines

'One day, a truck went into the side of the Red Cross quarters and exposed our underwear drying on a rack.'
Mary Carroll Leeds, American Red Cross girl, Attlebridge, June 1944 to May 1945

'Through my late husband, Bill Davies, who was a civilian electrician, I came in regular contact with the Americans who were welcome to my very modest home at that period. I was within 20 to 30 ft of what was called the "frying pan", where a

'plane was ready to go. Even on a rainy day I could be sure of my washing being dropped by it just revving up ... Another amusing incident. I had several electricians who were seeing to totem bobs, etc., living with me. Jack had drawn several hundred pounds to pay wages. I slept on that cash that night and next morning gave it to Jack to pay the men's wages in the wooden hut opposite the "frying pan". The Yanks knew Jack was busy with loose bank notes about so they revved up the plane, overturned the hut and scattered the notes on hedges, totem poles and telephone wires. That taught Swifty Jack a lesson, but they were good lads, and retrieved it all.'
81-year-old Mrs Linda Weston, who lived next to Shipdham airfield in World War Two

'The Mess Officer was to have the pleasure of flying back with us to the USA. He made sure we had the best of everything. Then we had a party in which us and our girlfriends had two-pound steaks and our own enlisted man servant, flowers and white tablecloths. That's when I got to thinking, "This guy's been eating like this throughout the war. I've been getting my butt shot off and getting no real food at all!" All we got for an 11-hour mission was a box of British hydrocarbates. It was useless and just got pitched out the 'plane.'
John Holden, navigator, 452nd BG

I painted what seemed to be a million A-2 jackets, some of them pretty weird, but what they wanted was what they got. (Alfred R. Lea, 452nd BG)

'They would almost go into hysterics watching me pick up the fork with my left hand, the knife with my right, then switch the knife to the right hand, fork to the left hand to "jab at my meat" while I cut with my knife, then lay the knife down, switch the fork to my right hand and once more jab at my food.'
John McClane Jr., navigator, 44th BG

'We went to Kettering to catch the train, and as we had an hour to kill the radio operator located a pub and we had plenty to drink. On the way to London he opened the window in the compartment, stuck his head out and lost his cap. In London we had to find him another cap because he wouldn't get by the MPs without one. He found another pub while he waited. On the way to the rest home he pulled the same trick as before and lost that cap also. By the time we got there he didn't know whether he was in England or the USA.'
Howard E Hernan, 303rd BG

'We would try to spin the sails of the windmill at the end of the runway with propwash on take-off. When the landing gear would not retract because the solenoid was stuck, we'd have to use an eraser to activate it and sometimes the drag of the late retracting gear would cause us to "straddle" the windmill.'
Vince Reed, 466th BG

'There always seemed an abundance of sprouts.'
Howard E. Hernan, gunner, 303rd BG

'After flying around we finally had to just drop our bombs through the clouds. Some cabbage patch or brussels sprouts must have been bombed under. Brussel sprouts were not my favourite anyway. We used to have them for appetizers, main course and dessert.'
1/Lt. Joe Wroblewski, pilot, Shady Lady II, 351st BG, 23 March 1944

'One of the waist gunners said afterwards: "I was dropping chaff (tinsel-like strips to confuse enemy radar) when I felt a lurch. I looked out the window and saw Smarinsky's '24 going down. Then I looked out of the right window and saw another going down. I began throwing the chaff out, a whole box at a time."'
John Stanforth, 713th BS, 448th BG, 1st mission, to Magdeberg

'I painted what seemed to be a million A-2 jackets,

some of them pretty weird, but what they wanted was what they got. I believe the paint job I got the biggest kick out of was when my pal Rocco talked some of the sheet metal guys on the flight line into closing the jeep all in. They did a terrific job except they left the painting to me. So, being of Irish background, I ended up with the brightest emerald green you ever saw, trimmed in black-out white. It was really something else. I had to go over to Ketteringham Hall and managed to pass in front of the hall just as Gen. Kepner and some other general were walking down the steps. Did he ever do a double take. Needless to say, I didn't stop to ask directions.'
Charles 'Bud' Doyle, 389th BG

'One day we were the only silver ship in the squadron and we got singled out and picked on by the German fighters. I didn't want that again so the next day we deliberately flew an olive drab ship. Wouldn't you know it, we were the only OD ship and we got picked on again . . . '
100th BG pilot

'We had this crazy radio operator. Who wasn't crazy, especially radio operators and navigators? Between missions Miller urinated in condoms, tied the tops neatly and securely, and stored the condoms on a shelf above his bed for future use. The future use was to take them along to Hamburg or wherever, freeze them, and toss them out here and there, shouting "Piss on you Bastards!"'
Bill Mulroney, 94th BG

'We dropped some agents in the foothills of the Alps near Munich. It was a "hairy do" because the only possible withdrawal manoeuvre was a "chandel" to avoid slamming into the mountains. A few nights later we were back to the same drop zone with a resupply drop. We made S-Phone contact with the agents on the ground and asked what other supplies they might need. The answer we received was obviously an expression of a "wry" sense of humour. I quote: "We want a bunch of bananas and a few packages of condoms!"'
Lt. Col. Robert W. Fish, deputy CO, 'Carpetbaggers'

'This day we had a new ball turret gunner, Peter P. Catozza, a 17-year-old boy who had been working in the armament shop. We trained him as best we could because he hadn't been through gunnery school. Over Le Mans we shot our 4 July fireworks off at the swarm of Focke Wulf 190s. Catozza fired

One day we were the only silver ship in the squadron and we got singled out and picked on by the German fighters. (Lockheed)

off all his ammunition before we got to the target in his excitement. I could always tell who was firing his guns and which ones. I knew our new gunner was firing at aircraft too far away and told him to conserve his ammunition. After that he naturally wanted to get out of the turret. But we made him ride it out in the ball turret the whole way because any German pilot who noticed that a turret was no longer turning would be invited to try and attack. That broke him of the habit of wasting ammunition.'
Claude Campbell, pilot, 303rd BG

'At Snetterton Heath the air raid sirens sounded so often that men, living in the air raid shelters, disregarded them and instead, continued their games of poker long into the night. One night the air raid warning sounded and they took no notice until someone ran along the roof rattling a stick. Thinking it to be enemy machine gun fire the inhabitants threw their playing cards in the air and fled from the shelter!'
Frank E. Moran, 96th BG

'On the way out we had our usual comedians. Tail gunner Scerrati called over interphone saying, "It's all off, it's all off."

'Excited navigator Perle asked, "What's off! What's off!"

The answer: "The hair off your head." '
Joe Wroblewski, pilot, 351st BG

'Their Officers' Mess was directly above our dining room and during lunch one day I saw smoke rising from my small son's pram in which he was sleeping outside. Rushing out, I found it had been caused by a cigar thrown out from above! There were profuse apologies, followed by lots of wonderful American goodies sent to atone. They were such a friendly crowd, but even so we were not allowed anywhere near the operations (or war room) centre; however, they used to entice the youngest daughter and my son into where all the secrets were and then give them sweets, much to Nanny's great disapproval.'
Mrs Angela Boileau, sister-in-law of Maj. Etienne Henry Tudor Boileau, owner of Ketteringham Hall, HQ, 2nd Air Division from December 1943 to 1945

'That horrible winter of '44 and '45 was one of the worst Britain has ever had. Our armies were in trouble and the weather was so bad we couldn't get a 'plane off. Our troops were in the worst humour I have ever seen and it stayed that way until we finally got a mission off.'
Col. Larry Thomas, CO, 453rd BG

'Due to a wind change the returning bombers used the short runway which actually ran downhill. It was just too short for our aircraft and one of them failed to make the turn in time, whereupon two others crashed into it. We were lucky no-one was killed and it became known as the "Grand Slam". Speaking of luck, one of the luckiest people I know was an English workman who was driving his truck on the perimeter strip and evidently not paying too much attention to the taxiing aircraft. In fact, he drove his truck right into one of the propellers, which subsequently cut the steering wheel off in his hand. When he was able to regain his composure, which was several minutes later, he marched over to the Adjutant's Office and demanded a new truck. Maj. Uttely offered him a

That horrible winter of '44 and '45 was one of the worst Britain has ever had. (Thorpe Abbotts Memorial Museum)

deal. We would get him a new truck and he would get us a new $10,000 propeller and a $15,000 engine. The case was closed!'
Bill Carleton, 351st Squadron Engineering Officer, 100th BG

'There was the time when Snyder and some others were visiting our barracks and the putt-putt bombs would come over – putt, putt, putt. The conversation would stop, everyone would listen to see if it fell before reaching our location or putted on past and then stopped. This particular night, the putt-putt stopped directly overhead. Everyone scattered. Even though it was serious, it was real amusing, for one great big old boy tried to crawl under the lower bunk. The board rail was probably five inches from the floor, so, of course, he could not get underneath there and it looked so silly to watch him head butt his head and continue to try to get under the bed!'
Emmett D. Seale, 446th BG, Flixton

'When my girl was in high school she had a project to write and wanted to know about my escape. I started off by telling her that "after we left the hotel ... "

'She interrupted and said, "What Hotel?"

'Of course, I had to explain to her about Turkey being a neutral country and so on ... she laughed and said she would be laughed out of school if she told a story like that. So I started off again: "I was given nothing but turnip soup for breakfast and an SS trooper dragged me for three miles trying to get the ring off my finger and I was beat every other day ... "

'She liked that much better.'
Earl Zimmerman, radio operator, 389th BG and Ploesti veteran

JOHNNY'S DEATH

*Do not despair
For Johnny-head-in-air;
He sleeps as sound
As Johnny underground.*

*Fetch out no shroud
For Johnny-in-the-cloud;*

*And keep your tears
For him in after years.*

*Better by far
For Johnny-the-bright-star,
To keep your head,
And see his children fed.*

'For Johnny', John Pudney

'I never knew him. He fell in battle when I was three. He gave me his name and his Irish heritage and little more; but perhaps, in the end, that is all there is to give. I remember feeling his loss but at age three I could not comprehend the enormity of it. Most of my knowledge about him was as seen through the eyes of others. They remembered that his well-to-do family spoiled him (he drove and wrecked a Cadillac convertible during the Depression years when many Americans considered themselves lucky to eat!). He took flying lessons and, when courting my mother, would "buzz" the church when she was at services. All would run out to see Johnny disappear in the clouds in a biplane

I never knew him. He fell in battle when I was three. (Dr. John McGlone)

... Here then is the last mission, on 5 January 1944, of the B-24 American bomber crew 38 of the 713th Squadron, 448th BG, and the last desperate hours in the life of John E. McGlone Jr., gunner and staff sergeant, USAAF.

'The target for today would be Kiel. The crews suffered the usual Army game of hurry-up-and-wait, as they were delivered to their 'planes by trucks, and then nodded off, huddled in their flying suits awaiting take-off. Finally, the 'plane began its lift-off, and cleared the end of the runway and the treetops. They climbed through the blinding overcast for thousands of feet before the nose gunner, Bob Hudson, observed that the overcast was beginning to thin out. Soon they broke through the clouds and reached the dazzling sunshine to see before them a huge fleet of bombers assembling for the raid. Two hundred and forty-five aircraft were to attack Kiel, 131 B-17s from the 1st Bomb Division, and 114 from the 2nd Bomb Division. From his left waist gun position, Johnny watched as the planes climbed, circled, and struggled to attain their assigned positions.

'The 1st Division had been designated to lead the raid, but somehow a group of B-24s had gotten into the forward position instead of the B-17 group. They departed the English coast over Cromer and headed out over the North Sea. The clearing weather revealed whitecaps on the ocean below. It looked cold and ominous. The long flight eastward over water kept them out of German territory as long as possible. An in-flight 360 turn by the B-24 group failed to correct the group alignment, and the B-24s would be the first to go in over the target. The entire formation turned 90 to the south for the downward thrust toward Germany. "Clyde" Maxton scanned the sky above his top turret position, John McGlone and Hank Gautier watched from the waist positions, while Malcolm Crow looked rearward through his sights at the trailing American bombers. The territory below was German-occupied, and the 'plane began to receive hostile fire. Bob Hudson in the nose position was the first to see the bursts of flak as they approached the islands off the northern coast of Germany and the Jutland Peninsula. The Germans were beginning to get the range. The planes themselves were so high they could not be seen with the naked eye, but the German anti-aircraft gunners were aided by radar and rangefinders which made them deadly accurate.

'Almost an hour of flying time remained before they reached the target when Major Squyres' 'plane was hit by flak and went down. The loss of a squadron leader was a bad omen. Tension mounted and stomachs tightened as flak bursts increased about them. From his waist gun position, Johnny could see the "little friends" who were escorting them that day.

'As they approached the target area, the utter chaos of aerial combat blinded all reality. They were now squarely over the Third Reich and approaching a heavily defended industrial city. The flak that had been previously experienced was a minor annoyance compared to that which was about to be thrown at them. Hundreds of German gun positions were now plotting their course, and fighter squadrons of the Luftwaffe were scrambling to meet the invaders. To make matters worse, one B-24 group was forced to make two runs over the target. This double jeopardy would cost lives. Forty per cent of my father's squadron would be shot down in the next few minutes. Aside from the deafening roar of four engines in an uninsulated bomber, the additional noise and confusion were almost unbearable. Gunners became excited and hollered into the intercom as they saw German planes approach or witnessed the loss of a fellow bomber. The noisy clatter of machine gun fire almost drowned out the sounds of exploding flak nearby, but no one failed to hear the rattle of metal against the side of the bomber from a near miss. Soon to this confusion would be added flames, explosions, and screams of pain. They approached the target at high noon.

'The first to die was Robert P. Hudson, in the nose-gun position. Prior to the final approach over the target, the bomber could take a certain amount of evasive action to avoid the flak but for the last two minutes of the bomb run, it had to fly straight and level for the bombardier to sight on the target. Lt. Leonard Feingold was in the nose area just behind the nose gunner, leaning over his bomb sight, when the bomber was hit. A burst of flak took away the nose turret and with it the life of Bob Hudson. Feingold was undoubtedly rattled at the sudden appearance of a gaping hole where only moments before there had been a friend and fellow crew member. The wind whistled through the bomber with tremendous force, scattering maps, charts, papers and people about.

'Feingold regained his position over the sights and opened the bomb bay doors. The weather was clear, and visual bombing was possible. At exactly 12 noon, the bomb load was jettisoned on the enemy city. Pilot Curtis and co-pilot Donald Clift,

A burst of flak took away the nose turret and with it the life of Bob Hudson ... Feingold regained his position over the sights and opened the bomb bay doors. Pilot Curtis and co-pilot Donald Clift, with the bombs away, could now begin to take evasive action and perhaps escape. 1st Row L-R T/Sgt. R. P. Hudson; S/Sgt. H. I. Gauthier; S/Sgt. M. C. Maxton; S/Sgt. J. E. McGlone; S/Sgt. M. C. Crow. Standing, L-R: S/Sgt. E. E. Higgins; 2/ Lt. L. H. Feingold; 2/Lt. E. J. Moore; 2/Lt. D. Clift; 1/Lt. J. E. Curtis. (Dr. John McGlone)

with the bombs away, could now begin to take evasive action and perhaps escape, even with the nose blown away. But it was not to be.

'Seconds after the bombs were dropped, and with the bomb bay doors still open, another burst of flak hit the 'plane, entering through the open bomb bay doors and exploding in the mid section of the 'plane, setting the aircraft on fire in that area, half way between the radio room and the waist gun positions. First one engine and then a second was hit as the mortally crippled bomber dropped out of formation and began to lose altitude. Sgt. Eugene Higgins, the radio operator, was having his own private hell dealing with the flames in the radio room. He reported to Curtis

that the whole ship was on fire and the pilot sounded the alarm bell, a signal for all to hear that it was time for those who could bail out to do so. The co-pilot was trying to help Higgins put out the flames and at the same time reopen the bomb bay doors as an escape route. Clift lost consciousness in the process but later reported he had seen that Higgins was badly burned, without a parachute on, and still struggling with the flames in the radio room.

'Meanwhile, in the rest of the 'plane, all was confusion, noise, burning and death. The book says that the 'plane was hit and exploded, but there were several minutes between these events, minutes which must have seemed like an eternity for men about to die. Lt. Feingold was last seen with a parachute on, crouched over the nose wheel opening, ready to bail out. Others in a similar position, Curtis, Clift and Moore, survived even the explosion of the 'plane, when they were thrown clear, but not Lt. Feingold. He never made it to prison camp with the other officers. In view of Larry Maxton's report that some were killed on the ground, it is easy to conclude that Feingold made it out of the ship but could not make it past Nazi hatred of Jews. With the name Feingold on his dog tags, he was the last person who needed to be bailing out over German territory, but he did and was never seen alive again. Ominously, German burial records show most of the crew buried on 6 January 1944. Feingold was not buried until 13 January. The stricken plane was travelling at hundreds of miles per hour and the difference of a few seconds or minutes in bailout time could make a great difference in where one landed. If the landing was near a regular army unit, a person might be treated roughly but fairly, whereas a landing near some farmer who lost sons in the war might end fatally from a pitchfork or scythe. A survivor on another 'plane lost over Kiel that day told me that the town where he landed was governed by a raving lunatic of a Nazi who would certainly have caused an American's death, but he was away that day and the other villagers treated him with sympathy. It was a draw of the cards.

'It also made a vast difference what kind of parachute one was wearing (or not wearing). Lt. Curtis and the other officers aboard the plane had been wearing back-pack 'chutes as they went about their business of flying and navigating the 'plane. All survived, save Feingold. The enlisted men had chest pack 'chutes which they carried with them and had to put on before bailing out. The few seconds involved in this procedure apparently spelled the difference between life and death for at least some of the men. The official reports are filled with comments stating that the crew did not have time to don their chest 'chutes. In a few minutes it would not have mattered anyway, for they were now attacked by German fighters intent on finishing off the crippled bomber.

'S/Sgt. John McGlone reported the coming attack over the intercom. "Fighters coming in at six o'clock low."

'The official report of operations, written two days later, states that the bombers were subject to heavy attacks by 100 enemy fighters, mostly two-engine aircraft. Jim Curtis later described their attack as "savage". In order for Johnny to see them approaching from six o'clock from his left waist gun position, he had to be looking at an extreme angle and upward from his side position. His final thoughts are known to God, but one can imagine a grim determination as he sighted through the cross hairs and down the long barrel of his single, .50 calibre machine gun at approaching death.

'That he was still alive and at his gun position surprised the pilot, who thought that all the crew had already bailed out. Perhaps Crow in the tail and Gautier at the right waist were sighting at the same approaching 'planes as Johnny, since their

bodies were later found with the wreck. Maybe they were already dead. Johnny was certainly wounded and may have been the last gunner left alive in the slaughterhouse that had been a B-24. Either he couldn't, or wouldn't, get out, and since McGlone sighted and reported the coming fighters, it may be presumed that he made his last best effort to blow them to hell. In the next few seconds, McGlone's fight in extremis would be over. Those last moments are shrouded in the confusion of the uncontrolled roar of damaged engines, the chatter of machine gun fire, the choking, oily smoke and the twisting gyrations of the dying 'plane undoubtedly seen through dazed, bleary and pain-wracked eyes. Then, in a blinding flash, all was over. Johnny's soul was freed with the speed of light.

'He, and the others, had gone to their God like soldiers.

'The 'plane crashed in an open field near Krempechide that was used by the German Army for manoeuvres. The next day, Nazi soldiers cleared the wreckage and found the bodies of the gunners who "rode her in", McGlone, Gautier, Hudson, Crow and Maxton. Curtis, Clift and Moore had escaped the burning 'plane. They were thrown clear by an explosion and had been able to parachute to safety, or at least to the relative safety of PoW camp Stalag Luft I, where they spent the rest of the war. Two were still missing, Higgins and Feingold. Their bodies, "carbonised" as the local burgomeister later stated, would eventually be buried with the original five. Later, mortuary reports would describe crushed skulls, missing limbs and bullet-riddled bodies.

'In 1949, Johnny's remains were brought home to his final resting place in a national military cemetery. The mementoes began to accumulate. The flag that had covered his coffin, the Purple Heart, a certificate attesting to his valour, and now his name etched on a headstone. None of this fooled his mother. She carried the pain for the rest of her long life. They had killed her darling boy . . .'
'Flight To Eternity' by Dr. John McGlone Jr.

They'll never take my son again
Johnny, I swear this to you!

'Johnny, I hardly Knew Ye' (Irish Folksong)

MIA

Way down in Ruhr Valley where black mushrooms grow
Way down in Flak Valley where B Two Fours go
You're briefed in the morning
No fighters, no flak
But the boys that go down there
Will never come back.

'The dogs left behind by MIAs were starving and had to be shot, as they were raiding the Mess Halls.'
Maj. Newton L. Mclaughlin, Special Services Officer, 448th BG

'Sixty per cent of crews had no parachute training.'
Maj. Jim O'Brien, CO, 68th BS, 44th BG

'I became friends with Rocky Starek and the day he was shot down, 10 July, 1944, was my 10th birthday.'
Patricia Everson

'His crew was hit over France near Paris. They bailed out, hit the ground OK and were grabbed by the Free French. Instead of being hidden in a farm house, six of the crew were taken into Paris and hidden in a house of prostitution. This fellow said that when he was 20 years old he weighed 160 lbs. Several months later, when they were moved, he weighed 140 lbs. He said they could not be confined without sampling the merchandise.'
Larry Goldstein, radio operator, 388th BG

'I was always fascinated by the sight of bombs leaving the nearby 'planes. We reached the drop point and the bombardiers released the bombs using an interverlometer, a device that let the bombs out one at a time. As they fell, it would appear the bombs were stacked one above the other, suspended in space in a long stream, especially when they were stacked 52 high. I was looking directly at *Northern Lass* when flak set off the bottom bomb. It exploded and set off the one above it which in turn set off the next higher, and so on until the last exploded in or very close to the bomb bay. The 'plane fell out of formation and began to go down. Five men bailed out before the 'plane was brought under control. Lt J.P. Ferguson brought the badly damaged aircraft back to England and crash landed at Attlebridge.'
Lt. John W. McClane Jr., navigator, 44th BG, St Trond airfield, Belgium, 9 May 1944

'Three of our men were killed in the 'plane and six more were killed by German civilians when they touched down. I was almost killed by a farmer but a Frenchman talked him out of it.'
Kenneth M. Peiffer, tail gunner, 491st BG, Misburg Nov 1944

'As for my parachute entangled in the tree, we never found it. They say that several little girls in the neighbourhood had new dresses for school the next year.'
Fred Becchetti, 445th BG

'Contrary to the usual stories, my past life failed to flash through my mind. I was too busy fighting to keep that life.'
Lowell Watts, pilot, 388th BG

'It's a remarkable thing what goes through your mind when you bail out. I recalled the time I had signed on at 17. My mother had been very upset

```
                    WAR DEPARTMENT              LSS/mrb
              THE ADJUTANT GENERAL'S OFFICE
IN REPLY                    WASHINGTON
REFER TO
AG 201 Patton, Ralph K.
   (15 Jan 44) PC-N 017062              22 January 1944.

 Mrs. Viola M. Patton,
     1417 Mill Street,
         Wilkinsburg, Pennsylvania.

Dear Mrs. Patton:

            This letter is to confirm my recent telegram in which you were
regretfully informed that your son, Second Lieutenant Ralph K. Patton,
0-680,283, Air Corps, has been reported missing in action over France
since 5 January 1944.

            I know that added distress is caused by failure to receive more
information or details. Therefore, I wish to assure you that at any time
additional information is received it will be transmitted to you without
delay, and, if in the meantime no additional information is received, I
will again communicate with you at the expiration of three months. Also,
it is the policy of the Commanding General of the Army Air Forces upon re-
ceipt of the "Missing Air Crew Report" to convey to you any details that
might be contained in that report.

            The term "missing in action" is used only to indicate that the
whereabouts or status of an individual is not immediately known. It is
not intended to convey the impression that the case is closed. I wish to
emphasize that every effort is exerted continuously to clear up the status
of our personnel. Under war conditions this is a difficult task as you
must readily realize. Experience has shown that many persons reported
missing in action are subsequently reported as being prisoners of war.
However, since we are entirely dependent upon governments with which we
are at war to forward this information, the War Department is helpless
to expedite these reports.

            In order to relieve financial worry on the part of the depend-
ents of military personnel being carried in a missing status, Congress
enacted legislation which continues the pay, allowances and allotments
of such persons until their status is definitely established.

            Permit me to extend to you my heartfelt sympathy during this
period of uncertainty.
```

and had said, "You'll probably end up getting shot down." '
Orlo Natvig, radio operator, 91st BG

'The ship was on fire. The pilot gave the order to abandon. Since I already had my chest pack on I probably was the first to get out. I kicked out the escape hatch and was gone. Four others managed to get out before the plane disintegrated.'
Clyde Crowley, bombardier, 95th BG

'I asked my co-pilot to unbuckle my seat belts before he bailed out. Just as he stood up to do so a 20 mm cannon shell cut him in half.'
William Bruce, 445th BG, Kassel, 27 September 1944

> *When you've feathered your third prop*
> *and there are Focke Wulfs up top*
> *Then it's time for you to stop*
> *Because friend – you've had it*
>
> *If you land in sight of Dover*
> *and some Nordic type sea rover*
> *Says 'For you the War is Over'*
> *Then friend, you've had it*

'I turned around and saw a German soldier on one knee with his rifle pointed at me. I threw up my hands. He came toward me, still holding his rifle on me and said the words I dreaded to hear.
   "For you the war is over." '
Lt. Loren E. Jackson, pilot, Crash Wagon III, *551st BS, 385th BG*

> *T'was May the ninth that I did spring*
> *from a B-24 with a burning wing*
> *Into the cold I leapt, nine thirty exact*
> *Midst a silence interrupted only by flak*
>
> *Belgium lay 20,000 feet below*
> *Dimly visible in the sun's early glow*
> *Jerry was thick there as everyone knew*
> *But nothing to worry about – so said S-2*
>
> *The farmlands near Liege awaited my descent*
> *I steered the 'chute as down I went*
> *A quick reconnoitre on reaching the ground*
> *Did not disclose the enemy around.*

'I told myself that I had better pull the ripcord. When my 'chute opened I looked for other parachutes and they were all tiny specks above me. One of the 109s flew past me at about 50 yds distant.

The pilot took a good look at me and flew on.'
Carl Grosshell, 491st BG

'I was helpless as the FW 190 streaked past. He couldn't have cleared us by more than six feet. We were in the High Right Squadron and I could see the fighters attacking the lead squadron like a swarm of bees . . . At this time I heard the bail-out bell ringing, so I got out of the turret and found the navigator, putting on his 'chute. The whole nose compartment looked like a sieve. Those exploding 20 mms had blown up right between us but neither of us were hit. By this time we were nosing down and the whole left wing was on fire. We opened the nosewheel door and bailed out. I hadn't really looked at the ground until I saw our ship crash. I then realised that the ground was coming up rapidly. We had been trained to hit going forward and roll up in a ball. However, I was unable to reverse my direction and hit going backwards. My feet and fanny hit just about like a machine gun. Had I landed as I had been trained, I'm sure I would have had three tongues in my shoes because I hit so fast and so hard.'
George M. Collar, 445th BG, Kassel, 27 September 1944

' . . . I noticed an unusual red glow in the sky around us. As I turned my head to the right, through my co-pilot's window, I saw a parachute floating down. Then the 'plane in front of us burst into flames. Other parachutes appeared on all sides. Suddenly, a FW 190 swooped in front of us from underneath and behind. At the same time my arm was being pounded by my co-pilot, Newell Brainard. One engine was on fire; while working to feather the prop, other German fighters came into view. All around us was on fire.. .black smoke . . . 'planes going down . . . more parachutes . . . machine guns firing . . . the shudder of 20mm . . . shells hitting . . . another engine gone . . . intercom out . . . 'plane out of control . . . a gripping fear – near panic . . . then, fire!'
1/Lt. Raphael E. Carrow, 445th BG, Kassel, 27 September 1944

' . . . In an orchard, there, lying on the ground, was the body of one of our fliers . . . The victim had obviously been blown out of the 'plane as he landed without a 'chute. Every bone in his body was broken . . . We travelled up and down the hills and forests all day, picking up approximately a dozen bodies, some of them horribly mangled. In the middle of an open field we came across a radioman. He had a bad leg wound but came down in his 'chute. He was lying in a pool of blood and was dead.'

George Collar, 445th BG, Kassel, 27 September 1944

'We were told that if we happened to be shot down in Germany to surrender to the first uniformed person we met, even if a postman. The Germans were very disciplined and respected anyone of authority, but the civilian population did not take kindly to airmen bombing the Fatherland, killing thousands of their relatives and friends. Many a downed airman was murdered before he could surrender.'

1/Lt. John W. McClane Jr., navigator, 44th BG

'We had just dropped our bombs and made a turn off the target. We received several hits by flak, then a direct hit in number three gas' tank. The 'plane caught fire immediately and Lt. Veal called, "Bail Out!" over the interphone.

'We started falling out of formation and the 'plane exploded. I was in the tail and it blew the tail off. I bailed out a little later. The navigator, Lt. Don Johns, was blown out from the nose; fortunately he had his parachute on. Just after I landed on the ground I was captured and taken to Wehrmacht HQ.

'I was questioned by a German officer. A little later I was taken and shown five of the bodies of the men I flew with. I recognized two of them. They were Lt. Veal and Sgt. Hord. The rest were too badly burnt and mangled to recognize. Later that night I was told that they found the other two bodies but they did not show me these. They told me that one other man had bailed out but wouldn't tell me which one it was so I couldn't be sure who got out. Next day I was taken to Pinneberg, Germany and put in the hospital for a severe back injury.

'On 4 April I was taken with 29 other men to Stalag Luft I at Barth. Lt. Johns was in this group of men. That is when I learned who was the other survivor. He did not know if anyone else got out or not.'

Sgt. Robert A. Herman, tail gunner, 832nd BS, 486th BG, Hamburg, 30 March 1945

'Write a big letter/Send it to me ... care of/ Stalag Luft Three.' (Ron Kramer)

KRIEGIE

'Write a big letter
Send it to me
Send it in care of
Stalag Luft Three.'

Second verse of 'Down In Ruhr Valley'

'An old woman asked the soldier if I was an Englander. When he said I was American she exclaimed, "American Devil!"'
Lee Gordon, ball gunner, 305th BG

'At Frankfurt (Oberussel) we were put in solitary confinement, interrogated and accused of being spies unless we gave the information our interrogators needed. I said my dog tags were proof enough and refused to answer any questions. Finally, I was handed a piece of paper with answers to most of the questions and told to sign it. I refused and was taken back to my eight ft by 13 ft cell. The truth was they knew more about what was going on than I did.'
William Sterrett, 100th BG

'A life sentence.'
Capt. Ronald V. Kramer, 448th BG on arrival on 29 May at Stalag Luft III

'One of my most poignant memories is of Christmas Eve 1944. The Germans permitted us to be out until nine o'clock that night (normally we were locked up in our blocks at 6:00 p.m.). We were visiting back and forth, greeting our friends and wishing each other a Merry Christmas. We expressed our strong conviction (and ardent hope) that the Germans just could not hold out much longer. One memory in camp during the Yuletide season is the Kriegie parody on the song "I'll Be Home For Christmas".'
PoW

We won't be home for Christmas,
Don't depend on us.
We'll have snow
But no mistletoe
Or presents on the tree.
Christmas Eve will find us
Standing at appell,
We won't be home for Christmas,
We know that very well.

'In the Stalag Luft I we were allowed to write very few letters and postcards per month. I received a few letters from my mother and aunt but none from my wife. Up to a year after I was released from captivity her letters were returning to us. It appeared that most of them had not left the US. I had received one book parcel from my wife with two books censored out.'
Dean H. Sanner, Mosquito pilot, 25th BG

'I have been living with a private since you are gone. Please don't cut off your allotment as he does not make as much as you.'

'I will be glad when you get home so I can make our divorce final. I've been living with an infantry Captain for a time as he is swell.'

'I'm sure they are treating you well because they tell me so here in the US.'

'You can consider our engagement at an end. I'd rather be engaged to a 1944 hero than a 1943 coward.'

'I went down to the Red Cross the other day to see what I could send you. They told me that you could probably send me packages as you have so much food and clothes over there now. They also said that you could go to school and learn a trade.'

'I know I should have kept you home and joined the Air Force myself. Even when you were a kid I expected you to end up in prison.'
Extracts of letters received by PoWs. Dean H. Sanner

'I'm sorry a prisoner of war received the sweater I knitted. I made it for a fighting man.'
Reply to a letter of thanks from the PoW after receiving the sweater from a woman through the Red Cross

Emily Post
c/o Daily Mirror
New York City

Dear Miss Post,

I am a P.O.W in Germany and one of the main foods that the Germans give us is barley. Often, due to the season, of course, one finds large worms in his barley. I would like to find the correct way of disposing of said worms. Some say to go ahead and eat them rapidly. If I do this, I vomit. Others say to nonchalantly place them on the side of the bowl. If I do this everyone else vomits.

Please set me straight.

Sincerely

P.O. Dubyu

Letter composed by a PoW as a joke

A crowd was there when he stopped his crate
'Where am I?' he asked, 'It sure looks great.'
'Why where,' they asked, 'Were you heading for?
This my boy is Stalag Luft IV.'

Willie Green's Flying Machine

When half parcels are the thing
And there will be no mail 'till spring
If it's verboten not to sing
My sympathy – you've had it

When the bells ring out the cheer
If the boat just left the pier
and you're still looking for a souvenir
Then chum – you've really had it.

'We received a little horse meat once in a while, a few potatoes, rutabagas, salt, German brown bread, ersatz coffee, some sugar and ground barley. The bread was extremely heavy even after the sawdust and wood slivers were brushed and picked off. It could be sliced less than a quarter of an inch thick. The ground barley was always a treat. We boiled it in a bucket all day so it would swell up to many times its original volume . . .

'We were so hungry that we could not keep our minds off food and recipes. We all became expert cooks in our minds and our conversations often centred on food. Everyone got out their little blue Red Cross books and wrote down marvellous menus. Our diet consisted of four thin slices of very black bread, only about an eighth of an inch thick, and a bowl of soup a day. As a consequence, I lost about 45lbs in weight.

'There was a period of six weeks to two months when Red Cross parcels were not delivered and things got pretty bleak. There was a cat that used to wander around the compound. It disappeared during this time. I was told it tasted like rabbit.'
Dean H. Sanner, PoW, Stalag Luft I

'The quarters in the South Compound at Luft III were terrible. Two hundred men were living in barracks containing 16 rooms with one night

latrine each. The rooms were dim, smoky and poorly ventilated. Several of the men went crazy from the confinement; others developed complexes.'
Karl Wendel

'I was given a bowl and spoon and cooked my meals in the washroom near my bunk. With others cooking, the room became quite smoky. We had no cooking stove at this time. We got hot water from the camp kitchen and the Germans gave us boiled potatoes or boiled rutabagas for our noon and evening meals. Sometimes we would get spinach or pea soup. The pea soup had bugs in it and we threw most of it out or gave it to the Russian PoWs. They were so hungry they ate it eagerly.

'Every day we got a ration of dark bread from the Germans. I would try a piece and put a slice of cheese and fried Spam on it. It was good. Sometimes we got blood sausage but I did not eat much of it. A few mornings we got barley for breakfast.'
John L. Hurd, ball turret gunner, 401st BG, shot down on his 11th mission, to Politz, on April 1 1944. Stalag 17B Krems, winter 1944

'Our barley ration to the kitchen has been cut 28 per cent and "spuds" 15 per cent. There are enough Red Cross parcels for a couple more issues and they are being given out one for two men per week. Most of the time we get spuds once a day. The other two meals we get hot water. Living conditions are poor. There is good news from the fighting fronts. Maybe we won't be here much longer.'
John L. Hurd, diary entry, March 9 1945

'The march was a nightmare. Our German guards were as miserable as we were and many wanted to escape with PoWs, but we had orders to remain together as a group. When Roll Call was taken at Stalag Luft VIIA, Moosburg, 31 South Compound men were missing, having escaped using "X" Committee maps, compasses and equipment distributed before the march began.'
Col. Delmar Spivey

'When we stopped for our five to 10 minute rest each hour, many of the inexperienced PoWs would kneel in the centre of the road and start rocking back and forth on their hands and knees, not knowing they were freezing to death. I and some others did everything we could to get them back on their feet. We dragged them, kicked them in the

"fanny", swore at them — anything that would cause a spark to get them moving.'
Frank Cotner, 466th BG PoW, on the 'Death March' from Stalag Luft III, winter 1945

'The Germans said they would shoot stragglers. Very tired, I kept numbly plodding like the others, concentrating on each step.'
Bob O'Hearn, 306th BG PoW, on the 'Death March' from Stalag Luft III, winter 1945

'A most wonderful day; the 609th day of imprison-

Behold, I will rain bread from heaven for you (Author's Collection)

ment. The war was still going on but for us, as the German lady wistfully said on the day I was captured, "For you der war is over."'
Bob O'Hearn, 306th BG PoW, day of liberation, April 1945

'So here's to happy days ahead,
When you and I are free.
To look back on this interlude
And call it history.'

J B Boyle, written in POW camp

'We were assigned to the Green Project — recovery of Allied PoWs from the west coast of France where camps had been set up and named Camp Lucky Strike, Camel and Chesterfield, etc., after cigarette packets. We flew over and if we could identify any 92nd personnel we could bring them back to the base. Every day we sent a B-17 over. One day I got to go. It was strange to see these men who had been PoWs for years. I heard that Maxwell, my co-pilot on my first tour, who I had gone overseas with and who had been shot down flying with another crew, had been liberated by the Russians. He had taken off and no-one had seen or heard of him since. Then it was decided that high point infantrymen were to be flown home by the 92nd from Istres near Marseilles. The airfield had been built by the Germans and there were many mines in the area. We drove flocks of sheep over the fields to explode them for us. The sheep herder was paid for the number of sheep that were killed. There were no barracks so we lived in tents. Seats were installed in the B-17 bomb bays and we could carry about 36 men from Istres to Cassablanca, where MATS took over to Brazil and Miami.'
Bill Rose, 327th BS, 92nd BG

MANNA

'Behold, I will rain bread from heaven for you.'

Exodus 16.

'A truce was arranged. We were ordered to reconstruct and strengthen the huge bomb bay doors in order that each bomber could carry 4,500 lb of canned "C" rations in 50-lb cases. They were to be dropped in a free fall from an altitude of 300 ft on a bomb-scarred airstrip west of Amsterdam.

Armaments were not to be carried.

'As the B-17s crossed the coast of the Netherlands, the 900 combat veterans were scared. Was it a trick? Was this to be where the propaganda machine of Herr Goebbels would bolster the Third Reich? By the destruction of 100 bombers in one blow? The dykes had been blown a few days before to bog down a possible land invasion by the Allies.

'At dawn this bright sunshiny morning a Flying Fortress named, *Not Today-Cleo*, lumbered with an unusual cargo – would its bomb bay doors hold the shifting weights of the canned delights? There was to be radio silence. As the B-17s approached the European coast, the 'planes were low enough that rolls of barbed wire could be seen, strung for miles along the beaches. Uniformed German soldiers were patrolling, but only glanced up at the aluminium birds. The airmen began to rest easier at no sign of the deadly ack ack guns. All of a sudden, the intercoms were alive with laughter and joy.

"Look at 3 o'clock!" someone hollered.

'The bombers were flying over thousands of tulips in full bloom. Some Dutchmen, or maybe lots of them, had removed part of the tulips in a huge field. Plainly spelled out so it could be clearly read from the air, but not on the ground, were special words which said, THANKS YANKS. The crews were exultant.

'As the four engines roared at full throttle over the airstrip, hundreds – no, thousands – of what looked like little matchboxes tumbled from the 'planes ahead. They were the "C" rations. As they hit, broke open, and scattered wildly, cheers could be heard. Thousands of people lined the roads outside the airstrip barriers; they were not to collect the food gifts until the drop was complete.

'A native was riding a bicycle on a dyke. He looked up, the cycle turned, he rode into a canal.

'In Europe, cows were staked on a chain 20 to 30 ft long to graze. One ran in fright. As she came to the end of the chain, she went tumbling head over heels. In England's eastern counties cows were used to low-flying 'planes, either landing or taking off. The noise would not have caused a stir.

'As the 'planes thundered over the city of Amsterdam, again the Germans were noticed, some on foot, some in tanks or other war vehicles. On the roof of a 10-storey building stood people waving and holding the "Stars and Stripes", all unseen by the enemy in the streets.

'What a glorious way for the Dutch to express their gratitude to a handful of Yanks. The 'planes turned northward across the Zeider Zee, the North Sea and back to base at Deopham Green in East Anglia. In a few days Churchill announced to the world that victory in Europe was at hand.'
Jim French, B-17 tail gunner, 452nd BG

'We flew three or four mercy missions to Holland until the end of hostilities, carrying food. One of them was before the Germans surrendered. They had promised us a corridor to fly across the country unmolested at low level. We could see German troops marching around in their black uniforms with swastikas flying.

'Our second mercy mission was on 5 May, the day the Germans in Holland surrendered. We taxied out in the usual manner when the hydraulic system on the ship stopped working. The ship in front of us stopped and it looked as if we couldn't avoid running into her. Ancinolli, the bombardier, and Robascowitz, the navigator, were having a fit trying to get out of the nose. The co-pilot was madly stamping on the brakes and I was having a fit reaching around trying to throw all the switches in the cockpit. Several gunners standing behind my seat were sweating blood. We finally restored the hydraulic system and stopped the ship in the last possible fraction of a second. Erwin Jones, a college classmate from my home town and a lieutenant in an air defence company at Thorpe Abbotts, was riding in the very front of the ship in the glass nose, oblivious to all our troubles. After we had finally stopped, he calmly turned around and innocently asked the navigator if we weren't awfully close. The navigator couldn't answer; he wasn't able to breath yet!

'We went in at 200 ft, buzzing a small sail boat on the Zeider Zee and blowing it over. We had orders not to drop unless we saw crowds of civilians, but the Dutch were lined up around the edges of the field waving and cheering. They had really turned out. Flags were flying everywhere and the streets were packed with people waving and cheering. It was a great day for the Dutch. We dropped our 4,000 lb of food after trouble with the improvised "drop doors" in the bomb bay. We buzzed Amsterdam a couple of times. O'Leary, who was riding up front in the nose where he could get a better view of the town, called over the interphone, "Church steeple coming in at 12 o'clock high!"

'I remember a little Dutch boy looking up and trying to race us on his bicycle. There were 'planes ahead of us who made their drops and people were

running across the target area to get the food, unmindful of the fact that they could be knocked to Kingdom Come with a can of Spam. [A German soldier threw a Dutch girl to the ground and shielded her with his own body on one such overshoot. The overshoot hit and killed him but the Dutch girl survived.] 'Planes all around us were starting to drop their food but our 'plane flew across the field without any salvo. The bombardier had gone to sleep! He awoke with a jerk and made the drop into the Zuider Zee. Such folly, but how typical. The best of intentions, the worst in execution. I hoped the forthcoming peace would be better than that!'
Bill Carleton, 351st Squadron Engineering Officer, 100th BG

THE LUCKY BASTARDS

'There was never a good war or a bad peace.'

Benjamin Franklin

The white ball goes up for entrance into The Lucky Bastard Club. (the late Marvin Barnes)

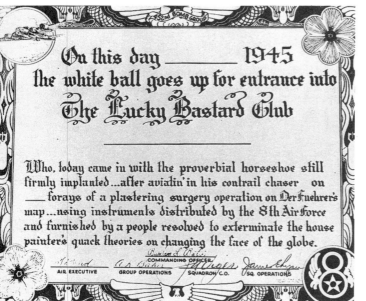

On this day _____ 1945 the white ball goes up for entrance into The Lucky Bastard Club

_____

Who, today came in with the proverbial horseshoe still firmly implanted...after aviatin' in his contrail chaser on _____ forays of a plastering surgery operation on Der Fuehrer's map...using instruments distributed by the 8th Air Force and furnished by a people resolved to exterminate the house painter's quack theories on changing the face of the globe.

'We were convinced that nothing could be changed about the outcome of the war. The war was completely lost . . . we knew it could only take a few more days. On the other hand, we had the most advanced, far superior aircraft . . . the first operational jet. We saw that the German population had to suffer under horrifying attacks without any hope day and night. Having the best fighters in the world ready to take off we couldn't sit down and tell the people, no . . . we won't take off any more because the war is lost. It was a moral question for us. We had to go into combat.'
Generalmajor Adolf Galland. CO, Jet Fighter Wing 44 equipped with Me 262s

'All wars are senseless and yet, World War Two was unavoidable. We had gained victory not necessarily through superior intellect but rather through the will to win and the belief that we were in the right. Like all human endeavours, we were fraught with frustration and at times, saddled with stupidity, but the love of man and the love of our country brought forth accomplishments and sacrifices beyond man's own comprehension.'
Bill Carleton, 351st Squadron Engineering Officer, 100th BG

'I cried as they fired rockets to celebrate VE Day. My mother explained they were so happy to be going home.'
Patricia Everson

'The 100th BG was known throughout the land not because we were superhuman but rather because we were human. Our fame and notoriety spread not just because of Regensburg or Berlin or the Russian mission, but also because of our losses, and yes, even because of our "faux pas". We were famous and to some of the new flyers, infamous both for what we did and what we gave. Mighty as we were with our 70 to 80 bombers and our 4,000 men, we were but a small fraction of the total force ultimately applied against the Axis Powers. We contributed our part and it was our knowledge and belief that others were making an even greater sacrifice that assured us of ultimate victory.'
Bill Carleton, 351st Squadron Engineering Officer, 100th BG

'Sacrifice cannot be transmitted into cold figures. We who are left can take pride in our work and efforts. We were part of a tremendous and magnificent cause. Many were with us who did not come back. We shall not forget them. We served

together at a great moment of history. Their sacrifice will light us down the years.'
CO, 96th Wing in a letter to Col. Shower, 467th BG

I cried as they fired rockets to celebrate VE Day. My mother explained they were so happy to be going home. (Pat Everson)

'I never had a bad conscience about it as the Nazis had no qualms about sending V-2 rockets into England that plummeted out of the sky at 3,000 m.p.h., exploding with no warning whatsoever. It's easy to say that what we did today was wrong but remember this was war and we were just young boys playing the game.'
Lt. John H. McClane Jr., navigator, 44th BG

THE OBSERVATION TOUR, BY AIR, OVER FRANCE, BELGIUM AND PART OF GERMANY IS TO SHOW YOU THE RESULTS, EITHER DIRECT OR INDIRECT, OF YOUR EFFORTS OF THE PAST MANY MONTHS FOR VICTORY FOR THE ALLIES. (Thorpe Abbotts Memorial Museum)

'Today I feel a sense of pride in having played a small part in the great drama of those days that truly belong to history. I formed friendships which have endured throughout the passing years with some of the finest men I have ever met. Many of our squadron mates suffered long imprisonment or gave their lives for our cause.'
Abe Dolim, navigator, 94th BG

'The US Army representatives didn't accept them, unfortunately.'
Generalmajor Adof Galland after he had offered the Allies two Me 262 units intact, located at Saltzburg and Innsbruck, Austria.

'THE OBSERVATION TOUR, BY AIR, OVER FRANCE, BELGIUM AND PART OF GERMANY IS TO SHOW YOU THE RESULTS, EITHER DIRECT OR INDIRECT, OF YOUR EFFORTS OF THE PAST MANY MONTHS FOR VICTORY FOR THE ALLIES AND THE FREEDOMS THEY REPRESENT. DURING THE TOUR THE NAVIGATOR WILL KEEP YOU POSTED AS TO THE AREA YOU ARE OVER. THE FOLLOWING IS TO FURTHER ASSIST YOU IN IDENTIFYING THE NOT-SO-LONG-AGO TARGETS ... THE RETURN IS VIA BRUSSELS AND YOU WILL DEPART THE COAST AT CAP GRIS NEZ, FRANCE. PASSING THE STRAITS OF DOVER THE ENGLISH COAST IS ENTERED AT DUGNESS [sic], SE FROM LONDON. NOTE WINDSON [sic] CASTLE AND THE BEAUTIFUL COUNTRY ESTATES AS YOU COME HOME TO BASE AROUND THE WEST OF LONDON. DO NOT CARRY YOUR CHUTE BY THE RED HANDLE'

Ruhr Observation ('Cooks Tour' or 'Trolly' mission) for ground crews of the 8th Air Force, May 1945

'After the final inspection, four American and four British airmen stood to attention at the flagpole. One lone bugler played and the American flag was lowered for the last time, and the British flag raised for the first. This seemed to me a very quiet and unpretentious ceremony to end the three years of occupation by the 44th BG of Shipdham. Three months after the end of hostilities, and several air bases later, our Chemical Company got aboard a rusty old Liberty ship at Liverpool for our trip home. It looked like a luxury liner to us.'

Roxy Marotta, 806th Chemical Company

Our Chemical Company got aboard a rusty old Liberty ship at Liverpool for our trip home. It looked like a luxury liner to us. (Author's Collection)

I flew a couple of aircraft to Lowry ... and the graveyard at Kingman, Arizona, where there seemed to be 5,000 or more. (USAF Official)

Goodbye G.I. Bud. Now you know the way
Come back and see us in a brighter day.
When England's free and the
Scotch is cheap but strong,
And you can bring your pretty wives along.

Goodbye G.I. don't leave us quite alone.
Somewhere in England we must write in stone
How Britain was invaded by the Yanks
And under that 'a big and hearty thanks'

A.P. Herbert, a famous English historian, for the opening of the American Red Cross Club in London in 1945

'I flew a couple of aircraft to Lowry AAF, Denver, Colorado and the graveyard at Kingman, Arizona, where there seemed to be 5,000 or more. Many more later I suppose.'
Seward M. Meintesma, ex-466th BG and trainee B-29 crewmember, USA, 1945

This ancient relic of the Second World War
Crept across the room and slouched at the bar
And in hollow tones from his sunken chest
He demanded a drink, and only the best

The people said nothing but watched the glass
As the beggar produced his bombsight pass
The glass to his lips they heard him say
'Bomb Bays open! Bombs Away!'

Right: *Goodbye G.I. Bud. Now you know the way/Come back and see us in a brighter day. (Frank Thomas [on steps with his sister, Geraldine and mother Lucinda Elizabeth Thomas; Evansville, Indiana, August 1945].)*

Then without a word he slouched through the door
And the last of the bombardiers was seen no more
But all through the years, the phrase has stuck
When you say 'Bombardier' you add, 'Tough Luck.'

THE TIES THAT BIND

The roar of planes and the sight of flares
This sound is still with us after all these years
You now have visited that same little spot
That none of you have ever forgot
With friends of old and some so new
It's been a pleasure meeting you

Pedar Larsen, 96th BG

The atmosphere was ghostly, building doors left open, some furniture still left in situation, curtains blowing in the wind, ashes in the tortoise stoves. (Author's Collection)

'The atmosphere was ghostly, building doors left open, some furniture still left in situation, curtains blowing in the wind, ashes in the tortoise stoves. Magazines on the floor, roadways deserted, the hospital empty; nothing remained alive ... Daily we visited our old haunts, the control tower, the fire station, where a few weeks earlier we had enjoyed coffee and eggs. All was silent. We walked the whole airfield hoping we were wrong; they would be back. Alas, it was not to be. Realization eventually came but still we visited our beloved Thorpe Abbotts.'

Billy Taylor, Suffolk schoolboy

'I was alone in the Tower in the ground floor front room, at about 1:45 p.m., paint brush in hand. A breeze came through the room, then noises started, with aircraft engines, radios (RT) followed by men shouting. I was oblivious to anything else other than the noise, but I must say that prior to this, five minutes before, I had glanced out of the window and thought what a wonderful day it was. What seemed ages, but was a few seconds or so. I left the Tower at 1:55p.m. and headed straight home. My wife Jane was surprised to see me home so early. I did not tell her at that time but did tell her later. Mike Harvey, Ron Batley and I have all experienced an unusual atmosphere at the Tower prior to the dedication.'

Sam Hurry (Diss schoolboy in World War Two), 100th BG Memorial Museum, Thorpe Abbotts

'September 1955. He got off the bus at the King's Head in Shipdham, looked around at what should have been a familiar sight. He walked slowly up the narrow dirt road towards the air base. The wind was damp and cold, the grey clouds scudding low, the fields already harvested, wet, forlorn and inhospitable. Just as it used to be in those memorable months.

'The grey, damp runway was silent and seemed to sulk. Through the seams of the concrete grew weeds. He stood at the end of the runway, looked up its length, felt the tears coming to his eyes. Only 10 years ago it had been full of life, engines roaring as the big bombers lifted off with their lethal loads, wings whistling, landing gear retracting. Now all was silent but for the mournful wind, now it seemed as though it were in mourning.

'Turning left, he soon came to the grove of trees where *Southern Comfort* used to stand. Shutting his eyes, he saw it again, men clustered around the silver ship, busily covering the flak holes, working on the engines, filling the gas' tanks, loading the bombs.

'At the corner where the Aero Club had stood there was nothing. Only the pool remained to mark the spot. The pool where they had thrown in the officers to celebrate the 200th mission. The Aero Club was one of the few pleasant places on the airfield, and it was good to remember it.

'Across the way his squadron huts had been cleared away, the land was now being farmed. His memory filled his mind with the comrades who had laughed and joked and played tricks on each other, the little stove that had barely heated a few feet of the cold hut but had been able to make their coffee and toast their bread.

'The hangars were silent, hostile. He walked past them to the control tower. All the window glass had been broken. Warily, he walked up the debris-filled stairs. Standing on the edge of the observation deck, his eyes slowly roamed around the desolate field, stopping at the dispersal stand across the runways where his ships used to sit. There he and his crew used to wait for the signal to fly or abort. There they waited while the sky to the east turned from blackness to a dull grey. There they had waited for the sound of a pop and a green flare to rise into the day, telling them the mission was "on", or a red flare to tell them the mission was "scrubbed". All the while they waited, the sky larks were singing their welcome to the dawn, rising up and up and then falling to a few feet above the ground, again and again, singing their hearts joy to the world.

'When the green flares would rise to tell them the mission was about to start, they would climb into the cold ship, shivering with fear, hiding their fear with forced smiles and laughter. The engines would be warmed, their roar rising and lowering like hungry lions. Then they would join the long line of bomb-laden ships waiting to rise into the sky while the men inside smiled and joked and shook with fear.

'Wiping his tears from his eyes, he descended the stairs and walked with quickened steps to the 14th Bomb Wing HQ area, trying to wipe his memories from his mind. Pushing open a door that leaned on one hinge, he walked into his former barracks. Standing in the doorway, his eyes roamed over the long room, the steel struts of the roof, gloom dripping from the bare rafters. The silence seemed to scream at him.

'The door to "Doc" Douglas's room was open beside him. He stepped into it, over some rusted window frames; his eyes quickly surveyed the dusty floor, the dirt streaked walls, the rain-stained roof. "Doc" used to be extremely tidy – he would be shocked to see it now. Then his eyes stopped on the graffiti. "Bloody Yanks, stay home with your filthy minds, your wads of money, your hands off our women. Rot in hellfire, damn you."

'It was as though he had been struck on the head with a heavy implement. His eyes blurred for a few moments, his blood surged through his brain, he felt a fever in his eyes. Turning, he walked out the door, his mind churning as he strode purposefully back to the King's Head.

'Inside the pub he ordered a pint of 'alf and 'alf', walked to the fireplace and sat next to the fire. His head bowed, he sipped on the beer slowly, but he could not erase the sight of the bitter graffiti. He finished his beer without enjoying it, placed the empty glass on the bar without looking at the barmaid and walked out the door silently.'
Jacob Elias, 44th BG, Shipdham

- - - - - - -

'There's a "GHOST American airfield" in England, just down the road from the modern US jet base at Alconbury, and it's fast becoming a favourite Yank tourist haunt.

'The installation – at Polebrook, 60 miles north of London – was a beehive of activity during World War Two, when it served as the HQ of an American outfit. Today, it is as deserted as a haunted house.

'Jet-age Yank airmen with a hankering to be transported back into history have only to visit the base to get a hair-raising reminder of how things

There's a 'GHOST American airfield' in England, and it's fast becoming a favourite Yank tourist haunt. The installation – at Polebrook, 60 miles north of London -- was a beehive of activity during World War Two. (Author's Collection)

must have been there during the war.

'Some 50 buildings stand empty and deserted on the erstwhile busy base, their windows shattered and their doors creaking eerily on rusted hinges.

'Pigeons dart insanely about the bare interiors, with bats and field mice their only company. Inside the barracks, grass has forced its way up through the warped floor boards.

'Out by the runway, a tattered windsock still flutters above the old wartime flightline but has fallen prey to weeds. The roar of B-17s has long since gone.

'Polebrook, like many of the RAF bases hastily erected during the early World War Two days, has lain idle and uninhabited since the war.

'Everything remains just as it was left back at war's end in 1945, the huge hangars standing black and foreboding amid their silent surroundings and scores of old bomb shelters dot the landscape like rows of tombs.

'Strange, incongruous signs like "Barbershop" and "Chapel" dangle from the pre-fabricated huts here and there, but the sounds of snipping shears and hymnal voices have long been silent.

'In a huge building that apparently served as the officers' Mess, the ghosts virtually come alive as paintings on the wall evoke memories of yesteryear.

'A sign over a dusty counter identifies one room as the "Oasis Bar" and the insignia identifies the last tenant as the 351st BG.

'On the walls are listed the raids the 351st participated in against the Germans, along with the date and number of Nazi aircraft destroyed. Names like Amiens and Hamburg and Berlin are repeated often and alongside a Schweinfurt raid on 17 August 1943 are painted 25 swastikas, one for each Messerschmitt shot down.

'Another insignia of the 351st hangs over the door – a golden eagle with bombs clutched in its talons – and against the opposite wall is the familiar emblem of the US 8th Air Force.

'The haunting atmosphere of the abandoned B-17 base so excites the imagination of some visitors that they swear they are able to detect the roar of Flying Fortresses coming in for a landing – mission completed.'
'Stars & Stripes', 6 October 1958

*St Andrews Church meant a great deal to me during the war and also played an important part in our missions. On our return we knew when we saw the church steeple that we were almost home safe. (*National Geographic*)*

'It was like a dream come true for me to go back to England and see the people who had meant so much. You become close to people very quickly when you're in a life and death situation.

'Now there are no 'planes on the hardstand at Snetterton Heath. The old runway is a racing circuit with the roar of racing cars and cycles replacing the roar of our engines as we lined up to take off on a mission. The living quarters have been demolished and that land is now used for farming. Only three bomb shelters remain. These were used when our field was strafed or when a buzz bomb engine stopped overhead – it was then that we ran for cover!

'The motor pool building, the parachute rigging silo, the operations building and a pile of large timbers stored in the woods are all that remain of the old base.

'St Andrews Church meant a great deal to me during the war and also played an important part in our missions. On our return we knew when we saw the church steeple that we were almost home safe.

'Snetterton Heath echoes to the roars of racing cars and the cheers of crowds, but the volume of all that will never drown those two years 40 years ago.

That's part of our heritage as much as it is yours. It's always going to be that way, and if you doubt that the association will ever fade, then go out to Snetterton Heath in the dark hours as dawn is breaking and the first light of day cracks the eastern horizon, and the mists wrap themselves around the old Norfolk oaks and there's a pinch in the air. Then, in your mind's eye, you can see them – you can see *5 Grand, Wabbit Tracks, Fertile Myrtle* and all the other bombers roaring their way into the sky over the Norfolk fields, carrying their lethal loads. That's an association that will never die – those ghosts will be there long after you and I have been gone for generations.'
Peder Larsen, 96th BG

'Dedicated to the men of the US Army Air Forces, Station 118, who
through their efforts, devotion and duty, aided in bringing
victory to the Allies in World War Two.'

Inscription on the 392nd BG memorial obelisk, Wendling, Norfolk

GLOSSARY

A Bag	barracks bag	Jug	short for Juggernaut, P-47
AFCE	Automatic Flight Control Equipment		Thunderbolt
Big-B	Berlin	Latrine	
big friend	bomber	Rumour	unfounded rumour
Bird Colonel	full colonel	Liberty run	night off into town
Bitch	to complain	light colonel	lieutenant colonel
Buzz job	'attack' base, etc., at very low level	little friend	fighter aircraft
CAVU	Ceiling And Visibility Unlimited	lucky bastard	one who has completed his tour of
Chow Hound	GI who likes to eat		missions (and given a certificate
Chow Line	mess queue		for the L.B. Club)
Chug-a-lug	drink vast quantities of beer	Lufberry	fighter manoeuvre
Dear John	a letter from a girl back home saying	Milk Run	easy mission
	she's found someone else	No-ball	V1 target
Dogface	infantry soldier	Non-com	NCO
ETO	European Theatre of Operations	Over the Hill	absent without leave
feather		PFC	poor f------ civilian or private first
merchant	loafer, lazy individual		class
First John	first lieutenant		
looie	lieutenant	Piccadilly	
Flak	Flieger Abhwer Kannonen	Commando	prostitute
Flak Alley	heavily defended bomb run	Pill roller	medic
Flak Happy	state of victim of combat fatigue	Poop	information
Flak House	rest home	POM	Preparation for Overseas Movement
Flak Shack	rest home	pubbing	
Funny money	pounds sterling	mission	pub-crawl
Furlough	leave	PX	Post Exchange – military shop
GI	Government Issue, American	Red-lined	cancelled
	fighting man	Re-Tread	old officer recalled to active service
GIs	diarrhoea	Sack	bed
Greenhorn	inexperienced flyer	Sack Time	bedtime, sleep
Happy Valley	Ruhr valley	Scrubbed	cancelled
Heavies	bombers	Second John	second lieutenant
Holy Joe	chaplain	Section Eight	discharge given for mental
Hot Crock	garbage, nonsense, untruth		breakdown, insanity, etc.
IP	Initial point at the start of the bomb	Shack Job	easy woman
	run	Shack Up	sleep with woman
Iron Ass	hard, demanding, tough officer	Shortarm	VD inspection
Jnr. Birdman	inexperienced pilot	Shuttle	long bombing mission via stop en
			route

Sky pilot	chaplain	TS	Tough Shit
Snafu	Situation Normal All F----- Up	V-Mail	a letter greeting card . . . written on
Snowdrop	Military policeman, so-called because		a special form, they were
	of his white helmet		photographed on microfilm, flown
Short Snorter	a bill of currency autographed to		to the States and delivered
	prove one had been in that	WAAF	Women's Auxiliary Air Force
	country	Wolfpack	fighter outfit
Tour	series of missions	ZI	Zone of the Interior (USA)
		Zoot Suit	flying suit

BIBLIOGRAPHY

A Minor Front	Robert Conquest
An Army Air Force Navigator	1/Lt. John W. McClane (unpublished)
Bawdy Barrack-Room Ballads	Hugh de Witt Universal-Tandem 1970
B-17s Over Berlin	Ian Hawkins, Brasseys/95th BG 1990
Castles In The Air	Martin W. Bowman, PSL
Chicks Crew	Ben Smith Jr. 1978
Classy Chassy	Ian Logan & Henry Nield, Mathews Miller,
	Dunbar 1977
Country Boy-Combat Bomber Pilot	Col. Robert H Tays, USAF (Ret'd)
Crew Sixty-Four	Gene Gaskins
D-Day Dodgers, 'Airman's Song Book'	Edited by C.H. Ward-Jackson & Leighton Lucas.
	William Blackwood & Sons Ltd 1967
Elusive Horizons	Keith C. Schuyler, Avon Books 1969
Fields of Little America	Martin W. Bowman, PSL
First Over Germany	Russell Strong, 306th BG
Flying To Glory	Martin W. Bowman, PSL
'For Johnny'	John Pudney 'Collected Poems'. Putnam
Flight From Boyhood, The	T/Sgt. Robert T. Marshall (unpublished)
Flight To Eternity, The	Dr. John McGlone Jr.
GI Memories of the ETO	Sgt. Jack M. Preston
History of Aircraft Nose Art, The	Jeff Ethel & Clarence Simonsen. MBI 1991
Four Miles High	Martin W. Bowman, PSL
Liberator Men of 'Old Buck, The	Gen. Andrew S. Low USAF (Ret'd) 1979
Story of the 453rd BG	
Lines to an American officer	Noël Coward
In Search of Peace	Michael D. Benarcik. Jostens, 1989
Mighty Eighth, The	Roger A. Freeman. MacDonald 1970
National Geographic	
Ploesti	James Dugan & Carroll Stewart. Johnathan Cape
	1962
Rackheath Memories	Edited by William G. Robertie
Second Air Division Newsletters	D. Van Den Bogaerde 'Poetry Review'
'Steel Cathedrals'	Paul Dehn 'The Day's Alarm' (Hamish Hamilton)
'St Aubin D'Aubigne	
Stars and Stripes	Simon & Schuster. New York 1943
Target: Germany	
Yank magazine	
'Vargas'	Alberto Vargas and Reid Austin, Plexus 1978